PARTICIPATORY PRACTICE

Community-based action for transformative change

Margaret Ledwith and Jane Springett

s d...

This edition published in Great Britain in 2010 by

The Policy Press
University of Bristol
Fourth Floor
Beacon House
Queen's Road
Bristol BS8 1QU
UK
Tel +44 (0)117 331 4054
Fax +44 (0)117 331 4093
e-mail tpp-info@bristol.ac.uk
www.policypress.co.uk

North American office:
The Policy Press
c/o The University of Chicago Press
1427 East 60th Street
Chicago, IL 60637, USA
t: +1 773 702 7700
f: +1 773-702-9756
e:sales@press.uchicago.edu
www.press.uchicago.edu

© The Policy Press 2010

Reprinted 2012

British Library Cataloguing in Publication Data
A catalogue record for this book is available from the British Library.

Library of Congress Cataloging-in-Publication Data
A catalog record for this book has been requested.

ISBN 978 1 84742 012 1 paperback

Cover design by Qube Design Associates, Bristol
Front cover: image kindly supplied by www.alamy.com
Printed and bound in Great Britain by www.4edge.co.uk

Dedication

For Grace, whose light shines in the world; with hope for a world worthy of her, and all children.

For Ian, who has been consistently supportive of my work in the world, and for my mother and father.

Contents

List of figures and tables

Figures

Tables

Acknowledgements

Margaret: Thanks to Liverpool John Moores University for supporting me to take on the editing role for this book. Thanks also to those studying the MA in Critical Pedagogy and Social Justice for wholeheartedly embracing the notion of critical space. Thanks to Peter Maddocks for *How to be a cartoonist* and John Byrne for *Cartooning*; these books helped me to discover a new dimension of knowing beyond the written word. Finally, thanks to Emily Watt and Jo Morton at The Policy Press whose enthusiasm has made the experience of writing this book a joy!

Jane: Thanks to Kristianstad University College, Sweden, whose respect for the purpose of academia gave me some space to write physically and intellectually, and where colleagues helped my learning.

Introduction[1]

This book is the product of a shared journey, influenced by the experiences of two very different lives. We have approached it in the spirit of the book itself, founding our approach on dialogue, on mutuality and respect for each other's ideas, and an openness to a dialectical challenge, locating dissent as central to knowledge creation within a frame of 'connected knowing' (Belenky et al, 1997). The consequence has been an organic, transformative process for us, a delightful outcome, but certainly not a foregone conclusion. There have been moments of trepidation along the way. At the outset we would like to say that our preparedness to be open, dialectical and empathetic is testament to the ideas we share with you, the reader, in the book. And this is the source of our delight: by working together, in the way that we advocate in this book, we have discovered that participation as a transformative approach works in diverse contexts.

In the book itself, we emphasise the use of story as a way of anchoring the process of change in lived experience. True to this approach, we share aspects of our own stories with you here. A participatory approach calls for us to acknowledge the ways in which our own life experiences have shaped the ideas that we share with you, and these vignettes give you insight into critical moments that have influenced our theory and practice over the years.

We met in 1992 and became firm friends who recognised our shared values long before we recognised shared academic interests. That recognition surfaced in 1996, when we both attended one of the participatory action research conferences at Stroud, organised by Peter Reason and Judi Marshall. It was a coming together of the personal and professional at an event that aimed to do just that: understand life as a connected form of knowing.

Jane's story

When I met Margaret, I had already moved my focus from geography to health promotion, and through the latter had become attracted to the ideas of Paulo Freire, introduced to me by Nina Wallerstein at a chance meeting at the University of Liverpool. Nina, who is now a professor at the University of New Mexico, had been using Freirean approaches in her work with marginalised young people in New Mexico as well as in her previous work in South America. This approach to popular education resonated through my work as a part-time tutor with The Open University, helping me to gain much greater practical understanding of how adults learn to be questioning and confident. Over the years, both in my work with The Open University and elsewhere, I saw people blossom when they gradually gained insight into new ideas about themselves in their world.

At first glance, a move between geography and health promotion might appear strange and disconnected. Yet the two are more closely linked than it appears on the surface – many of the ideas in this book were first introduced to me as an undergraduate geography student, and they have resurfaced time and again in different contexts. It was during my time as an undergraduate that I became aware of ecology and our place in it. We debated 'A blueprint for survival', published by *The Ecologist* (1972), the first time the environment and our impact on it reached a wider audience. Inspired into action, we collected and dumped non-returnable bottles on Schweppes' factory doorstep.

It is easy to think back and identify crucial turning points in one's life that at the time seemed to have no great significance. One such turning point found me sitting in a lecture theatre at the first Healthy Cities conference in Liverpool in 1987 thinking, as I was listening to the various plenary speakers, "But this is urban geography!". A chance conversation over coffee with a colleague had brought me here. He talked about his partner, a landscape architect working with a community in Vauxhall, Liverpool. That community, which came to be known as the Eldonians, was hailed for its community action in rejecting the city council's plans for regeneration. Instead, they developed their own Eldonian village in partnership with community architects. Here was my first taste of participation and both my heart and my head wanted to know more. Healthy Cities was and is an initiative spearheaded by the World Health Organization (WHO) Regional Office in Europe aiming to engage local government in health and well-being. In order to create healthy communities, it is important to see health and well-being as influenced by a range of dimensions. This notion of 'healthy cities' struck a chord, not only because the approach emphasised the need for an interrelationship between humans and their social and physical environment, but because it acknowledged that without peace, shelter, education, food, income, a stable ecosystem, sustainable resources, social justice and equity, human flourishing is just not possible. These ideas resonated with me as a human ecologist, a geographer for whom notions of the interrelationship between humans and their environment is core. It was an understanding that was second nature to me: notions of reciprocal maintenance, caring for each other, our communities and the natural environment, and central was the empowerment of communities and individuals to take control of their lives. The Healthy Cities/Health for All movement, whose origins lay in an opposition to the Thatcherite policies of the 1980s that denied the existence of health inequalities, attracted me. Albeit often described as a social movement in bureaucratic clothing (Stevenson and Burke, 1991), it was at this time starting to roll in the UK, and I rolled with it, so starting my journey from pure theory to an integration of theory and practice, and from geography to health promotion.

Having been drawn to new approaches to inquiry, intellectually engaging with the ideas of John Heron, John Rowan and Peter Reason in the 1980s, the experience of putting these ground-breaking ideas into action followed later. I was working with a local community worker on an outer estate in Liverpool to pioneer a participatory approach to evaluation across a whole range of initiatives in one neighbourhood. It was agreed that the community worker would train local people in research skills to enable them to do their own evaluation. He began by asking them to think about how they would celebrate their success in a year's time. By making the experience relevant to them, he released passion, energy and enthusiasm. This, in turn, was transmitted beyond the boundaries of the room, with the result that even more people turned up to the next meeting.

The reference to heart and head is important here: passion as well as intellect need to be integrated. I remember visiting a health centre for Native Americans in downtown Berkeley, California. A peripatetic 'medicine man' happened to be visiting that day and agreed to meet us. He talked about health problems involving drug and alcohol abuse faced by Native Americans in relation to spiritual health, and the importance of a holistic approach to life. Taking a book, he placed it laterally level with his throat. The trouble with western society, he said, is that the head is cut off, like this, from the heart. I can still see that picture in my mind's eye. It made so much sense in relation to health promotion. Here was a principles and values-based approach to practice which encapsulated not only notions of ecology, but also notions of wholeness. This was a concept of health that had been with me since my childhood, and which, as I was starting to discover, underpinned other worldviews.

At around the same time, as I started to change my focus, I also started to seek changes in myself. I grew up into a shy and sensitive young adult, whose fear of people led me into the world of academia. From here, personal circumstances then jettisoned me into a world on the fringes of life, on boats on the canals and in the docks in different parts of England. Here, living off the land with very little money, estranged from my family because my mother did not approve, had a profound effect on my attitudes to the material and the social.

I started questioning reality and my place in it, and increasingly became self-reflective, more self-aware. Just as the health promotion movement enticed me out of my academic ivory tower, personal life experiences were drawing me into an inner journey, along *The road less travelled* (Peck, 2002). Indeed, it was a colleague giving me that book that started the process off. It was at this juxtaposition, between a movement of increasing inner and outer awareness, that my path crossed with Margaret's. We met at the same series of spiritual development workshops. The reflective process involved working in groups and pairs, and we only found ourselves together once, towards the end, during a workshop focused on shamanic practices. In this exercise we were asked to try a self-managed shamanic inner journey encouraged by drumming. Our partner's role was to record the journey as we described it during the process of deep self-reflection. In this way, I recorded Margaret's story of her journey and she recorded mine. And so began our story.

Much has happened both personally and politically since this time in the early 1990s. I discovered that the values and principles underpinning community-based practice that attracted me to health promotion were shared by others engaged in other practices with other foci, such as adult education, housing, environment, the arts, community development and many more. What connects us are those deeply held values and principles that provide not just a foundation for practice, but a foundation for life – values of respect, trust, dignity, mutuality, reciprocity. This book revisits those values that drew the two of us together, which were shared by those in the Health for All movement and by many other social movements around the world, not only to reinstate them at the centre of our practice, but to reinvigorate and develop them to new levels by putting participatory practice at the centre of all that we do to promote the well-being of all.

Margaret's story

I began life as the daughter of Grace Constance: I now find myself the grandmother of Grace. It feels like the wheels have turned full circle. Reflecting back on those austere but optimistic post-Second World War years, life welcomed me into the bosom of a loving extended family headed by adoring grandparents and surrounded by a stable community. So much of my sense of self was formed in that Birmingham suburb, nestling at the bottom of the steep hill that led to Erdington Parish Church, a church that witnessed all our family births, marriages and deaths. I can still name our neighbours and local shopkeepers, can still picture Mr Shute, the chemist, in the High Street, who would make up a 'cough bottle' when I was 'chesty'. Opposite was Dr Treadwell's home and surgery, Coton Cottage, tucked behind a little picket fence. He was the doctor who nursed me through polio when my mother was too scared to hear the word, let alone let me go to hospital. The village green at the other end of the High Street, where I stood to attention in my new guide uniform on Sunday mornings for church parade, had the Victorian public library and baths to one side, and Wrenson's, the local grocers, to the other, the delivery boy's bicycle parked up against the wall outside. All these remain symbols of my early stability.

I did not know the meaning of schooling as hegemonic at the time, but this concept has retrospectively been key to my experience of schooling as a child, and to triggering my critical consciousness as a teacher in young adulthood. Picture 1972, with me in the frame, a newly qualified classroom teacher, nervously facing a class of 36 eight- to ten-year-olds, looking out across a sea of faces eagerly weighing me up. The school building was Victorian, with classrooms leading off a central hall. Inside, the classrooms had fixed desks and windows were set too high for anyone under six feet tall to see a world outside. On first examination, the only resources available to me were geography textbooks, 20 years out of date. These were stacked in enormous cupboards that flanked the long wall opposite the windows. As the days went on, I was perturbed by what I saw acted out before my eyes. Three years of teacher training had reinforced over and over again that politics should be kept out of schools; classrooms were apolitical spaces. What I witnessed, of course, was hegemony in action: power acted out in this microcosm of wider society, and relations of 'race', class and gender reinforced. I did not know what hegemony meant at the time, but very simply it refers to the way that dominant ideas resist change, in this case by classrooms acting as places where children get silenced and learn their ranked status in the world, according to the status quo.

In the culture of the staff room, I listened to pronouncements that diminished the life chances of young children, just as I had experienced as a child. I had no analysis to give me any understanding of how to make an intervention in this process of disempowerment; I just knew that it was profoundly wrong.

From the primary classroom, my search for insight and understanding led me in a number of directions, from adult literacy to educational psychology. In the early 1980s, I worked with Vietnamese refugees, those known as the 'boat people', who risked death and abandonment on the South China Sea to escape tyranny in their own country, only to find a different kind of tyranny in the West. As I listened to their stories of separation from children, of giving birth on the high seas on rusty old landing craft that offered no dignity and no protection, of facing death as boat after boat from the West abandoned them to starvation and dehydration, we held each other for comfort; we became friends in our common humanity, as they taught me more than I could ever teach them. I began to realise that my quest for critical insight was out there in the real world, in community, where everyday lives are shaped. That was the point at which I chose to study for a Master's degree in Community Education and Development at the University of Edinburgh, and it proved to be the context in which my search for a critical analysis of power was realised. David Alexander, with great passion, introduced me to the ideas of Antonio Gramsci, the Italian Marxist who was imprisoned and died under Mussolini and the rise of fascism simply for teaching people to think, and Paulo Freire, the Brazilian adult educator, who was imprisoned and exiled for teaching people to read and to question. Such is the power of ideas! As I read about Gramsci's concept of hegemony, and began understand his analysis of the way that power is threaded through our everyday lives from our time of birth, it became so obvious, it was hard to believe that I had not spotted it myself. But the way we are taught to see the world is so powerful that it permeates the essence of our being and influences the way we act in the world. Gramsci felt that false consciousness is so pervasive that it takes external intervention from 'traditional intellectuals', as he called them, to act as a catalyst in the process of demystifying power. My experience was certainly testament to that.

The political context of the time saw the New Right in ascendance. Thatcherism took hold, poverty escalated and my life became one of activism. The miners' strike of 1984–85 brought support from alliances all over the world as we witnessed hegemony at work: while the power of persuasion was asserted through control of the media, convincing the country at large that the miners were undermining the very moral fabric of society, freedom of movement from mining communities was blocked by the police who were, cleverly, drafted in from other parts of the country to avoid mixed loyalties. The women of the mining communities took immediate action, to the shock of Margaret Thatcher who had expected that she could appeal to them to force the miners back to work. Women Against Pit Closures became their organised action as they rose up in support of their families and communities, threatened in their survival by starvation tactics. Initially they set up soup kitchens to feed families whose benefits had been cut. Many of these women had never been outside their mining communities, built round the pithead to serve the interests of the industry; their role was one of unpaid labour. Their outrage at the burgeoning threat of the government's desire to dismantle the last large union of organised workers gave them the confidence to give public talks all over the country and abroad, seeking support. Alliances across difference emerged, and at many demonstrations coachloads of supporters would swell the numbers. This was the heyday of new social movements, and women, gay and lesbian groups, greens and others stood together against injustice. This was the stamping ground of my political activism.

Participatory democracy in Nicaragua captured the hearts of those who stood for a just and peaceful world. The Nicaragua Solidarity Campaign was central to my life. In Nicaragua, in 1985, living with the people of Puerto Cabezas in particular helped me to experience participatory democracy in action. Under the Sandinistas, advised by Paulo Freire, literacy and health campaigns swept the country, led by young people, filling hearts with hope. As part of a twinning campaign between Manchester and Puerto Cabezas, we organised for John McDonald, the well-known health educator, to go to Puerto Cabezas to develop a health centre. He wrote saying, 'How could you do this to me?'. Even for someone like John, with many years' experience in Africa, Puerto Cabezas was at the edge of the world – all those who could get out had left, and the town was under constant threat. Frequent attacks were made by sea from Honduras and overland routes were landmined by the Contra. It did not stop those of us whose vision of a democratic future lived in the hope of Nicaraguan success. Yet this little country, striving to achieve true participation, was perceived as such a threat to the US that sonic booms were heard every day over Managua, creating fear in the minds of everyone. On a bus trip to Bluefields, we were almost swept up into a Contra raid – attacks like this were commonplace. The Contra, trained in terrorist tactics in Florida, would descend from the cover of the rainforests of the interior and abduct local women, rape children in front of their fathers, cut off the fingers of husbands and force wives to drink the blood. It was terrifying for someone like me who had had such a sheltered upbringing. We worked to support workshops for those 'dis'abled as a result of the war, to twin schools with those in Manchester, to set up women's sewing projects as local economies with the support of women's groups in the UK, and to support a community artist to use wall murals with local people as a way of telling their stories. Nicaragua inspired hope in all of us that a harmonious and just way of life, founded on participatory democracy, was possible. In relation to becoming critical through border crossing (Giroux and McLaren, 1996), this was a transformative experience for me. I saw life from an altered perspective. Recently, in Katharine McMahon's novel *The rose of Sebastopol*, I read, 'What good is their reference out here? Can't you see? We are in a different place, where we have to think differently and find ourselves a new way of being' (2007: 218). Just as Mariella was faced by this stark fact by her lady's maid, Nora, in the Crimean War, I quickly learnt the meaning of changed thinking leading to changed doing. One particularly critical encounter was when we were invited to meet the head of the army battalion defending the northern region, a dangerous area bordering onto Honduras. He willingly agreed to talk to our little group about the struggles they faced on a daily basis, but then took my breath away: "We send money to support your miners' strike. Tell me how you have used this struggle as a way to true democracy." In the face of the courage shown by the Nicaraguans, how could I explain that the false consciousness fostered by dominant hegemony had persuaded popular opinion against the miners, who were seen as undermining, rather than acting for, democracy.

Back home, I was very involved in the women's movement. We were active in our local groups reflecting on our lived experience, building practical theory from grassroots action. It was visible and powerful. We organised Greenham support groups to maintain the women's peace action. It was a time of organised activism: we marched the streets carrying banners to say who we represented – Quakers, gay groups, civil rights activists – all joining together as one, singing, 'Free Nelson Mandela!'. We joined with the anti-deportation campaigns of the civil rights workers. We loaded lorries full of supplies for War on Want, supported Médecins Sans Frontières, the list went on. It was a time of inspiration and hope.

In this period, I first worked in Old Trafford, bordering Moss Side in Manchester, with multicultural inner-city communities, then with the people of Hattersley, a Manchester 'overspill' or 'peripheral' estate invented to house people from 'slum clearance' areas of inner-city Manchester, built on damp land that was no good for farming, on the foothills of the Pennines in North West England. My new-found praxis, a unity of reflection and transformative action, gave me a critical lens through which to see power acted out in everyday lives, in tangible ways before my very eyes. This not only helped me to understand life on the margins, but it gave me insight into who was destined to occupy this space outside the mainstream. I began to understand the way that poverty is a tool that reinforces discrimination, and that the process is not indiscriminate, but targets very specific social groups. From experience, I began to understand that knowledge is power, and that ideas sold as 'common sense' make no sense whatsoever, but are internalised and obscure the blatant contradictions that we live by in the West. Theories of power gave me conceptual tools to see and understand the world in more critical ways. The theories on their own in the academy would have remained academic, but they came alive in my practice in the community, building knowledge in action from lived experience, a living praxis.

I hit a point of dissonance in the theory/practice divide when I decided that my practice would evolve more critically if I developed it within a PhD framework working with the internationally respected adult educator, Ralph Ruddock. I struggled to make sense of research methodologies that attempted to decontextualise the lives of the people with whom I worked until my colleague, Paul Jones, handed me a copy of Reason and Rowan's *Human inquiry* (1981). This was another critical moment in my politicisation. I read: 'this book is about human inquiry ... about people exploring and making sense of human action and experience ... ways of going about research which [offer] *alternatives* to orthodox approaches, alternatives which ... do justice to the humanness of all those involved in the research endeavour' (1981: xi), and my eyes lit up. This revolutionary book, the product of new paradigm researchers' action for change, was transformative in my thinking. It gave me insight into participatory action research as a liberating practice, and profoundly influenced my approach to knowledge creation in everyday life. The approaches to research I discovered here were consonant with the value base of community development practice, and offered an integrated praxis, a way of building knowledge in action and acting on that knowledge. A basic model that has stayed with me ever since this time is Rowan's cycle model which offers a structure for integrating theory and practice as an ongoing dialectical cycle of action and knowledge generation (Rowan, 1981: 98).

In 1992, when I met Jane, I had just made a move from grassroots community development practice into the academy. I faltered on the interview day, questioning the relevance of moving to such a cloistered context after being at the heart of community life for so many years. In my mind's eye, I could see myself sitting in Mottram Churchyard, having a picnic lunch with Paul. Our partnership was so good for so long, and we thrived on the challenges of Hattersley life, "Could there ever be life after Hattersley?", we asked ourselves. But, life moves on, and my challenge was to locate myself where I could make most difference to the process of change, to keep community development critical. In my new role as a community work educator, my life was woven together with Paula Asgill, a woman of Jamaican heritage, who became my close friend and colleague. Through shared experience, we became aware of differences in our lived realities as two women, divided by racism. We worked together on research into alliances between Black and White women in order to gain deeper insight into the process of sustaining alliances for change, and I began to touch at the edges of White power as it manifests itself in daily encounters. She died at the age of 47, 14 years later.

During this period, a young student came bursting into my office, waving a call for papers for the 'Pedagogy of the Oppressed' conference in Omaha in 1995. He had been excited by my passion for the work of Freire, and was urging me to submit a paper. I did, and I found myself beginning a long connection with what is now known as the Pedagogy and Theater of the Oppressed organisation. In 1996, Doug Paterson from the University of Nebraska at Omaha invited Paulo Freire and Augusto Boal to the conference, where it was my great pleasure to meet them just a few months before Freire's death. This was the context for my engagement with such radical educators as Ira Shor, Peter McLaren, Antonia Darder, Peter Mayo, Michelle Fine, Maxine Green, Chris Cavanagh and many others significant in the critical pedagogy movement.

Our joint story

Now, 17 years after we first met, this book has been influenced by all these significant experiences in our lives. Our inspiration for writing it came from our commitment to a participatory worldview as a way of life that is predicated on peace, cooperation, social justice, diversity and sustainability. Here we present you with the results of the process we have shared, and the ideas that have emerged from that dialectical engagement, in the belief that participatory practice is the path to participatory democracy.

Note
[1] Throughout, we have used 'race' and 'dis'ability to emphasise the socially constructed nature of these concepts, and White and Black to indicate the political nature of these broad categories.

Section One
A participatory paradigm

ONE

Participatory practice

> To be denied the capacity for potentially successful participation is to be denied one's humanity. (Doyal and Gough, 1991: 184)

Participation

Participation is a transformative concept. It is a way of life, a way of seeing the world and a way of being in the world. We say this to emphasise that it is not simply an approach to working in community; it has far-reaching implications for practice when the thinking behind it is more fully understood. Its philosophy is founded on principles of peace, justice and equality, a profound belief in the worth of everyone and the sanctity of the natural world. Our purpose in this book is to take you on a journey that transforms your thinking about participation. Our aim is that, in turn, this should transform your practice in the world. Our belief is that, in becoming more critical in our thinking, our perceptions of the world around us change. In other words, becoming critical, developing a questioning approach to practice, challenges the taken-for-grantedness of everyday life. Attitudes that have been sold to us as 'common sense' no longer make any sense at all, and we begin to see beneath surface-level symptoms that often distract practice to discover an interconnected network of power relations that create inequalities. This is a hopeful and inspiring process; we become more aware that change is possible, and how it can be achieved.

'Participation is fundamental to the nature of our being, an *ontological given*' (Reason and Bradbury, 2001: 8). We are inextricably connected by the web of common humanity, but more than this, we are woven into all forms of life on earth. The concept of life as an ecosystem, held in fragile balance, helps us to understand that by harming anyone or anything we are violating this interdependence, and so endangering the well-being of the whole. This was captured recently in a television documentary in which a Tibetan Buddhist came out of her door to share some of the meagre rations, on which she was barely surviving the freezing, high altitude, winter conditions, with the wild geese that were starving around her. This vignette captures the essence of a world that runs counter to the top-down, competitive values of the western worldview, to demonstrate how seeing our world in a more connected and cooperative way influences how we act. For these reasons, participatory practice begins in lived reality, in our being in the world. And it is questioning this everyday experience that leads to changed understanding. Freire refers to this as liberating education, but:

> Some believe that the notion of education for emancipation is utopian …
> [T]his sort of 'realism' breeds acceptance of social evils. It offers docility
> and compliance with the powers-that-be. (Kemmis, 2006: 463)

Peter McLaren, in a discussion of *disutopia*, states that 'our internal and external worlds seem to have been split apart', a disconnection he links to the process of disutopia as 'not just the temporary absence of Utopia, but the political celebration of the end of social dreams' (Dinerstein and Leary, cited in McLaren, 2000: xxv). We want to offer you an insight into a participatory approach to practice that restores hope from hopelessness, connects the unhappy times that we live in to the fractured state of our external world, and situates critical agency as a form of autonomous being in the world that leads to action for transformation. Think of it as a *practical utopia*: a way of shaping a better world impassioned by outrage over the injustices that we have created in the present. This releases the energy of possibility. From our disenchantment with what is, we become enchanted with what might be.

Participatory approaches to practice involve restoring the essence of our being through living cooperatively, developing projects that are founded on mutuality – from LETS (Local Exchange Trading Systems) to recycling, and from community gardens to carnival – the examples are endless, but they all have well-being at their heart. For such practice to be successful, the thinking behind the practice has to be rigorous and critical. For this reason we now take you through the key ideas that you will find woven throughout this book; these are crucial for your understanding of participation.

Participation as practice

Within the term 'participatory practice' we embrace a diversity of roles, but we locate community development at the heart of the process. The key purpose of community development is collective action for social change, principled on social justice and a sustainable world (see Community Development Exchange's [CDX] website www.cdx.org.uk). As an increasing number of people are required to have the skills, knowledge and understanding to practise good quality community development, it is vital that the process is fully understood. To begin with, the foundation of this work sits in the carefully defined core values and principles that frame its practice. The values that underpin every aspect of the practice are those central to what we would call an ideology of equality: dignity, respect, trust, mutuality, reciprocity, cooperation and so forth. This value base provides a system of checks and balances that ensure the validity and integrity of the work. The values can be developed into a series of quality questions, and these elicit evidence in the process of evaluation. In other words, if we say that the work is reciprocal, what evidence is there that there are equal, respectful partnerships in place? In this way, if I claim my work involves trust, what does that look like in practice? How does it manifest itself? What is the evidence that it is taking place?

In a lengthy consultative process with those involved in community development at every level, National Occupational Standards for Community Development Work have been established in the UK. These are subject to ongoing review, and currently the Federation for Community Development Learning (FCDL) is working with the Lifelong Learning Sector Skills Council (LLUK) to undertake a revision that will build on the standards currently in place (available at www.cdx. org.uk). The values and practice principles defined by the National Occupational Standards for Community Development Work are, at present, expressed as:

- social justice
- self-determination
- working and learning together
- sustainable communities
- participation
- reflective practice.

In the wider contexts of participatory practice, it is poorly understood that there are nationally agreed frameworks in place for community development, and for this reason we draw these to your attention. We have a deep concern for the incomplete and somewhat confused approaches to practice that result from this lack of coherence, this lack of understanding of the wider purpose of community development.

Participation became acknowledged as a key, transformative concept in community development in the early 1970s, influenced by the pedagogy of Paulo Freire. As Taylor and Mayo note, participation 'emerged almost as a prerequisite for any community development initiative and became the subject of "mainstreaming" by many local, national and international agencies' (Taylor and Mayo, 2008: 264). Participatory practice treads the fine line between transformative change and maintenance of the status quo. So, a word of warning: when the transformative potential of concepts such as participation are not fully understood in practice, there is a danger that they become diluted and therefore dangerous. By this we mean that our practice could be hypocritical, claiming to be emancipatory while, in reality, doing quite the opposite. In this respect, Cooke and Kothari (2001) boldly name participation as the 'new tyranny' to emphasise the way in which key concepts reduced to buzzwords can flip transformative practice into serving the interest of the powerful and maintaining the status quo. If participatory approaches to practice are to justify a position on social justice, environmental sustainability and collective well-being, then participation has to be understood as a transformative not ameliorative concept. The political dimensions of participation need to be framed within participatory democracy, a worldview in which communities are in control of the decision-making processes that affect their lives, giving voice to the most marginalised, giving greater power to local governance to influence policy making thereby making institutions accountable. This approach is central to all forms of participatory practice, not only those overtly labelled community development, but those associated forms of practice that fall under health promotion, adult education, schools, youth work, social work, conservation, regeneration, local economic development and many more. Transformative change for a world that is cooperative, diverse, equal and flourishing calls for an understanding of the interrelatedness of the three core dimensions of our work – social justice, environmental sustainability and collective well-being – because they are central to everything about everyday life. This insight is the key to unlocking the transformative potential of participatory practice.

Big ideas, but how do we engage with them in grassroots practice? Dialogue with local people focuses on the action that needs to happen to address the immediate and pressing issues faced by the community. Each specific local intervention is inevitably linked by a myriad of connective pathways to the bigger picture issues of social justice, sustainability and collective well-being. This realisation is what inspires local initiatives to reach beyond the boundaries of community: everything about community life is part of a whole system, that of life on earth. The practical projects that are developed in a community are diverse, but always identified in dialogue with local people as relevant to their needs. In any one community, these can range from anti-poverty strategies (such as credit unions), to housing projects (such as insulation or damp proofing), to identity politics (such as women's projects, anti-racist projects, youth projects), to safety, health, literacy and many more. All are interlinked in the process of community development in cycles that give more and more local people voice and the confidence to take autonomous control of their lives. The collective dimension builds steadily outwards, from issue to project, from project to alliances/networks, gathering momentum towards movements for change. In this way, projects, rather than the discontinuity of 'project-ism', become vital and connected stages in the process of change. Strategies that help to support this level of organising are community-wide democratic bodies, such as forums, and beyond-community connections with regional and national campaigns, networks, alliances and other collective organisations and watchdog bodies, such as Child Poverty Action Group. In these ways, participatory practice extends from local to global, gathering momentum for collective action for change.

Barriers to participatory practice

Let us take a look at some of the tangible barriers to transformative approaches to practice at this point. We are living in times where short-termism is the order of the day, where funding bids for practice to develop are based on competitive tendering, often to criteria that insist on 'new' projects rather than developing those already in operation, with practitioners increasingly on temporary contracts and preoccupied with meeting policy targets at the same time as chasing funding for their own continued existence. The new managerialism, with its top-down culture of bureaucracy, results in distracting levels of permission-in-triplicate, eroding the autonomy of practitioners who work at the cutting edge of change;

theory is divorced from action, with the consequence that practice becomes 'thoughtless' (Johnston, quoted in Shaw, 2004: 26) and policy-led (Craig, quoted in Shaw, 2004).

Michael Pitchford (2008) levels some hard-hitting challenges at community development: incorporation of community development into government agendas has distracted us to the extent that we have lost our way and consequently have little sense of direction, let alone any clarity of overarching purpose. We need to listen to this, and become more focused, more vigilant in our approach to practice. Pitchford argues that even the term 'community development' has been muddied; it is not understood to be significantly different from either community involvement or community engagement agendas, therefore it has lost its distinctiveness as a process for facilitating social change. 'The case can and should be made for how community development can deepen democracy', but will not happen if practitioners' minds are colonised by top-down policy from above which results in 'herding communities into structures and forums they neither own nor relate to' (Pitchford with Henderson, 2008: 94-5). A culture of anti-intellectualism has created an even deeper theory/practice divide, discouraging practice that is either critical in approach or which extends into a collective form beyond the local project. The result is fragmented practice that attempts to engage with the symptoms of oppression, with no attention to the root causes, one that gets swept up into policy-driven agendas of improved service delivery. A plethora of policies have emerged that absorb, conceal and dilute such transformative concepts as social justice, participation and empowerment, de-radicalising their potential by reducing it to improved service delivery. At the same time, in relation to 'actionless thought' as underlined by Shaw (2004), there are many who would say that 'the "postmodern turn" in the current theory of much European and North American adult education seems all too often to cut it off from its historical roots in social purpose, political engagement and the vision of a better world' (Martin, 2008). Rennie Johnston (2008: 6) cites Mamet: 'Whether they like it or not, current defectors (from the intellectual left) are seeking to provide a vocabulary for the progressive intelligentsia to abandon the poor'. This is part of a burgeoning debate on '"how all the Marxist have become post-modernists" ... [with the result that] many university adult educators have been seduced (and reduced) by inward-looking academic reference points that get in the way of both social commitment and a wider world view' (Johnston, 2008: 2-3). We believe there is an important line between embracing insights into difference and diversity, and resisting the full sway of postmodernism's preoccupation with the personal/psychological that undermines any sense of the collective whole.

A participatory approach calls for collective action, and our belief is that this needs to happen in alliances across difference that build on compassion and empathy (Ledwith and Asgill, 2000, 2007). This awareness has led us to re-vision Freire, taking the dichotomous notion of oppressor/oppressed into understanding oppressions as a plurality of multilayered, intersecting forces. The idea that different ways of knowing provide routes to multiple, subordinated truths places us in opposition to the overarching dominant truth embodied in global neoliberalism, a truth that reifies market competition above life itself.

Participation as critical education

> Education, or the act of knowing as Freire calls it, is an ongoing research programme into aspects of people's experience and its relationship to wider social, economic and political factors. (Kirkwood, 1991: 103)

Participatory practitioners are popular educators. Working in equal partnership with people in community on projects that may be practical, creative, aesthetic or economic, we use liberating education (Freire, 1972) to teach people to question the issues affecting their lives. What is happening here? Why is it happening? In whose interests? The process of questioning leads to a greater critical awareness of the root sources of social issues, and is threaded through practical projects in an integrated way. This is embodied in the 'but-why?' method (Hope and Timmel, 1984: 59). Capturing an issue in a familiar scene from everyday life – Freire used line drawings, but photographs or any other art form serves the purpose – the issue becomes decontextualised, or coded, and can be seen more critically as a result. In a community group, through dialogue, the animator aims to get the discussion to go as deeply as possible, from surface reaction towards the root causes of the issue, simply by asking questions (see Chapter 9). This places the emphasis on critical consciousness as the basis of autonomous learning at the heart of Freirean pedagogy (Freire, 1972). The liberating potential of critical education is based on mutual, reciprocal, horizontal relations of dignity, trust and respect, the antithesis of dominant, top-down vertical relations of superiority/inferiority, and therefore an intervention in the way that practitioners and the community relate. Freire's pedagogy runs counter to *banking education*, sometimes known as the jug-and-mug approach – pouring facts into unquestioning minds. It starts in people's lived reality, questioning everyday life, ensuring that every encounter is a liberating experience.

Reflexivity is central to the process of becoming critical. This simply means the ability to reflect on our reflections, going ever deeper under the microscope to examine our own attitudes, assumptions and prejudices in order to open ourselves to new insights and understandings. We could see this as an inner dialogue, knowledge as the exploration of both an internal and external reality. We propose that it is impossible to engage critically in the outer world without this inner, self-critical reflection. For instance, in relation to practice, we need to be aware of the impact of our own identity and its power dimensions across the diversity of people with whom we work, whether this be rooted in 'race', class, gender, or any other form of difference. If we fail to understand our own power in relation to our partnerships in community, and power relations within the groups with which we work, we are unconsciously reinforcing the same divisive structures.

In these ways, participatory practice becomes a tool for a more critical knowing in the world based on practical knowledge. By using a narrative approach to addressing knowledge in action, and action as knowledge (Reason and Bradbury, 2001), we offer tools for practitioners not only to explore the world, but also to examine the lens through which they perceive the world, and in so doing local practice begins to be seen within bigger social issues.

Participation as empowerment

> As historical and social beings we find ourselves already in a linguistically structured lifeworld. In the forms of communication through which we reach an understanding with one another about something in the world and about ourselves, we encounter a transcending power. (Habermas, 2003: 10)

Empowerment is closely tied to the process of becoming critical. Critical consciousness involves understanding the nature of power and the way in which it permeates our lives. Around the same time as Freire's *Pedagogy of the oppressed* was translated into English, so was Gramsci's *Selections from prison notebooks* (1971), and this had a massive impact on our understanding of power. Gramsci's concept of *hegemony* in particular helped us to understand the subtle nature of power, and the way that the dominant ideas of society infiltrate our minds through the diverse range of institutions in civil society – family, school and all formal and informal groupings – to persuade us that the interests of the powerful are the natural order of things. The power of Gramsci's insight into the role of *consent* in the process of false consciousness helps us to see that civil society also offers an opportunity for liberating interventions through a process of critical consciousness, beginning in questioning the status quo. This process of becoming critical leads to autonomy, and autonomy leads to empowerment. True empowerment, however, is not an individual state, but a collective state, which is why Freire stressed that true liberation involves a collective process if it is to be transformative (Freire, 1972).

Critical theory provides a passionate and motivating force that empowers people to act. Changed awareness of the injustice of existing conditions is sufficient to empower a collective movement for change, but this cannot be left fluid and intuitive. Fay suggests that our goal can only be achieved when 'all three phases of the tripartite process of enlightenment, empowerment and emancipation are completed' (Fay, 1987: 29). We like the way that he structures this into a 'complex of theories which are systematically related' (Fay, 1987: 31):

I A theory of false consciousness

a) This needs to explain how people's understandings of their life experience are incomplete or contradictory;

b) it also needs to explain how people accept these understandings without question;

c) at the same time as offering alternatives that make greater sense.

II A theory of crisis

d) This needs to spell out what a social crisis is, and in Chapter 2, 'Troubled times', you can see the bigger picture evidence for a crisis of social justice and sustainability;

e) this evidence is substantiated by statistical analyses of child poverty, its class, 'race' and gender connections, and the resulting social divisions that threaten not only social cohesion, but the future stability of the world, and how this is embedded in the existing social order;

f) a historical account of how both false consciousness and the structural forms of discrimination came into being is also necessary, and we trace this with the help of theories of power.

III A theory of education

g) This needs to offer insight into the educational context necessary for critical consciousness;

h) and it also needs to identify the approaches, skills and methods needed for critical pedagogy.

IV A theory of transformative action

i) This needs to focus on the particular aspects of society that need to be changed in the current context;

j) there must be a strategic plan of action that at very least identifies the catalyst for social transformation, for example Gramsci's concept of *the intellectuals*.

(Adapted from the basic structure offered by Fay, 1987: 31-2)

Fay suggests that it is only when these four theories, together with their sub-theories, are consistently interrelated that there is a structure capable of explaining, criticising and mobilising for transformative change.

In this way, we see empowerment as only possible when part of an integrated praxis, in which theory and action are in symbiotic relationship, building knowledge from experience. Yet, the anti-intellectual times we have created lead to practice that is driven by policy, and even though the policies emphasise empowerment through participation, nothing is changing. In fact, all the evidence points to the fact that we are becoming more divided than ever. For instance, poverty for children and older people is increasing in the UK, and the gap in life expectancy and ill health between richest and poorest communities is at its greatest since Victorian times, and growing (see websites for the Child Poverty Action Group [CPAG] and the New Economics Foundation [nef]: www.cpag. org.uk and www.neweconomics.org/gen/ respectively). And, disturbingly, these patterns of division and alienation are reflected around the globe. The fallacy is that, while the developed world is getting richer, it is becoming more divided and less happy. Empowerment is a product of being critical, and cannot be understood without insight into the way that power works in society. 'The self and society create each other' (Shor, 1992: 15), and therefore change for a just and sustainable future is based on questioning the status quo, becoming curious about the way that the form of democracy that exists in the West is creating privilege for some at the expense of greater inequalities for others.

Participation as theory

An analysis of power is central to participation as an emancipatory practice. In Ira Shor's words, being critical involves 'extraordinarily re-experiencing the ordinary' (Shor, 1992: 122): participatory approaches to practice are about teaching people to question answers rather than answer questions. From the time we come into the world, we absorb a way of making sense of what is around us to such a degree that we take it for granted, and cease to see the contradictions acted

Teaching to question

out in everyday life. Our lived experience invades the very essence of our being, and we do not spontaneously see the world in a critical light unless something triggers our consciousness. Only then do we begin to question what we have previously accepted unquestioningly. This *false consciousness* sells us a *common sense* that is nonsense. We internalise the contradictions of life as a natural state of affairs and so are persuaded not to challenge what is unjust but simply to accept it as the given order, as inevitable. In this way, people are persuaded to consent to their own oppression. Unequal social relations formed out of subject/object interactions produce and reproduce domination and subordination according to the dominant order. Social status determines which social groups are dominant and subordinate in ways that are reinforced through prejudice (personal and cultural attitudes) and discrimination (the way that the structures of society embed domination and subordination as social divisions). Class, 'race' and gender are major social divisions, and are compounded by age, 'dis'ability, sexual orientation, religion and ethnicity. This process is mutually reinforcing at every level, from social relationships to poverty-related life chances. In these ways, the forces of discrimination are threaded through everyday life experience, and the result of this is oppression.

When Paulo Freire's seminal work, *Pedagogy of the oppressed*, was first published in English in the US in 1970 and in the UK in 1972, it had an immediate impact on not only community development, but also on adult literacy, liberation theology and popular health campaigns around the world by helping practitioners understand the nature of oppression, and how empowerment begins in questioning the status quo. Freire's thinking was also instrumental in the participatory action research movement, which challenged the controlling assumptions of traditional research and its role in reinforcing the dominant interests in society. The pioneering work of the New Paradigm Research Group came to fruition with the publication of *Human inquiry* (Reason and Rowan, 1981). It offered an eclectic range of methods within an action research approach that involved understanding and working with people in a process of mutual research, of action and reflection as a cycle of co-creating knowledge and acting together to transform situations.

Emancipatory action research is action research that is overtly committed to social justice. It is a vital component of participatory practice generating knowledge in action, which:

- is founded on an ideology of equality – dignity, respect, mutuality, reciprocity, compassion, conviviality;
- adopts a methodology that is collaborative and so attempts to work *with* not *on* people as a process of empowerment for all involved;
- uses methods grounded in everyday narratives, giving voice to silenced voices, and being open to ways of knowing that extend beyond the intellectual. For example, it uses self-reflexivity and dialogue, but may also use story, music,

drama, poetry, drawings, photographs and any other medium that gives rise to different ways of knowing;
• is committed to action for transformative change.

Its commitment to human flourishing brings together the emotional, spiritual, intellectual and physical dimensions of being human, in order to develop emancipatory, transformational knowledge that leads to different ways of being in the world. This might sound a tall order, but it ripples from the self, to others, to communities, organisations and cultures, organically and collectively gathering momentum until it reaches the potential for a movement for change.

This approach to research involves four interlinked stages in the process of transformational practice:

• questioning the status quo and dominant ideology
• identifying the key sites of intervention in the process of disempowerment
• creating new ways of seeing and making sense of the world (epistemology)
• creating new ways of being and acting in the world (ontology).

In these ways, it is an evolving praxis, a living process of creating knowledge in action and action as knowledge in cycles of development.

Stephen Kemmis talks about the necessity for emancipatory action research to tell unwelcome truths that people do not want to hear (Kemmis, 2006). These are necessary tools in 'being critical'. Without this denunciation or truth-telling our work lacks a critical edge and is unlikely to be transformative. So, in Quaker conceptualisation, we need to 'speak truth to power', connecting local issues to broader questions. If our work only aims to improve the efficiency of practice without examining the consequences of these practices, if it unquestioningly aims to implement government policy, if it fails to engage the voices and perspectives of all those involved, or if it is conducted alone without those whose lives are affected by the practice, it is not emancipatory action research (Kemmis, 2006: 460).

Emancipatory action research builds on theories that engage with multiple truths, multiple ways of knowing. In the search for a single truth, a White, male, Eurocentric way of seeing the world became accepted as the dominant truth. We now understand that there are many diverse truths, many ways of seeing the world from different realities. For example, working with the idea of multiple truths, or counter truths, a Black feminist epistemology was developed by Patricia Hill Collins as an alternative epistemology (1990):

1. using concrete experience as the basis of meaning, an ontological basis for knowledge;
2. using dialogue to explore knowledge;
3. using an ethic of caring as the basis of social relations;
4. using an ethic of personal accountability.

Based on the idea that 'every idea has an owner and that the owner's identity matters' (Hill Collins, 1990: 218), we all become agents of knowledge, seeking truths that emerge from dialogue that engages with lived reality. Knowledge of everyday experience is vital to the process of transformative change, and Hill Collins notes that dialogue has its roots in cultures of an oral tradition and is the antithesis of western dichotomous thought which makes sense of life by Othering subject/object. The African worldview, she suggests by contrast, is holistic and searches for harmony, seeking that which is more fully human through connections and interactions, and dialogue is central to that process. bell hooks notes that 'dialogue implies talk between two subjects, not the speech of subject and object. It is a humanizing speech, one that challenges and resists domination' (1989: 1312). Similarly, in their seminal contribution, *Women's ways of knowing*, Belenky et al (1986) emphasise that the use of dialogue in assessing knowledge claims is predicated on connectedness rather than separation.

Critical reflection and transformative action are not separate processes: they are inextricably integrated as a unity of praxis. However, the trivialisation of theory in current times (Noffke, 2005) presents us with a problem. Without theory there is no praxis, and without praxis our work becomes 'thoughtless action' (Johnston, cited in Shaw, 2004: 26); it lacks criticality. Through dialogue we are able to begin the process of questioning the taken-for-grantedness of everyday life. This is not only the starting point for critical consciousness, but also the motivation for collective action. As we become skilled in the practice of dialogue, we deepen our capacity for critical thought, questioning everyday experiences, challenging false consciousness to reach new insights into the political nature of personal lives. As we begin to see the world in different ways, we change how we act in the world. People join together to act collectively for social change, fired by a sense of justice and hope for a better world. In this way, the critical public spaces needed for local dialogue move through increasingly collective contexts to global dialogue as the basis of movements for change – 'a supraterritorial space' (Scholte, 2000: 199).

As local, grassroots, community-led organising began to challenge centralised, top–down, external interventions, the early 1970s saw a new theorising of participation as a practice based on social justice and true democracy. As we have already mentioned, the seminal work of Paulo Freire, *Pedagogy of the oppressed*, and Gramsci's *Selections from prison notebooks*, had an instant impact on participatory practice, emphasising the role of education in liberation. Practice based on education and action, the investigation of social reality with critical consciousness in cycles of action and critical reflection, became 'prerequisites for participation' (Tandon, 2008: 288).

Participation as social justice

We are painting a picture that locates participatory practice at the interface of domination and liberation, identifying the profoundly political nature of everyday life. This is the essence of Freirean pedagogy. Taking aspects of life's experience as the focus of dialogue and reflection, the dehumanising elements of everyday life are identified and used as the basis for transformation (Freire, 1985). Mo Griffiths talks about the 'little stories' that link voice to narrative making that vital connection between the deeply personal and the profoundly political 'by taking the particular perspective of an individual seriously; that is, the individual as situated in particular circumstances in all their complexity [and linking this] to grander concerns like education, social justice and power' (Griffiths, 2003: 81). In order to situate little stories within collective narratives we need to provide statistical evidence of social trends. For example, in Chapter 2 we draw on the evidence of a UNICEF report on child well-being in rich countries, in which the UK is ranked bottom of 21 countries (UNICEF, 2007). A simple poverty analysis in the same chapter reveals that not only are one in three children in the UK growing up in poverty, but that structural discrimination skews those figures according to 'race', class, gender and 'dis'ability, making the interconnectedness of risk much higher for children whose families fall into specific social groups. Damian Killeen, consultant on social justice and sustainable development, asks 'is poverty in the UK a denial of people's human rights?'. This question is based on the fact that poverty and discrimination contravene the Universal Declaration on Human Rights, and that a refusal to incorporate the International Covenant of Economic, Social and Cultural Rights into UK law has entrenched discriminatory attitudes against the 'undeserving poor' that resist popular support for anti-poverty policies (Killeen, 2008). For instance, while UK children in general stand one chance in three of growing up in unacceptable levels of poverty, a child of Bangladeshi or Pakistani ethnicity living in the UK is at over twice the risk.

We are concerned that rafts of anti-poverty policies are not reducing inequalities and improving life chances for people in poverty. Recent research into child well-being in the UK attempts to isolate child poverty and child well-being in order to influence more targeted policy interventions using two sets of measures (Tomlinson et al, 2008). The first measure is at household level, on dimensions of financial strain, material deprivation, the physical environment, psychosocial strain, civic participation and social isolation, combined into a weighted poverty index. The second measure attempts to isolate four dimensions of child well-being: home life, educational orientation, low self-worth and risky behaviour. All these dimensions are interrelated, but by identifying those aspects that have most impact on a child's well-being, it is possible to target interventions. Research such as this focuses on the cost to the child during childhood, rather than the costs to the economy when the child becomes an adult, a failing of much current UK policy. Developing holistic narratives about the impact of child poverty with children, giving voice, taking seriously and making connections helps to give insight into the costs of poverty to our children. In other words, it is research that is ethically rather than economically driven. Ironically, while 'progress' continues to be measured as synonymous with wealth, the resources needed for the world to live at western levels of consumption would take three planets (www.neweconomics.org), suggesting that our western worldview is creating lifestyles that are not only unhappy but also destroying the natural world at the same time. Participation is about collective well-being based on social justice and environmental sustainability; current practices are creating an unhappy, alienated world that is not thriving.

It is not possible to work in a participatory way without understanding the bigger political issues that shape people's personal lives – just as we have begun to do here. Participation implies democracy; a state where everyone has a voice in the decisions that affect their lives, and acts collectively for a common good. In order to work in a participatory way, we need to understand that subordination and discrimination dehumanise and destroy hope, and everyone pays the price, rich and poor alike. Participation involves creating hope out of hopelessness, and as 'hope is an ontological need … we need critical hope the way a fish needs unpolluted water' (Freire, 1995: 8).

What tools can we look to to help us with this analysis? A simple model which is widely used to aid understanding of prejudice and discrimination is Thompson's PCS (personal, cultural, structural) model (2003, 2006) (see Figure 1.1). Three concentric rings indicate levels of interaction between the individual and society. It is particularly helpful because it effectively symbolises the ways in which these different levels mutually reinforce each other. Too often analysis stops at the P-level – that of individual, personal prejudice. Challenging sexist comments or even tackling the behaviour of racist groups in a community is not enough to bring about change on a structural level without being part of a groundswell movement for change.

Figure 1.1: The PCS model

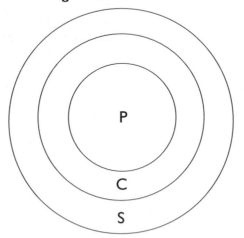

Source: Thompson (2003, 2006), © Palgrave Macmillan, reproduced with permission

To illustrate this, Thompson embeds the P-level (the personal or psychological – a level of thoughts, feelings, attitudes, action and prejudice) within the C-level (that of the cultural, shared ways of seeing, thinking and doing – a level of commonalities, consensus and conformity); which in its turn is set within the S-level (the structural level where social divisions are sewn in to the fabric of society and oppression and discrimination become institutionalised – the socio-political power base) (Thompson, 2006). All these levels interact in ways that mutually reinforce prejudice and discrimination. This understanding is essential. It indicates why it is impossible to counter oppression by targeting one level at the exclusion of the others. Personal prejudice, cultural attitudes and structural discrimination form an interactive dynamic that constantly maintains social divisions and serves the power relations in society. This dynamic is so powerful that it negates any action that fails to address the whole. In this respect, it is a reminder that local practice, in order to be transformative, needs to extend beyond community to change the structures of society.

Participation as democracy

Tandon poses three aspects of the re-imagining of the theory and practice of participation: power, citizenship and democracy. 'Participatory democracy has been shown to be a process of enhancing representative forms of democracy, on the one hand, and rejuvenating its institutions on the other … participation is thus an input to as well an output from democracy' (Tandon, 2008: 294).

Dialogue involves questioning, reflecting and analysing in a process of becoming critical. The spaces needed for this sort of critical dissent dialogue are what Mo Griffiths refers to as 'political public-spaces', where people can come together to 'argue, agree, discuss and decide what to do … where people respect each other and, through communication with each other, help to develop the kinds of people they will all become' (2003: 126). John Elliott reminds us, 'the space for the exercise of such agency will not come simply as a gift from government. It will be wrought out of a political struggle by teachers and others within society, to create the material conditions for a free, open and democratically constructed practical discourse to emerge as a context for professional action' (2005: 363). It is only when our individual outrages at injustice find collective political expression that there is sufficient force to act for the common good. And, as Mae Shaw says, 'an open culture of debate is one of the best ways to protect community development and democracy' (2004: 28)

In order to bring about transformative change for a more fair, just and equal world – a system of participatory democracy in which people are involved in decisions which affect their lives – we need to understand the way that discrimination reaches into everyday lives prescribing a pecking order based on class, 'race', gender, age, ethnicity, religion, sexuality, 'dis'ability or any other form of difference in complex and interconnected ways. 'Democracy is no longer a political concept but an economic metaphor', warns Antonia Darder (2002: 12). This market-led imperative has led to an ideology of disposability, with greater importance being put on some lives than others, driven by profit. Freire saw racism and sexism as central to capitalist relations (Shor and Freire, 1987), and we were exposed to the worst aspects of this politics of disposability when Hurricane Katrina hit the Black communities of New Orleans in 2005 (Giroux, 2006a, 2006b). Antonia Darder challenges those of us 'committed to antiracist struggle and social justice [to] become fully conscious [of] an all-consuming capitalist system that is everywhere at work in sustaining, perpetuating, and exacerbating all forms of social discrimination, economic exploitation, cultural invasion, and systematic violence again women, gays and lesbians, working-class people, and racialized populations' (Darder, 2002: 13).

Consciousness of the personal as political becomes the basis for informed action for social change. This is the key to understanding the political nature of personal or local issues. It stops us from personalising failure, helping us to grasp the complex interconnected dimensions of oppression. In this way, our practice becomes more considered and we resist surface-level reactions that blame the victims of poverty, placing responsibility at their feet. Whatever the diversity of local projects, this political-educational dimension is threaded through our work in cycles of development, giving people confidence in their own ability to act together on the issues that affect their lives.

Participation as biodiversity

The process of globalisation has accelerated over the past two decades, creating 'a human crisis as well as a threat to the entire planet' (Cannan, 2000: 365). Alienated lifestyles that elevate the right to consume over the responsibility to live in balance with the earth have led not only to crises of global poverty, but crises of environmental sustainability. John Ruskin, who lived the last decades of his life at Brantwood on Coniston Water in the late 19th century, not so far from where we write this, situated spirituality at the heart of economics: 'There is no wealth but life' he wrote in his collection of essays published as *Unto this last*. His challenge to economics was to identify 'that which teaches nations to desire and labour for the things that lead to life: and which teaches them to scorn and destroy the things that lead to destruction' (Ruskin, 1862, in Rosenberg, 1998: 259). This emphasis on putting people and planet first is at the heart of new economics. Ruskin understood that wealth is synonymous with well-being and that an economy that exploits nature and humanity can never bring about sustainability and human flourishing. Economics can only be understood when situated within the wider ecosystem that is dependent on diversity. His thinking had a profound influence on future thought and action, including Gandhi and E.F. Schumacher, both of whom placed people at the heart of economics, rather than deifying the market over life on earth. As feminist thought developed, so the interrelatedness of the control over the environment and the control of women emerged in eco-feminist thought. The central argument from eco-feminism is that 'a historical, symbolic and political relationship exists between the denigration of nature and the female in Western cultures' (Spretnak, 1993: 181). Eco-feminism is rooted in principles of 'harmony, co-operation and interconnection' that challenge the perceived male principles of competition, 'discrimination, extremism and conflict' (Young, 1990: 33).

What we see here is a need for the maintenance of harmony and balance in all systems if the world is to thrive. As Reason says, 'The conscious mind alone necessarily fragments the whole … the experience of wonder and awe is at the core of our participation in the cosmos, and through beauty we can feel our sense of belonging' (2005: 39). It is this sense of 'walking in beauty on the earth' (Reason, 2005: 41) that gives rise to a reverence and gratitude for all that is living and part of the whole. In the words of Ruskin, 'There is no wealth but life, life, including all its powers of love, of joy, and of admiration. That country is the richest which nourishes the greatest number of noble and happy human beings' (Ruskin, 1862, cited in Rosenberg, 1998: 270). The idea of beauty is vital in the poorest communities – celebration, festival, environment, but the one I (Margaret) would like to tell you about here is a community garden. My eyes filled with delight as I rounded a corner between tightly packed miners' houses to find a beautiful oasis, a community garden, nestling in stark contrast to the harsh angularity of darkened red brick and the absence of space for anything green. The garden was built as a cooperative community project, on derelict land where houses had disappeared down a subsiding mine shaft. The stories I heard were testament to the healing beauty of the natural world: "When life gets too much and I can't face the day, I come and sit in this garden, quietly, and gradually I find the strength and confidence to go out into the world again." Not only do people look out on beauty where there once was dereliction, but they are drawn to it, get to know each other as never before and come together as a community to celebrate throughout the year, carols at Christmas, barbecues on summer evenings.

Similarly, in the early 2000s, community police on Merseyside initiated a process that came to be known locally as 'alleygating'. This involved knocking on the doors of terraced houses to get local agreement to put gates at each end of their shared back alleys. These alleys were often full of litter and night-time activity. The process brought the community together in a common space for the first time, and after the gates were put in place small community gardens emerged and shared activities became established. The Merseyside Health Action Zone funded the original pilot and commissioned a study looking at the impact on people's health. Based on the findings a video was produced in which people talked about its impact on a general sense of well-being.

These simple local examples of community action are the beginnings of bigger picture ecological perspectives of a reconnection of humanity with the whole.

Community Garden, Scholes

Photo: Grace Gregory-Pike

Participation as a worldview

Participation operates from an altered worldview. From critical education to participatory democracy, participatory approaches to practice express a worldview that heals the alienated aspects of life as we have created it on earth: 'an unhappy planet' (www.neweconomics.org). A participatory worldview is one founded on cooperation not competition, on diversity not disempowerment; it is a belief that we can co-exist in the world in harmony and diversity in ways that enable everyone and everything to flourish.

The interdependence of life on earth has been fractured, resulting in a separation of the internal self, self and other and separation of humanity from the natural world, or 'the more than human world' (Reason, 2005: 39). This process is accelerating with the escalation of globalisation, reaching into traditionally more diverse cultures with the same competitive, exploitative and discriminatory worldview. The result is that the structures of discrimination that are so destructive in the West are becoming a globalised phenomenon. Modern western consciousness has taught us to see the world as functioning separately – public/private, emotions/ intellect, Black/White, good/bad, right/wrong, male/female – and has attached behaviour and values to this dichotomous, split way of seeing life, resulting in the validation of individualism – a denial of the unity of life on earth. A profound understanding of the interconnected whole that is life on earth gives a spiritual dimension to participation, and it is 'the purpose of education and inquiry ... to heal the wounds brought about by the dualism in which we have been marinated' (Reason, 2005: 39). The challenge for us, as we co-create happier and healthier possibilities, is to measure personal well-being as a component of collective well-being, as real wealth with social and environmental values at its heart.

This calls for a new way of seeing the world:

> We need, I believe, a way of knowing which helps us to heal this split, this separation, this alienation. We need a way of knowing which integrates truth with love, beauty and wholeness, a way of knowing which acknowledges the essential physical qualities of knowing. We need a new story about our place in the scheme of things. (Reason, 1994: 14)

Everyday spirituality is located in participatory practices in which we approach life as sacred, in all its interconnectedness, and seek a way of creating life on earth based on human flourishing. This is a form of participation that is self-aware, reflexive, critical, autonomous, at the same time as maintaining both diversity and unity in the name of a common good. It embraces concepts such as conviviality as a way of being and love as a passionate caring for all humanity. It begins with simple respect for people and the natural world, and it resonates outwards. As Paulo Freire says, 'there is no way to transformation, transformation is the way' (from his keynote lecture at the 1989 Changing Identities conference in London, organised by Lawrence & Wishart; see Griffiths, 2003: 125).

For Freire it was impossible to conceive of a liberating practice without a profound commitment to humanity: 'his notion of humanity was not merely a simplistic or psychologized notion of "having positive self-esteem", but rather a deeply reflective interpretation of the dialectical relationship between our cultural existence as individuals and our political and economic existence as social beings' (Darder, 2002: 35). We have to look beyond the personal. 'There is no question that in today's world, no authentic form of democratic life is possible for the future without a revolutionary praxis of hope that works both for the transformation of social consciousness on one hand and the reconstruction of social structures on the other' (Darder, 2002: 30). For Freire, feelings, dreams, wishes, fears, doubts and passion are part of a pedagogy of hope, one in which a profound love for the world is an energy for change. This is essentially predicated on a horizontal way of seeing the world, a view that is juxtaposed to the top-down, vertical relations that lead to exploitation (see Figure 1.2).

Participatory practice inherently believes that another type of world is possible, a holistic worldview in which the concept of *participation* represents a wholeness founded on equality in diversity, cooperation rather than competition, mutual respect rather than false status, and the profound well-being that leads to human flourishing in the world. As we move towards these ideals, the full transformative potential of *participation* becomes released. This seeking for wholeness, connectedness, balance and healing in a fractured world is everyday

Figure 1.2: Juxtaposed worldviews

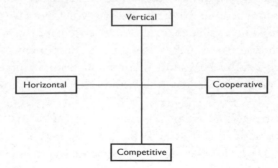

spirituality, as 'we are called to work together in community with others who are also struggling for justice' (Reason, 2000).

Participation: a multi-dimensional model

Building on Peter Reason's (2005) ideas, we have developed a model (Figure 1.3) to help you think more clearly about participation as interconnectedness, as a whole.

Figure 1.3: Living as part of the whole: a multi-dimensional model of participatory practice

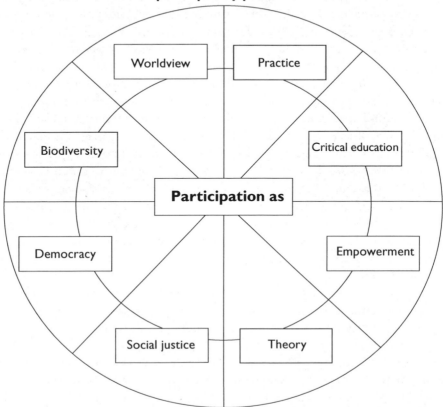

Participation begins in everyday life

Lived experience is at the heart of participatory practice, and this book is about trying to understand experience by locating it in dialogue generated from the stories people tell about their everyday lives, locating stories in collective narratives and situating these within the bigger picture of our political times. Our challenge is to convince you, the reader, that participatory approaches to practice are straightforward and infinitely possible.

> Men and women make history from the starting point of given concrete circumstances, from structures that already exist when they are born…. The future is something that is constantly taking place, and this constant 'taking place' means that the future only exists to the extent that we change the present. It is by changing the present that we build the future, therefore history is possibility, not determinism. (Freire, 1993: 84)

Paula Allman talks about the need to understand and use concepts more fluidly, more critically, more dialectically, if we are 'to engage in authentic local and global social transformation' (1999: 65). By making sense of our social reality, understanding the critical connections between our histories, cultures and differences, gaining insight into the relations of power that have shaped who we are in the world, we begin to grasp the links between ideology and alienation, and this helps us to dismantle the 'common sense' that has led to a dominant ideology that divides and alienates us from our natural participatory place in the web of life on earth.

> When we share our differences within dialogue, listening carefully to one another and helping each other to examine the origins of our thinking, we usually come to a sharing of values and commitments, and the process that has led to this means that what we share really means something significant … the dialogical process helps to keep our minds open and questioning, enabling us to be curious and reflective about our developing, critical consciousness. (Allman, 1999: 140)

Participatory approaches are committed to locating knowledge in everyday life. In our practice we bring ideas and knowledge and action together to produce *practical knowing*. Doniger (1998) talks about looking through a microscope at the thousands of details that bring our stories to life, and through a telescope to see the unifying themes. Classed, racialised, gendered and all other social differences that define our experience provide us with moments to engage deeply in the work of dismantling oppression. In a process of reflection–dialogue–action we question the ways in which lives are expanded or limited according to who we are. In this sense, anyone's experience can become a beginning place for inquiry, where, in challenging privilege, we challenge the boundaries of our understanding.

The ideas that we have introduced in this opening chapter are threaded throughout the book. They are all interlinked to a fully integrated whole. In order to present them in a more coherent way, we have taken key themes as the focus for each chapter, while keeping the threads of the whole narrative woven throughout. Imagine the chapters as weft threads in a tapestry, with the long warp threads weaving in a connectedness with the whole. We conclude with Chapter 9, 'Becoming whole', which situates participatory practice in relation to democracy in crisis: a troubled world in which divisions within the self, between ourselves and between humanity and the natural world are leading to escalating crises of social justice and sustainability. With the view that life on earth is an interdependent web, we present a model for practice based on practical theories for a practical utopia.

TWO

Troubled times

> The universal is in the particular.... We are all part of one another, interconnected beyond the separations made by the mind. (Quinney, 1998: xi)

This chapter examines the political times that frame our local practice, placing particular emphasis on the way in which fragmented thinking is fragmenting policy and practice. The dominant way of seeing the world is influenced by those who are most powerful, but it has a massive impact on ordinary lives in community. This is why it is so necessary to understand how ideas influence public attitudes and, subsequently, social policy in order to analyse power and disempowerment. This is the basis of effective practice interventions. The opening quote emphasises our fundamental principle, that life on earth is an interconnected whole, and that social divisions and the destruction of biodiversity have created fractures in the health and well-being of the web of common humanity that is at the heart of our practice. Individualism does not encourage a way of life that takes a collective responsibility for the well-being of all. It is more likely to justify why some people are privileged while others are in poverty. But even more dangerous is the way that consumerism driven by market forces has justified levels of exploitation that increase social divisions and deplete natural resources, with the consequence that life on earth becomes disconnected. This has some far-reaching implications. Biodiversity and cooperation are concepts based on a reverence for the earth and all humanity. This perspective comes from an awareness that there is a balance to life on earth, that we are all part of a complex ecosystem that can only flourish in its interconnectedness. Here, we want to explore the ways in which our singular western worldview leads to behaviour that throws this out of balance.

Dominant ideology in the West is predicated on competition. Competition is seen as a 'good thing': it not only reifies the economy, but it is absorbed as an ideology into our personal relationships, our education system and everything else about the way we live our lives. It is a top-down view of life on earth that justifies exploitation, subordination and domination, and inevitably leads to divisions of poverty and privilege. We are living in worrying times in which social divisions are widening and our relationship with the natural world is out of sustainable balance. It is this worldview that has led to what Peter Reason (2002) refers to as the twin global crises of our times – social justice and sustainability. As globalisation escalates, fuelled by neoliberalism's hold in the West, the most vulnerable of the world are being exploited to meet the greed of rich, western markets, and the fragile ecosystems that sustain life on earth are being destroyed. In order to meet the challenge of practice interventions, it is vital that we explore some of the complex ideas that lead us to a deeper understanding.

Alienation is a consequence of a competitive worldview, one that justifies the minority living at levels of unsustainable greed while the majority are denied the right to meet their basic needs. In other words, it is a greed-over-need worldview which holds the inherent notion that some people are superior, and deserve to consume excessively, and others are inferior, and responsible for their own suffering. The rationalisation of a free market economy has elevated the economy over the rest of life's reality as a prime force beyond our control. We are persuaded to believe that the unfair life chances it deals to some social groups while privileging others are inevitable, and therefore beyond change. This gives rise to exploitative practices that are justified in the name of keeping the economy buoyant, distracting us from noticing that life on earth is a living system, and that all actions have an impact on its intricate balance. Reason talks about our need to re-enchant the world, to see humanity as a vital part of the whole system of life on earth if we are to bring about transformative practices for justice and sustainability (Reason, 2005).

Now at this stage you may be questioning what these bigger picture issues have got to do with community-based practice. Our response is clear and concise: by fixing our gaze on local and specific issues, our practice floats on the surface, engaging with the symptoms, failing to go down deep enough to identify the sources of structural injustices. This renders practice tokenistic rather than transformative, as placatory rather than participatory, as ameliorative rather than just. We find that transformative concepts, such as *participation, empowerment* and even *social justice* have been incorporated into mainstream policy, but reading the small print we discover that this radical intention stops short at 'improved service delivery'. Improving service delivery to poor and marginalised people does not change the structures of injustice that made them poor in the first place. It simply pats them on the head, and makes life just a little bit better around the edges. The danger, of course, is that we are complicit, that our practice is reinforcing the very structures of injustice that we claim to transform.

The image of prosperity that comes with global capitalism obscures the realities of poverty and discrimination that it creates, giving the illusion that everyone benefits. We find that people generally react with disbelief to the fact that one in three children are growing up in poverty in a rich country like the UK, and question the yardstick by which this is measured, suggesting that the figures are manipulated rather than real. The power of this thinking is so persuasive and the outcomes so corrupt that new ways of critiquing the bigger political picture and new ways of organising democracy are called for if we are to challenge a world situation that is running headlong into crisis. The rest of this chapter takes on that challenge. Community-based practice with a social and environmental justice commitment needs to engage with current political times and the way that structural power creates a divided reality if practice interventions are to realise a transformative potential. To pave the way to a more critical understanding of community-based practice, it is vital that we critique our political times. In this way, we are more likely to steer a course towards a participatory democracy founded on principles of social justice and sustainability.

Structural power and local practice

An analysis of power is central to any form of participatory practice. By remaining local and depoliticised, we run the risk of making life just a little bit more tolerable, but leave the power relations that create inequality intact. For these reasons, it is important to understand the ways in which power is constantly re-forming, and how dominant ideas persuade us to accept these changes as *common sense*. Critical theories offer conceptual tools by which we can identify power at work and question the way that this impacts on everyday lives. This is vital to any practice that attempts to bring about change, and we discuss this in more detail in Chapter 7. Here, to illustrate power relations and the way in which ideology influences policy, we trace three key political periods in the UK since the end of the Second World War during which there have been major changes in approaches to social policy that have impacted on child poverty in particular. We then explore neoliberal globalisation as a major thrust in the development of capitalism, and make links between local–global issues related to social and environmental justice. Finally, we consider the ways in which this paints a picture of democracy in crisis, and explore why a progressive re-politicisation of community is needed to pave the way forward to a just and sustainable future. To introduce our theme of 'troubled times', we begin by considering how a western worldview influences the way we have constructed our world.

Western worldview

A worldview is a paradigm for framing the way we see the world, the way we think about the world and the values that inform this perspective. These ideas have a profound influence on the way we act out our everyday lives. The roots of critical consciousness lie in questioning taken-for-grantedness, the unquestioning acceptance of the way life is, and we offer some practical ways of teaching people to question later, in Chapter 8. As we become more questioning, challenging our assumptions and exposing contradictions, we find that dominant ideology has permeated our minds, persuading us to accept the status quo as inevitable. This dominant way of seeing the world influences the way we think and therefore the way we behave, but often it is acting against the best interests of the majority of people by creating a reality which privileges the already powerful. So, by exploring the ideas implicit in a western worldview, which work on class, cultural, ethnic, religious, racial, gendered, sexual and many other social differences, we begin to identify the structural roots of discrimination. Our identities, a sense of who we are in the world, are formed within this complex, interconnected hierarchy of poverty and privilege.

A worldview is not fixed. As Reason (2002: 4) says:

> The worldview of a culture changes from time to time … worldviews
> are not simply rational things, they are about the mood of the times,
> the metaphors we use without knowing we are using them, the spirit
> of the times. A worldview encompasses our total sense of who we
> are, what the world is, how we know it. It encompasses our sense
> of what is worthwhile and important, what are the moral goods to
> pursue. It guides our sense of the aesthetic and the spiritual. And it is
> the basis of our social organisation and political, personal, professional
> and craft practices.

In this respect, we have seen more rapid change since the latter part of the
20th century than could have been imagined prior to this. Not only has the
technological revolution made communication on a world-scale immediate, but
absolutes have been dismantled before our eyes, and in our minds at this moment
are such iconic examples as the Soviet Union, the Berlin Wall, Apartheid in
South Africa with Nelson Mandela freed after 27 years' imprisonment to become
president and world peacemaker, and more recently the 'twin towers' at the
World Trade Center in New York, which prompted the West's 'war on terror'.
The illusion of stability in the West has now been replaced by instability, and
the banking crisis that triggered a global recession in 2008 has added to this by
hitting hard in people's daily lives. Boundaries of nation states no longer offer any
protection from global phenomena, and issues such as HIV/AIDS and climate
change place social and environmental justice at our feet, rather than distant and
in someone else's backyard. Global justice is now a preoccupation of governments,
non-governmental organisations (NGO) and people in general, particularly young
people who are moving towards adulthood with very different views of the world
(Piachaud, 2008). In turn, this is bringing about related local/global action, for
example the fair trade movement, which operates in schools, in towns, nationally
and internationally, to change attitudes and behaviour. Social justice is increasingly
becoming embedded in policy at national and global levels. For instance, the World
Health Organization (WHO)/Commission on Social Determinants of Health
(CSDH) (2008) call for closing the health gap in a generation, saying:

> social and economic policies have a determining impact on whether a
> child can grow and develop to its full potential and live a flourishing
> life, or whether its life will be blighted. Increasingly the nature of the
> health problems rich and poor countries have to solve are converging
> … reducing health inequities is … an ethical imperative. Social injustice
> is killing people on a grand scale. (CSDH, 2008)

Our western worldview is in a period of crisis, challenge and change. The
Enlightenment, the philosophy that developed in western Europe in the 17th and

18th centuries with its emphasis on an objective, rational, unemotional, scientific knowledge embedded in masculinity, has formed the basis of our ways of making sense of the world by seeking a single, scientific truth. At this point, we would like you to engage with the social and political theorist John Gray's comment:

> In the Western cultures, the foundations of Christian and Enlightenment humanism are now wholly eroded but the universalist project which they animated is still far from being abandoned. The idea that Western civilization is simply one set of cultural forms among others remains as alien and unfamiliar as the idea that liberal regimes must expect to share the earth with others which will never adopt their institutions or political culture. In truth, the perception in the public cultures of Western societies that they in no sense constitute the germs of a universal civilization, if and when it comes to pass, will signify a major discontinuity in Western cultural history, since it will represent the acceptance that the West's foundationalist claims, on which its sense of privilege and superiority in respect of other cultures was grounded, are hollow.... To attempt to prescribe for a recovery from Western nihilism is merely another form of Western humanist hubris. We can nevertheless discern a few of the steps we need to take, if we are to have any chance of opening a path through the ruins in whose shadows we presently live. (Gray, 2007: 268-9)

By problematising the western worldview in these ways, we can begin to engage with the notion of alternative ways of seeing the world and the role of epistemology in ontological change. In other words, our worldview in crisis offers an opportunity to explore different ways of seeing the world that create better possibilities. Groundswell action for change always comes from grassroots, so reflecting on these bigger issues helps us to become more critical in challenging our practice and its purpose. Gray's bigger issue perspectives offer us food for thought in the process of action/reflection. It is a form of problematising that helps us get to deeper levels of reflexivity. What precisely is he saying? Do you think there is any truth in it? Does it help you to see things differently? What does it suggest to you about your practice? We address the possibilities opened up by exploring alternative worldviews in Chapter 3. Here, we are critiquing the foundations and consequences of our current western worldview and the way that it has ultimately created crises of social justice and sustainability.

Enlightenment thought has given rise to a monochrome world in which everything has been defined in simplistic relation to its opposite as either right or wrong, Black or White, male or female, superior or inferior, good or bad, and so forth, obscuring more complex interconnections. Within that frame, dominant ideas have shifted over time, and here we use UK examples to explore how, since the Second World War, the way we make sense of the world has changed. This has been much influenced by technological developments, but structures of discrimination have become so embedded in our consciousness that they weave their way through emerging ideologies. We now examine three distinct political phases in the UK: the welfare state, Thatcherism and New Labour. Within a discussion of the ideology informing these three distinct changes in political thought, we situate them within the escalation of globalisation, and use child poverty in particular as a means of investigating the complex and contradictory nature of poverty as it has been allowed to manifest itself today.

Dominant ideology and the construction of poverty

The post-war welfare state

Popular consensus changes the face of policy. The welfare state was created in 1948, and was a major landmark in social justice thought, acknowledging the need for a collective responsibility for the consequences of poverty and ill health. The Beveridge Report (1942) formed the basis of the modern welfare state, aiming to eliminate the five giant evils as they were perceived at that time – Want, Disease, Ignorance, Squalor and Idleness (Timmins, 1996: 23). According to Timmins, the term 'welfare state' was popularised by the Archbishop of Canterbury, William Temple, in the early 1940s, and popular consensus was influenced by a country united by war. A changed ideology of welfare emerged based on the idea of people having a right to be supported by the state in times of hardship. This was revolutionary thinking, but today we are aware that it 'hid the giants Racism and Sexism, and the fights against them, behind statues to the Nation and the White Family' (Williams, 1989: 162).

In 1965, Peter Townsend and Brian Abel-Smith (cited in Mack and Lansley, 1985) produced a seminal work demonstrating by uncovering the stark impact of *relative* poverty in the UK that the welfare state had not achieved what it set out to do. It was out of this new awareness of the damaging impact of relative poverty that the Child Poverty Action Group (CPAG) was formed, co-founded by Peter Townsend, who died on 7 June 2009 and whose analyses of relative poverty in the UK and globally have inspired practice for decades. CPAG, as with all good democratic organisations, has provided an ongoing dynamic between grassroots projects and collective movements for change by offering a structure for ongoing action. In my (Margaret's) own grassroots practice, CPAG formed an essential source of information on up-to-the-minute statistical analyses of poverty, as well as a link for local-national campaigning. It is when we synthesise insights into poverty and its repercussions with the campaigning to organise for change that we see movement (Dorman, 2008).

In over 60 years since the formation of the welfare state, Britain has got much richer but income inequality and relative poverty have grown: 'in the 1960s and 1970s real income rose *without* increasing poverty – so there is nothing inevitable about rising inequality in a growing economy' (Dorman, 2008: 130). We emphasise this notion of 'nothing inevitable about rising inequality' as we explore what happened under a new regime.

The New Right and Thatcherism

A global economic recession after 1973, together with the expansive welfare spending of the 1960s, created a crisis in welfare funding which offered a niche for change. Thatcherism erupted onto the British political scene as an intellectual and political power more akin to the neoliberal ideology central to Reagonomics in the US, the Pinochet regime in Chile and the International Monetary Fund (IMF) and World Bank programmes in the developing world (Mayo, 1999) than the rest of Europe. It was a revolutionary move to the Right. During this period, United Nations (UN) documentation evidenced ways in which the World Bank was not only a corrupt ally of dictators, but also questionable in the way it managed its funds: 'In pressurizing governments to accumulate money to pay back debts, the Bank forces them to cut public spending, even on basics like health, education and subsidies on the price of food' (Kane, 2008: 196).

In order to understand the development of neoliberalism in the UK it is important to understand the way that these global forces were creating a world context for an ideology based on a free market. In doing so, we uncover fundamental contradictions. For instance, the World Bank promotes free trade for poor countries at the same time as those countries are cutting public spending in order to repay debts to the World Bank. This can mean that a local farmer is forced to compete in the global market where producers from the rich countries of the 'first world' are still subsidised. These are profoundly unequal and unjust relations that keep the developing world in poverty. In similar ways, deregulation and privatisation of a state's economic activities, called for by the World Bank, create a space for multinational companies to gain control over national economies, thus condoning an approach to economic development that benefits the corporate interests of the wealthy North at the expense of the vast numbers of the poorest of the world. Kane likens this activity to that of 'a kind of international loan shark' (Kane, 2008: 196). In these ways, we are able to understand that the global activities of capitalism are connected to grassroots communities, reaching into the poorest communities to siphon out local money for corporate interests.

Those of us in grassroots practice in the UK at the time did not realise that Thatcherism heralded a tide of neoliberalism, promoting free market policies. Neoliberalism is a political philosophy that embodies free market principles, minimal government, economic individualism, acceptance of inequalities, moral authoritarianism, nationalism, low ecological consciousness and the welfare state as a minimal safety-net (Giddens, 1998). It is at the heart of globalisation, and globalisation accelerated from this point on increasingly colonising cultures of the world as a major ideological force. We will explore these ideas later in the chapter. For now, let us examine the impact of Thatcherism in its time.

New Right ideology paved the way for a welfare revolution in the UK. Hegemonic change was sold to the general public as *common sense* on the ticket of the undeserving poor, the 'welfare scrounger'. Margaret Thatcher's claim that 'there is no such thing as society, only individuals and their families' wiped out civil society in one fell swoop, undermining working-class solidarity and creating the terrain for individualism. A strange justification for the simultaneous increase of poverty and prosperity was that rich people needed to become richer in order for that wealth to 'trickle down'. It was a powerful form of *false consciousness*; nothing trickled down and those carrying the burden of poverty as society became more unequal and divided were children, young people and their families. For those of us working in grassroots practice, the impact was immediate and alarming.

Women as lone parents were demonised as threatening the moral fabric of society, just one component in the tapestry of undeserving poor that was being woven through popular consciousness. Somehow, nobody questioned the right to impoverish the children of lone-parent families in contrast to the Scandinavian model that embraced lone-parent families as legitimate in their own right. The punitive approach of the UK reflected that of the US, which, for instance, developed massive social control programmes based on arresting absentee fathers for failing to pay child support and coercing young women onto Depo-Provera, a long-term birth control injection that had been controversially trialled in the developing world. At the same time, there was a strong move towards centralisation of decision making, a strategic move on the part of Margaret Thatcher who was aware that democratic processes of participation and local leadership had begun to give a voice to some of the most marginalised communities, with a groundswell of organising through the community forum movement. Rate capping the socialist councils most committed to participation clawed back this local democratic movement, resulting in the Thatcher government creating one of the most centralised governments in Europe. Town halls were stripped of their funds and the power to continue the participation programmes that had been underway in their communities. It was a clever move: local people directed their anger at local government as funding was withdrawn, not realising that central government was pulling the strings.

Grassroots practitioners witnessed dramatic changes. The working-class solidarity that had held poor communities together gave way to an 'I'm alright, Jack' attitude, 'Just look after yourself and your own'. Paul Jones, my colleague in Hattersley at the time, and I (Margaret) saw the warning signs and set up a soup kitchen in the precinct. We saw it as a way of alerting people to the impending policy changes, thinking that it might trigger some critical debate leading to action: the response was, "You must be joking; life couldn't get much worse than it is." It could, and it did! The ascendance of the New Right wrong-footed us all; it was sudden and transformed life as we knew it. I remember Stuart Hall, one of the few social and political commentators to offer an incisive critique of what was happening at the time, announcing bemusedly in a radio debate, "Thatcher may not know the meaning of hegemony, but she sure knows how to do it!". This provided the ideological backdrop for change.

Social welfare quickly became perceived as a burden rather than a collective responsibility and a moral right. Notions of collective social responsibility, which had formed the bedrock for the post-war welfare state, gave way to a competitive culture driven by individualism and consumerism. The 'Thatcher revolution', fuelled by social, political and economic change, was committed to a 'dismantling of the protective elements of state welfare, to breaking the power of the organised labour movement and to a reaffirmation of market forces that would bring poverty and unemployment to unprecedented levels' (Novak, 1988: 176).

This changed ideology paved the way for a welfare revolution, and it came in the form of the 1986 Social Security Act. Benefits became means tested and there was a shift from grants to loans administered through a local Social Fund. These were dealt with on an ad hoc, first come first served basis from a limited budget. People were also means tested for their ability to repay the loan, thereby creating a hole in the safety-net for the poorest of the poor. The results were devastating, forcing vulnerable groups further onto the margins of society while the rich got richer (Cohen et al, 1996). The Thatcher government, in these ways, rendered poverty distant and invisible. Paul and I, at this time, found ourselves in homes where people were forced to buy takeaway meals because they had no cooker, no pots and pans; some were sitting in overcoats because they could not afford to heat their homes; and some were sitting on bare mattresses on the floor of their living rooms unable to buy the basics for a decent life. Martin, unable to pay to heat his home adequately, resorted to wearing a black bin bag with holes for his arms, underneath his pullover. People became bowed and anxious, aged and ill before their time. A young woman pushing a pram through the shopping precinct looked ill with worry. "Is it really true that they are going to charge for water next? I have already stopped baths for the kids and just give them a wipe down. I just don't know how I'll manage if it gets any worse." In these ways, the suffering of poverty worsened through the Thatcher years, and predatory loan sharks knocked on the doors of the desperate to meet the needs not covered by new policies.

The ethical contradiction of transferring wealth from the *poor* to the *rich* not only created massive social divisions, but it also plunged our children into becoming the single group most vulnerable to poverty, replacing older people (Oppenheim and Harker, 1996). This is not peculiar to the UK. The strange phenomenon of extremes of poverty in rich countries is a consequence of the flawed ideology of neoliberalism and free market principles that took hold so forcibly at this time. Globalisation acts in the interests of the most powerful corporate concerns to siphon profit out of local communities into global pockets. Conversely, localisation rebalances the economy by redirecting profits back into rebuilding local economies worldwide rather than serving global competition in which the poorest and most vulnerable lose every time. This does not end world trade, but that which can be produced locally or nationally serves the interests of the environment and social justice by being more sensitive to local needs. As we argue later, this rebalances biodiversity, a concept that embraces both environmental justice and social justice. Colin Hines says, the first step is a 'mindwrench'; we have to critique the unquestioning acceptance of globalisation in order to understand its inherent 'economic, social and environmental nonsense' (Hines, 2000: vii). This opens minds to viable alternatives based on fairer, more environmentally sustainable principles in which re-diversification leads to participatory democracy – a world based on cooperation in which local control of the economy leads to basic needs being met and local environments respected. Local economic development, supported by organisations such as the New Economics Foundation, provides interventions in this process by redirecting local money back into local communities. So in this period, as poverty escalated in the UK, we witnessed local activism in the form of credit union development and LETS schemes that formed part of a grassroots anti-poverty movement. It was out of these desperate times, as loan sharks roamed through Hattersley seeking out the most vulnerable, that Hattersley Credit Union was born, the first community credit union in North West England.

During the 18 years of the Thatcher/Major governments, 'the British ... lived under a regime whose leaders [did] their best to eliminate the word poverty from the English language, along with all talk about inequality and social injustice' (Donnison, 1998: 196). The health correlations of poverty were also wiped off the agenda, and 'health variations' replaced health inequalities. The stark reality, while this smokescreen was in place, was the rapid escalation of child poverty. By the end of this 18-year period, child poverty had risen from one in ten to one in three. The imperative behind this thinking was that poor people need to be made poorer in order to get them to work, and that rich people need to be made richer in order to get them to stay. The rich became richer and the poor became poorer, creating a legacy of social divisions that we still struggle with today.

Hegemony in action, we witnessed government cash incentives offered to the very poorest in our society with a hotline to 'snitch' on neighbours and friends for benefit fraud. People in poverty were set up against each other, and boundaries were defined between the 'deserving' and 'undeserving' poor. Single mothers and young men, particularly Black young men, were demonised as 'welfare scroungers', while senior citizens fell into the ranks of the 'deserving poor'. This conceptual paradox, that people in poverty could be divided in this way, made an immediate impact on communities. When Paul used the opportunity to apply for surplus from the 'European beef and butter mountain' created by European Economic Community (EEC) farming policies, we struggled with our ethical position. To qualify, people had to be on Income Support, creating an insidious division between deserving/undeserving. Once it had been agreed that the beef and butter would come in tins and packets, rather than whole and unpacked, we felt that we had to respond to the abject need of local people. We arrived at the community centre on the day of the first delivery to see a queue stretching twice round the precinct and up the road as far as the medical centre. People waited for hours, clutching benefit books in case of spot checks by local inspectors, and we hastily made sure cups of tea were freely available. At the checkpoint there were hostile confrontations when the sheer indignity of queuing was met by rejection. "Me a war veteran refused a ****** handout, and you a ****** single parent ripping off the state, it's disgraceful!". "Abandon the book check", said Paul, throwing bureaucracy to the winds.

> Poverty is not only about shortage of money. It is about rights and relationships; about how people are treated and how they regard themselves; about powerlessness, exclusion and loss of dignity. (Archbishop of Canterbury's Advisory Group on Urban Priority Areas, 1985)

The Third Way and New Labour

A landslide election in 1997 heralded the dawn of New Labour. After the harshness of the Thatcher years there was a rapturous welcome for the Blair government. However, it was not evident in that moment that this marked the end of socialism and the beginning of neoliberalism as a unifying factor between parties of Left and Right. At the time, Peter Mayo wrote, '[Neoliberal ideology] is now also a feature of parties in government which have been historically socialist. The presence of this ideology on either side of the traditional political spectrum in Western democracies testifies to the hegemonic nature of neo-liberalism' (Mayo, 1999: 2). A subtle change of emphasis was taking place. While maintaining the neoliberal principles of a free market, New Labour and its embrace of the Third Way located community and civil society as the interface between people and the state. This marked a distinct shift from Thatcher's attempt to convince us that there is no such thing as society. Not long after his election, Prime Minister Blair wrote: 'we all depend on collective goods for our independence; and all our lives are enriched – or impoverished – by the communities to which we belong …' (Blair, 1998: 4). This new approach to government was informed by the thinking of Anthony Giddens and the Third Way (1998, 2000), which we critique is some depth in a moment. New Labour combined strands of communitarianism – community as a life with meaning based on the mutual interdependence of individuals – and the role of the state in partnership with community in creating a quality of life. For the first time we find the language of partnership with community, of bold anti-poverty statements, of a preoccupation with regeneration projects, of widening access to education. In this context, community development has gained more policy recognition than it has known before, but with more worrying consequences.

The Blair government inherited a divided Britain with social divisions that had escalated during the 1980s under Thatcherism. In March 1999, at Toynbee Hall, Tony Blair delivered a speech on the legacy of Beveridge, the unanticipated high spot of which was his own personal and political commitment to end child poverty within 20 years. Going public on poverty was applauded by the social justice lobby, and a social policy programme was set to tackle child poverty, unemployment, neighbourhood deprivation and inequalities in health and educational achievement. CPAG found themselves working for the first time with a government that acknowledged the unacceptability of one in every three children growing up in poor families, and was encouraged by a raft of anti-poverty policies directed at children and poor families. But just below the surface, clear contradictions lurked between the interests of the state and the rights and responsibilities of parents. As Tess Ridge rightly points out, a state interest in children as future workers leads to policies that are qualitatively different from those which are concerned with creating better childhoods:

> Children who are poor are not a homogeneous group, although they are often represented as being so. Their experiences of being poor will be mediated by, among other things, their age, gender, ethnicity, health and whether or not they are 'dis'abled. In addition, children will interpret their experiences of poverty in the context of a diverse range of social, geographical and cultural settings. (Ridge, 2004: 5)

Let us take a glance at the world stage, where similar changes were being mirrored. In 1999, the World Bank and IMF also took a new focused approach to reducing poverty in which, in just the same way as the Blair government, participation in civil society was key, and the poor became written in as players in their own transformation. Insightfully critiquing this new move, Kane (2008: 197) cites Arundhati Roy's comments that while the World Bank policies are now written in 'socially just, politically democratic-sounding language … they use language to mask their intent … the language of dissent has been co-opted' (Roy, 2004: 74). This last point, the co-option of the language of dissent, is vital to understanding the struggle for participatory democracy in every context. In the UK, the transformative concepts at the heart of community development have been hijacked, diluted with intent and incorporated into government policies with impunity. The radical concepts related to an equalisation of power in society now become peppered through policies as a means to improving service delivery in communities. Laying the responsibility for poverty at the feet of the victims of injustice has nothing to do with lessening the divide between the poor and the privileged, and we are deluded if we think differently. Here we are identifying linked processes operating at national and global levels, informed by the same ideology, mutually reinforcing one another – with the biggest impact of all being on the poorest communities. This empty rhetoric of change simply obscures the reality that poverty is the fallout of neoliberalism.

The ideology around 'deserving' and 'undeserving' poor has become embedded in the public consciousness to such an extent that it is seen as a resistance to redistribution of wealth by the government (Killeen, 2008). In this way, we find that this notion of the 'undeserving' poor that justified transference of wealth from the *poor* to the *rich* under Thatcherism has created enduring resistance to redistributing wealth, even to pre–Thatcher levels. Poverty is much more than individuals managing on low incomes – we all pay the price: 'the health and wellbeing of all members of society are affected by the experiences of those living in the worst deprivation' (Dowler et al, 2001: 4). More than this, Killeen argues that poverty and discrimination contravene the Universal Declaration on Human Rights and that successive governments' refusal to incorporate the International Covenant of Economic, Social and Cultural Rights into UK law has entrenched negative public attitudes to people in poverty, and so undermined public will to eradicate poverty. At the same time, discrimination against people in poverty is becoming structured as 'povertyism' akin to racism or sexism, a view based on the belief that poor people are of lesser value (Killeen, 2008).

Anthony Giddens and the Third Way

Giddens attempts to present a practical politics based on proposals for the 'redefinition of social democracy after the death of socialism' (Mouffe, 2005: 56). He identifies five dilemmas that call for radical rethinking: globalisation; individualism; loss of the Left/Right political divide; relocation of politics outside the mechanisms of democracy; and ecological problems. This is an argument based on the end of socialism as the antithesis of capitalism, suggesting that there is now no alternative to capitalism. He accuses Social Democrats of seeing individualism as problematic and failing to grasp it as an opportunity for a greater partnership between the state and civil society, that individualism heralds the end of collectivism and calls for a new definition of rights and responsibilities, an opportunity for greater democratisation. Third Way politics, according to Giddens, aims to 'help citizens pilot their way through the major revolutions of our time: *globalization, transformations in personal life* and our *relationship to nature*' (Giddens, 1998: 64). He sees globalisation as positive, extending far beyond the global market. And, as a proponent of free trade, paradoxically, he suggests that we can offset globalisation's more destructive aspects by concerning ourselves with social justice. In these ways he set the stage for a fundamentally changed New Labour that found expression in the Blair government's attempts to create a new democratic state.

A powerful critique of Giddens comes from Chantal Mouffe (2005), who challenges the contradictions inherent in a 'post-political' vision of a world beyond Left and Right, beyond hegemony and beyond antagonism. This is a world in which all public space for critical dissenting dialogue has been removed: we are all on the same side, the state and civil society in partnership to 'widen democracy'. At the very least we need to question the power relations that underpin such partnerships when 'organisations that are well-resourced in human and financial capital have expected ill-resourced community groups and relatively poorly resourced voluntary organizations to engage with them on equal terms' (Craig and Taylor, 2002: 142). Giddens sees the Third Way as 'one-nation politics', as non-conflictual, that any disagreements can be overcome by dialogue and education. His attempt to renew social democracy as beyond class politics requires an acceptance of the benefits of globalisation. A fundamental contradiction in his thinking, however, is the refusal to identify the links between global market forces and the acceleration of world crises of justice and sustainability. This presents a dangerous obscuring of the real challenges facing democracy. For instance, McLaren and Jaramillo identify 'a central antagonism of the current historical moment [as] that of empire': in the name of global democracy, the 'transnational ruling elite is being afforded a rite of passage to scourge the earth of its natural resources while besieging the working-class, women, children and people of color' (2007: 63). As with many of us, they raise the issue of Hurricane Katrina as global exposure of the 'race', class and gender warfare in the US, and importantly direct attention to the fact that, post-Katrina, fundamental questions about democracy have not been raised. Giroux critiques the twin Gulf crises, that of Katrina and Iraq, highlighting the escalating *politics of disposability* as a product of neoliberal times that heralds a crisis of democracy. The politics of disposability is a concept central to any anti-discriminatory practice, capturing the way in which some lives are seen as 'disposable' in political times in which we are defined by the contribution we make to the economy. These strange paradoxes, a war fought in the name of peace and a domestic crisis in which a whole population is abandoned to the consequences of flood, mask the 'race', class, gender and 'able-bodied' dimensions of injustice.

Giroux problematises the racist dimensions of the 'politics of disposability': a pair of Black feet with cardboard 'shoes' held in place by rubber bands is photographed on the front cover of his book (2006a). It poses questions of who? where? what? why? how? in the minds of anyone who sees it, defying the reality that it could capture the racism inherent in life in the US today. A new dominant ideology of the market sells to us as common sense a morality much more dangerous than the New Right's demonisation of the lone mother. It is a politics that justifies lives that are more valuable based on our roles as producers and consumers. The unproductive are considered expendable and abandoned to fend for themselves as they cannot be justified economically; investment in the public collective good is 'dismissed as bad business' (Giroux, 2006b). Giroux warns that these are 'dark times' in which our struggles should challenge war as a political act in the name of peace and markets as a measure of democracy. Interestingly, these are the times in which we welcome the first African-American president of the US, Barack Obama, elected to office just a couple of years after Hurricane Katrina, and the humiliation of George Bush on the world stage as he abandoned the lives of the mainly Black people of New Orleans to the floods.

Let us return to look deeper beneath the surface of ideas sold to us as 'post-political'. The picture painted is that of a non-adversarial context, a vitally important point to grasp. Mouffe suggests that Giddens and Beck use the term 'post-political' to suggest that we no longer have collective identities formed out of we/they dichotomies; we are in times in which political frontiers have evaporated under individualism, and we are 'now expected to live with a broad variety of global and personal risks without the old certainties' (Mouffe, 2005: 48). Adversarial politics is obsolete in this view.

> Individualisation destroys the collective forms of life necessary for the emergence of collective consciousness and the kind of politics which corresponds to them. It is therefore completely illusory to try to foster class solidarity, given that the main experience of individuals today is precisely the very destruction of the conditions of collective solidarity. The growth of individualism undermines trade unions and parties and renders inoperative the type of politics which they used to foster. (Mouffe, 2005: 49)

Within this perspective, the enemy becomes those who dissent; those who challenge this view are seen as hindering progress, as illegitimate and 'must be excluded from the democratic debate' (Mouffe, 2005: 54). The end of the adversarial model of politics, central to Beck and Giddens' argument, thus denies the importance of both 'antagonism' (conflict between enemies) and 'agonism' (conflict between adversaries), the latter identified by Mouffe as central to the transformation of existing power relations necessary to the counter-hegemonic process. This lack of understanding of the role of the adversary in transformative change is missed by Beck and Giddens. Mouffe is a pluralist, she believes that power is held in multiple contexts and should not be seen as solely a class struggle. She acknowledges Marxism as key to our understanding of capitalism, as crucial to our understanding of the role of economic power in the structuring of a hegemonic dominance. But we need to widen the political frame – evidenced by the praxis of the new social movements that have transformed how we understand the world. In other words, within a class analysis we would not have developed the thinking which led to the liberating action associated with civil rights, women's rights, children's rights, gay rights, 'dis'ability rights and ecological responsibility. Class is crucial to our understanding of hegemony and the forces of subordination, but as a metanarrative it subsumes the complexity of a plurality of oppressions. Mouffe's key challenge to Third Way thinking is in its total oversight of any analysis of the structures of power, so vital to the success of a counter-hegemonic process. She accuses Beck and Giddens' dismissal of the adversarial model as a consequence of them being unable to conceptualise 'the hegemonic constitution of social reality' (Mouffe, 2005: 54).

In Third Way politics, the shift to self-help fudges the issue of redistribution of resources. The myth of 'social capital' leading to social cohesion is naïve. It rests on the false assumption that communities are homogeneous spaces without diversity. Communities are living systems where conflict and cooperation co-exist, and they are inextricably bound up in the web that connects us all to a social, political and economic macro-structure. An ideology of self-help places the responsibility for a just society at the feet of those who are most targeted by injustice, neatly absolving any collective responsibility for the forces of structural discrimination which create the injustices in the first place. If we allow ourselves to be persuaded that our practice can be based on self-help we overlook the forces that continue to privilege the few and marginalise the many: 'self-sufficiency, the ideas that "left to their own devices" (and their current resources) poor communities would lift themselves out from poverty just fine, makes for an attractive myth but a regressive policy' (Berner and Phillips, 2005: 23).

The state of our children

> The true measure of a nation's standing is how well it attends to its children – their health and safety, their material security, their education and socialization, and their sense of being loved, valued, and included in the families and societies into which they are born. (UNICEF, 2007: 1)

This statement offers us a sound basis on which to consider the UK's standing. A UNICEF report on childhood in rich countries, produced in February 2007 (available at www.unicef.org.uk), ranked the UK at the bottom of 21 countries on an overall measure of child well-being. It produced a collective gasp of disbelief, but nothing more on the part of the general public. Such a massive contradiction as a rich country like the UK destroying the hopes of its future generations is readily dismissed as unrealistic. Child poverty in the UK remains hidden beneath the surface of prosperity, and justice remains blinkered. Yet poverty is still the single biggest determinant of educational failure, situating New Labour's rally cry, 'Education! Education! Education!', as a stark contradiction of terms as a route out of poverty for children. It seems that poor children are caught in a chicken-and-egg predicament. For this reason, we will focus on an analysis of child poverty.

As we approach the milestone to *halve* child poverty by 2010, activists are joining together under the Campaign to End Child Poverty banner to increase public awareness and to assert pressure on the government to 'keep the promise'. The Campaign to End Child Poverty is an alliance of more than 150 organisations including children's charities, child welfare organisations, social justice groups, faith groups, trade unions and others, concerned about the unacceptably high levels of child poverty in the UK. In October 2008 the Campaign organised a demonstration: 10,000 people marched through London demanding that the 2010 target be met, calling for milestones along the way to keep progress on target. The Department for Children, Schools and Families has called for a consultation on the Child Poverty Bill aimed at embodying in law the 2020 target to *eradicate* child poverty, which is progress, but unless analyses of child poverty are taken to more complex levels the outcome will be fruitless. We need to get our thinking inside the links between distributive justice and cultural justice, so that gender and 'race' are understood in relation to the traditional class struggle, not as competing with it, but as interacting with it to continue to privilege Whiteness and maleness (Lister, 2008).

When he made his promise to end child poverty by 2020 in the Beveridge Lecture in March 1999, Tony Blair stressed that social justice is about merit and that life changes should depend on talent and effort, on rights and responsibilities; he failed to address prejudice and discrimination and the experiences that rob certain social groups of their right to dignity and self-esteem. His aim was to break the cycle of disadvantage by ending social exclusion and deprivation so that 'being poor should not be a life sentence' (cited in Gordon, 2008: 159). New Labour has been the first government to go public on child poverty, 'giving child policies greater prominence than any in 100 years' (Gordon, 2008: 158). But when children are not placed at the heart of the matter, childhood well-being is sacrificed for 'wholly inadequate' social justice policies that miss the point. We have become stuck in an ongoing struggle trying to 'keep the promise' for 2020 based on deferred gratification that children can wait for adulthood in order that their lives improve. But by then it is too late. The legacy of child poverty has taken its toll.

So how do we perceive poverty and how is it measured? CPAG uses Peter Townsend's definition of poverty based on individuals, families and groups having access to an adequate diet, participating in activities and having living conditions typical to their own society. This is a measure of relative poverty that is based on marginalisation or the resources to participate in society. Consensus on how to measure this is still disputed: the government uses a measure without adjustment for housing costs, whereas CPAG use a more realistic yardstick to indicate real disposable income by adjusting for housing costs. Clearly, the latter allows families with children to be more visibly at risk.

The global banking crisis that led to a global recession in 2008 has created a massive rise in unemployment, falling house prices, house repossessions and debt in the UK. The crisis of credit created by the unfair practices of the banking system before the recession resulted in borrowers' vulnerability to debt as the impact of the downturn hit home. Ironically, the recession falsely lowers child poverty levels by reducing median income, but it is vital for the government in recession not to cut public spending on child policies as the impact of straitened times hits poor families hardest (Brewer et al, 2009). Adrian Sinfield echoes Smith and Middleton's (2007: 13) warning, 'Loss of employment is the single most significant cause of entry to poverty' (2009: 6), and those in low-paid and marginal jobs are at risk, with less savings and less redundancy pay. For this reason, policies that reverse rising levels of unemployment are vital to keeping poverty levels down.

Social mobility has been the preoccupation of New Labour policy, but the reality is that it has worsened. Since wider concerns about child well-being were triggered by the UNICEF report highlighting the extremely poor quality of life for UK children, Tomlinson and Walker (2009) have constructed a model of child well-being to work alongside a model of poverty so that the complex causal links between the two can be better understood. They challenge the limitations of 'one-track' policies when the multi-dimensional indicators suggest that poverty needs to be tackled along all its dimensions if children are to benefit. For instance, it is apparent that the well-being of parents has a massive impact on their children, and that neither income nor employment alone is sufficient to eradicate the impact of poverty and diminished childhood well-being. To capture the complex interrelationships, first they measure poverty at the household level along the following dimensions: financial strain, material deprivation, the physical environment (a combination of housing and neighbourhood), psychosocial strain, civic participation and social isolation. Second they measure four dimensions of child well-being: home life, educational orientation (attitude to school and teachers), low self-worth (anxiety, depression, self-esteem) and risky behaviour (smoking, truancy, drug-related behaviour). It is particularly important to understand these complex dimensions if policy is to be able to target the aspects that most seriously impact on childhood as these are likely to most seriously affect

Child poverty in 'Black and White'

Moss Side, Manchester (UK), 2008

life chances throughout the lifespan. The most important impact of this research is that it prioritises 'child poverty and well-being in the here and now' rather than the policy emphasis we have seen on deferred gratification to adulthood. We need to get to grips with the unacceptable burden of poverty that we have placed on children today (Tomlinson et al, 2008).

> Until politics engages effectively with the wider struggle against racism, it is impossible for the demands of social justice to be met. (Craig et al, 2008: 245)

The racialised dimensions of child poverty leave those from minority ethnic families at most risk. Whereas 30% of all children are growing up in poverty, a different picture emerges when we look at ethnicity: 27% of White children are growing up in poverty, whereas this figure escalates to 36% Indian, 41% Black Caribbean, 56% Black non-Caribbean and 69% Pakistani and Bangladeshi children, based on 2006/07 statistics (CPAG, 2008). Similarly, 'dis'abled children or those with a 'dis'abled parent are much more at risk of poverty, inadequate housing and social exclusion from public and community services (Flaherty et al, 2004). In addition to this, we begin to see anomalous concentrations of poverty. For instance, London, with a thriving economy that has generated 620,000 jobs in the past 10 years, has a child poverty rate of 39% (Oppenheim, 2007). We know that poverty creates ill health and premature death; in the UK, children of those in the bottom social class are five times more likely to die from an accident and 15 times more likely to die in a house fire than those in upper social classes (Flaherty et al, 2004). So you begin to see that when we dig beneath the surface, we begin to make more critical connections that provide us with a complex picture of the interlinking dimensions of poverty. The correlation between unemployment, poor mental health, homelessness, school exclusions, children in care/leaving care and high levels of youth suicide add further depth to that picture (Howarth et al, 1999). This is not only a profound social injustice, but its cost is immense to society as a whole.

Widening this deliberation, UNICEF, in its report *State of the world's children 2005: Childhood under threat* (2005), provides evidence that more than one billion children, one in every two children in the world, are denied the healthy and protected upbringing defined by the Convention on the Rights of the Child (1989), and are reduced to growing up in poverty. These are consequences of neoliberal capitalism and therefore a choice that profit is more important than justice.

In relation to the interface of social and environmental justice, Crescy Cannan emphasises that not only is the environmental crisis a crisis for us all, but it disproportionately affects both the poor and the South, and so 'intensifies forms of inequality and threatens collective goods – thus it is a human crisis as well as a threat to the entire planet' (Cannan, 2000: 365). Too few people are consuming too much. Our challenge is to change the unsustainable living habits of the West.

Sustainability and social justice involve the wealthy examining the destructive nature of consumer lifestyles in much the same way as anti-discriminatory practice involves Whites understanding the nature of White power and privilege. First, it is vital to understand that 'humanity has the ability to make development sustainable – to ensure that it meets the needs of the present without compromising the ability of the future to meet their own needs' (Brundtland, 1989: 8, cited in Adebowale, 2008: 251). This concept of *trusteeship*, central to the thinking of Ruskin and subsequently Gandhi, who was profoundly influenced by Ruskin's ideas, emphasises our collective responsibility to hand over the world to successive generations in better working order than we inherited it. This calls for better-developed theory and action on the interrelationship between the economy, environment and society. Our point here is that if we allow ourselves to become depoliticised, we fail to notice that social divisions are polarising, and the natural world has been thrown out of balance. This evidence must be set against our social justice and sustainability principles, and be considered in relation to local practice and global action.

Our consciousness remains partial if we focus our analysis on a personal/local level and fail to notice the ways in which these are social trends that are linked to structural injustices. Our practice will address the symptoms and overlook the causes. In this sense, it is vital that these trends are set within wider issues of world poverty and its gendered and racialised dimensions. Peter Townsend, as a critical commentator on world poverty and on behalf of UNICEF, talked about the UK escalation in child poverty as a 'neglect-filled Anglo-American model which unless there is massive investment in children we will head for economic catastrophe' (Townsend, 1995: 10-12). It seems that his prediction had substance.

Globalisation

Globalisation is not a new phenomenon; it is the force that provided the foundations for empire and slavery. But while the beginnings of globalisation are rooted in colonialism and the drive for wealth and power of European nations to exploit the raw materials and labour of indigenous people, the last three decades have seen that process accelerated by three major influences: computer technology, the increased power of multinational corporations and the dismantling of trade barriers under a neoliberal, free trade approach. The result has been the increased destruction of indigenous cultures founded on biodiversity, increased polarisation of poverty and privilege and widespread environmental degradation. Self-interest has replaced common responsibility, and Seabrook refers to the Western poor as the 'dead souls of democracy': 'the US and Europe have performed a vanishing trick on their own poor [and] ... this makes poor people harder to see in the rest of the world as well' (Seabrook, 2003: 10).

Simply speaking, capitalism has re-formed on a global level, exploiting the most vulnerable people and environments of the world in the interests of the dominant and privileged. It is important to understand that not only is this a form of corporate capitalism where the most powerful systems of the West dominate the world economically, but it also carries with it cultural implications. The western worldview, with its embedded political, cultural, racial, patriarchal, heterosexual, ecological and epistemological attitudes, is beaming its message across the world within the free trade process to reinforce structures of oppression based on 'race', gender, age, sexuality, faith, ethnicity and 'dis'ability.

> Neoliberal globalization is not simply economic domination of the world but also the imposition of a monolithic thought ... that consolidates vertical forms of difference and prohibits the public from imagining diversity in egalitarian, horizontal terms. Capitalism, imperialism, monoculturalism, patriarchy, white supremacism and the domination of biodiversity have coalesced under the current form of globalization.... (Fisher and Ponniah, 2003: 10)

It is in respect of this statement by Fisher and Ponniah that we suggest an understanding of the concepts of hegemony and counter-hegemony are vital. We say this because all sites of oppression also offer key sites of resistance, intervention and transformation, and it is this counter-hegemonic purpose that is of vital consequence to participatory practice if it is to maintain a commitment to social justice and sustainability. Borg and Mayo (2006) remind us of the centrality of this idea to critical practice by introducing de Sousa Santos's analysis of counter-hegemonic globalisation to their analysis of globalisation's impact on adult education policy in Southern Europe. Counter-hegemonic globalisation is a form of resistance to hegemonic globalisation. It reaches from grassroots participation through networks and alliances in movement for change for justice at a global level and is committed to countering the impact of globalisation. This is acutely relevant to our argument for transformative change. Without this insight, practice is not even touching the edges of injustice. Rooted, as it is, in anti-discriminatory analysis, transformative practice cannot justify an approach that focuses on the local and overlooks global perspectives on oppression. Unregulated markets, a free market economy and globalisation do nothing to protect the natural world and the most vulnerable people of the world from the drive of capitalism to produce at lowest cost and maximum profit. We are witnessing the rise of a counter-hegemony that emphasises shared responsibility for all in common humanity, that a globalised world connected by technology and trade must also be connected by shared values and accountability. You can investigate how to link your local practice to this movement for ethical globalisation through the New Economics Foundation website (www.neweconomics.org).

The International Forum on Globalisation is an alliance of North–South activists, economists, scholars and researchers providing analyses and critiques on the cultural, social, political and environmental impacts of economic globalisation. It was formed in 1994 out of a common concern that we were being led into a period of historic change more significant than any since the Industrial Revolution without discussion of the liberal, free trade principles on which it was built by the World Trade Organization (WTO), the IMF, the World Bank, the North American Free Trade Agreement (NAFTA) and other such bureaucracies. The aim was to stimulate new thinking, collective action and popular education about this changing state of world affairs. Vandana Shiva, a director of the International Forum on Globalisation, offers an eco-feminist perspective on the urgency for a global analysis to inform local practice:

> As the globalization project unfolds, it exposes its bankruptcy at the philosophical, political, ecological and economic levels. The bankruptcy of the dominant world order is leading to social, ecological, political and economic non-sustainability, with societies, ecosystems, and economies disintegrating and breaking down. (Vandana Shiva, quoted in Fisher and Ponniah, 2003: 1)

Ecological thought emphasises biodiversity and the way that indigenous cultures have evolved in harmony with their natural environments. Cultural diversity thus becomes essential for biological diversity and histories based on local economic development offer alternatives for the future that reflect values other than consumer lifestyles. Eco-feminism takes this a stage further, identifying a gendered difference in the way that women use principles of 'harmony, co-operation and interconnection' to challenge male principles of competition, 'discrimination, extremism and conflict' (Young, 1990: 33). On this basis, for decades women of the world have been organising and theorising an alternative worldview based on harmony and cooperation, non-violence and equality to create a new way of knowing which 'integrates truth with love, beauty and wholeness' (Reason, 1994: 14).

Participatory democracy

So, let us gather our thoughts together at this point and consider how we can progress this search for a new way of seeing the world. So far in this chapter we have concentrated on the troubled times in which we find ourselves. This has taken us from worldview issues, such as John Gray's critique of western civilisation with its claims of superiority over other cultures, to the manifestation of such a worldview, a world divided by poverty and privilege. Gray's challenge is that we find 'a path through the ruins in whose shadows we presently live' (Gray, 2007: 268-9). The global crisis over issues of social justice and sustainability presents a pattern in which divisions are increasing. In the rich countries of the West this presents a picture of disproportionate divisions of poverty and privilege; in other words, rich people are getting richer and poor people poorer. The strange paradox is that within this trend, poverty targets children in particular, and most particularly children from Black and minority ethnic (BME) families. The 2007 UNICEF report accused the UK of creating unhappy childhoods, and the US has been exposed for abandoning mostly Black lives in the crisis caused by Hurricane Katrina in 2005. Without doubt, we see a worldview that is struggling to make sense of its reality. At the same time, the process of globalisation is magnifying these values across the world as a whole. Vandana Shiva says: 'Capitalism, imperialism, monoculturalism, patriarchy, white supremacism and the domination of biodiversity have coalesced under the current form of globalization' (Shiva, quoted in Fisher and Ponniah, 2003: 1).

Reassuringly, Adebowale (2008) reminds us that we have the ability to create a sustainable and just world while meeting the needs of future generations. Not only do we have the ability, we have the moral responsibility, if we frame this within the notion of *trusteeship* as embraced by Ruskin and Gandhi, to pass the world over to our children in better working order than we inherited it. But if you find these big ideas somewhat daunting, the encouraging fact is that transformative change begins in community and collectively gathers strength. Our emphasis is that the change we work with in our everyday practice must be situated within these bigger global challenges if it is to be relevant. Let us picture the story of Barack Obama, who started his working life as a community worker in Chicago, and is now the first African–American US president. We would remind you that this is living evidence of the change brought about by local anti-racist action, expressed collectively through the civil rights movement.

Restating our position, participation is a transformative concept, it is the antithesis of isolation, marginalisation, exclusion, powerlessness and alienation. We advocate working with this concept at every level, from worldview to community projects. Here, we want to consider its relevance when applied to democracy as a way of re-visioning our way forward. As a counter-hegemonic force, action for participatory democracy is becoming evident. The Learning for Democracy Group (2008), discussed in Chapter 9, has taken the initiative forward in Scotland, and this has had an impact on the consciousness of others outside Scotland. Participatory democracy, if it is to have a transformative, radical dimension, and if social movements are to successfully launch a challenge to neoliberal definitions of democracy, calls for principles of *freedom* and *equality* to include concepts of *dissent* and *difference* (Laclau and Mouffe, 2001). Building democracy on dissent and difference foregrounds discriminatory power relations, enabling them to be more visibly challenged and changed.

So, in order to make that fundamental leap from treating people as the objects of policy to developing people's role as active subjects in politics, we must see the challenge as both intellectual and political (Shaw and Martin, 2000). In other words, it is imperative that theoretical analyses embrace both structural power as well as identity and difference at the same time as action in civil society opens up critical public spaces for a new citizenship, a thinking, confident, autonomous approach to democracy, for 'in order to "democratize democracy" ... there is an urgent need to politicize politics' (Shaw and Martin, 2000: 410). Working together with people to create new forms of collective identity through consciousness is the basis of a re-politicisation in which collective action from community calls for a new form of democratic participation. We now move on to consider how this can be framed within a participatory worldview.

THREE

A participatory worldview

> The human being is essentially a holistic being who lives in integrated totalities. When the human being is forced to lead a fragmented life, he/she shrinks, is frustrated, diminished.... (Skolimowski, 1994: 91)

Skolimowski (1994), in *The participatory mind*, cogently argues that in order to change the world we have to change the way we think about it and the way we view it. The nature of our mind is the nature of our knowledge, the nature of our reality. In other words, he argues, ontology, a theory of being, and epistemology, a theory of knowledge, are intimately related; the way we see the world affects the way we act in it. This chapter explores the way we view the world and in particular how the forces of domination and subordination, outlined in Chapter 2, are supported by a particular worldview that has been increasingly challenged over the past 30 years. To do this we want to focus specifically on scientific thought, which may seem far away from the problems of alienation and fragmentation in the contemporary world, but is nonetheless a crucial piece in the jigsaw puzzle of how we think and act in the world, and the consequential nature of the world we have created.

We have already talked about the alienated nature of our times, including the fragmentation of the self, mind, body, heart and soul. This fragmentation does not make sense in any way, even physiologically. As Pert (1999) has shown, peptides, the biochemical manifestation of emotions, are not just found in the brain – all bodily functions are emotionally connected. Cognition, or our understanding of the world, is a phenomenon throughout the body, operating through a system that integrates mental, emotional and biological activities. This is why Ayuverdic, Chinese and other indigenous medicines are underpinned by more holistic approaches that integrate mind, body, spirit and emotions. A visit to a qualified practitioner will involve questions relating to a person's symptoms, including those other than physical. Diseases, within this view, are seen as dis'ease', or lack of balance, so physical symptoms may be reflecting emotional or psychological imbalance. Relationships within the self, between people and with nature lie at the heart of the participatory worldview that underpins participatory practice for community development as a practice for human and environmental well-being.

Although the challenge to current worldviews, particularly within western thought, has been more noticeable in recent years, it can be found much earlier in the work of writers and scientists such as John Dewey (1925) and Jan Christian Smuts (1926) during the early part of the 20th century, and reflects a paradigmatic shift in western thought that has been developing for at least a hundred years. Yet our democratic institutions, organisational structures and educational practices remain resilient to the changes that these new forms of thinking imply. Indeed, in the UK in recent years many appear to have become further entrenched in old thought processes and have become even more alienating. We will examine the basis of this challenge to existing worldviews, and then look at what it means in terms of the way we act in the world. Seeing the world from an integrative or participatory perspective has implications for our practice. Even those of us who think we have moved towards a participatory view of the world are often not aware how the western ideological perspectives pervade the very essence of our existence. This is a crucial part of the form-shaping ideology (Bakhtin, 1984) that has implications for our practice, through what Shotter (2006) calls a monological approach to the world.

The dominant worldview: the western mind

Most writers who critique the non-participatory nature of our worldviews point their finger at two figures in scientific history: Newton and Descartes, the former charged with creating a mechanistic or reductionist view of the world, the latter with the dualistic separation of mind from matter, subjective from objective. However, both represent a way of thinking that goes back to Plato and Aristotle, and certainly represent a different worldview from that which was developed by other philosophers in other civilisations, in India, Japan or China, for example. In many ways, the notion of West, implying the opposite of East, is a mental construct that developed from around the 1600s onwards in the minds of Europeans and subsequently their former colonies such as the US and Australia (Agnew, 1998).

A key element of this thinking is the notion that reality can ultimately be explained in terms of basic laws, discovered only through precise measurement. In other words, there are objective facts about the world that do not depend on interpretation, and it is improved forms of measurement that will lead us to the real 'truth'. The difficulty with this approach, however, is that in doing this you also strip away the essential nature of things and their meaning. It fails to acknowledge humans as whole beings that not only think but also feel, and need to experience meaning. Indeed, Dimasio (1994), the neuroscientist, has shown how those who have no emotion act irrationally and that emotional engagement is essential to how human beings make decisions and live in the world. Also essential is a human connection with nature. Dewey (1925) explored this in his book, *Experience and nature*, where he argued that under a dualistic perspective experience is dismissed as irrational and that nature becomes defined as separate from experience. However, to really understand nature we need to look at the world in an integrative way, combining different perspectives and knowledge, including science. For Dewey, knowledge is derived from embodied intelligence, not from mind alone. We can see from this how decontextualising humanity from the natural world creates internally alienated selves, as well as ecological problems (Heron, 1992).

The phenomenologists Husserl (1989) and Merleau-Ponty (1962) were also highly critical of the dualist perspective. They saw subject/object and world/nature as internally related: human consciousness and nature mutually constitute each other. The assumption is often made that the objects of, for example, mathematically formulated physical laws are more real than the phenomena they are describing. In other words, the abstract models for the supposedly hidden reality behind experienced phenomenon take on a higher ontological status than the experiences themselves. We could relate this to our comments on the reification of the economy within neoliberal ideology in Chapter 2. As Bateson (1972) said, 'the Map is not the Reality': it is like taking an Ordnance Survey map which shows symbols of roads, rivers, churches, and then believing and acting as if certain roads are red, others are brown and churches all have crosses on their towers. Merleau-Ponty (1962) talks about the primacy of perception, that the experience of perception is our presence in a moment when things, truths, values are constituted for us. For him, perception is a *nascent logos*, it teaches us outside all dogmatism, and in his sense 'perception' is knowledge being born. Such perception is holistic and almost pre-thought. Heron (1996) calls this 'being in the presence' of something, and sees it as a process of engaging all the senses, visual, auditory, tactile, kinesthestic, and that anything we experience is interrelational, interdependent and correlative. As soon as we try to describe an experience in words, which themselves are abstractions, we often lose its essence. Even when we tell the story, the telling in itself changes the perception of the experience, and is limited by the very nature of language. This is why images are so powerful and account for the success of communicating through multisensory media, like Facebook. Senge et al (2005), in *Presence*, see a participative experience as that point before which transformation takes place, and draw on the analogy of the experience as of being at one with nature. Much of the time we do not engage in such a 'perception' of the world: perception in everyday life is second-order perception (Merleau-Ponty, 1962). In other words, we look at the world through a prism of habitually established meanings rather than engaging with the experience itself. However, when our experience creates meaning, this results in a more participative mode of experience. This offers a different approach to science, sometimes known as the Goethean approach. 'The organising idea in cognition comes from the phenomenon itself, instead of from the self assertive thinking of the scientist themselves. It is not imposed on nature but received from nature' (Bortoft, 1996: 240; see also Haila and Dyke, 2006). Indeed, it has been argued that if we neglect our senses and perceptual capacities, this will lead to a lopsided development of human beings in general (Zeki, 1999; Goguen and Myin, 2000).

For the fundamentalist scientist, any way of understanding reality other than through 'objective' science is dismissed as 'magic' or 'biased'. There is an overall failure to recognise that 'reality' is only a reflection of how we look at it and a particular 'spiral of understanding'. The dominant worldview presents not only a straitjacket on how we think and act in the world, but also separates us from ourselves and how we express our understanding of the world. Of course, the western worldview is not alone in this. Historically, religion and other dominant systems of thought have done likewise. However, it is important to recognise that certain aspects of contemporary scientific thought are embedded in our culture. This is not to say such thinking is wrong: it is an extremely useful tool if used with awareness. For example, in understanding poverty we need statistics, and in understanding causes of problems we need systematic analysis. Our argument here is that such a view has come to dominate our systems as part of a grand narrative, and this thinking has become fundamentally unbalanced.

Take, for example, the current preoccupation with evidence-based practice and accountability in the public sector. Many voluntary groups, communities and public sector organisations spend much time and money on producing numbers that are deemed to measure the effectiveness of an initiative. This has the advantage of reducing complexity to simple terms so that someone not involved can deal with the information about what is happening in an abstract form. The belief is that such data are a reasonable reflection of the reality of the issues with which they are dealing. There are advantages to be gained in simplification and detachment, but if data are used alone in making decisions, the results can be irrational because something important has been missed out. It is about much more than just providing qualitative data, although this can help. When findings are presented not only through data but also through the stories of those involved, told by them directly to the decision makers, they respond with their whole being and often come to different conclusions. I (Margaret) remember the difference this action brought about when we managed to persuade local authority councillors to re-create their council chambers in the community centre for meetings related to our community. They heard the stories, trod the pavements, saw the sights and smelt the smells of our community, and experienced their decision-making powers differently as a consequence.

Of course, the notion that scientific knowledge or evidence is something created separately and is then 'translated' or 'transferred' into practice lies at the heart of this current preoccupation by those in public sector management with the perceived inability of practitioners to engage with that knowledge. The very problem is created by a dualist way of thinking; it sees practice as separate from science. In the evidence into practice or translational science debates is a failure to realise that the evidence that is being transferred into practice is only partial; real understanding can only come from an interactive process of engagement with practical reality, involving what Polanyi (1958) calls 'subsidiary awareness'. This is intuitive or first-order perceptual knowing. Instead of seeing the world as something out there, we need to view ourselves as embodied participants of a greater whole, and thereby become more responsive. In other words, our inner and outer worlds are connected and cannot be treated as unrelated. This notion also puts a different spin on the issue of generality. The craving for generality in a traditional scientific sense, when applied to society often leads to an imposition of general principles in inappropriate contexts, for example, we have tested this solution in Salford, so we can apply this to the whole of the UK. This ignores the necessary variety of human experience in specific contexts. As we see later, diversity is important for the survival both of humanity and of the planet.

Control through the application of blanket rules and measurement has been a key feature of current public sector approaches to management. The result has steadily reduced the spaces for creativity and engagement and a sense of authentic autonomy (Goodson, 2007). We have to have a sense of who we are in order to engage successfully in equal relationships (Doyal and Gough, 1991). Feeding 'the beast' or 'the suits', as interviewees described it in one evaluation, I (Jane) was involved in, not only takes up valuable time, but also reduces time to reflect and engage with people as essential feeling human beings. Thus, as March and Simon (1993) pointed out many years ago, the bureaucratic need for control creates the problems of client dissatisfaction that it seeks to solve. In relation to this, Goodson (2007) shows how such need to control has reduced job satisfaction in education and healthcare in such a way that it has taken away the passion and vocational element that originally motivated teachers and nurses in the first place. Those who have not retired early 'just do the job', and withdraw their hearts and minds from a sense of collective public purpose and meaning making.

Pirsig explores these ideas in the 1970s cult book *Zen and the art of motorcycle maintenance* (1974). He compares some organisations with a motorcycle and argues that they share systemic qualities in that they are sustained by structural relationships, even when they have lost their meaning and purpose. However, to tear down the organisation, like pulling apart a motorcycle, is to deal with the effects and not the causes when the real cause is the system of thinking. If you tear down an organisation but do not change the thinking, the patterns of thought that created it will repeat themselves. For the character in Pirsig's novel, the separation of subject and object is an artificial interpretation imposed on reality that destroys its quality or essence. In the case of the motorcycle, this is embedded in the craft that created it:

> Man [sic] is not the source of all things, as the subjective idealists would say. Nor is he [sic] the passive observer of all things, as the objective idealists would say. The quality which creates the world emerges as a relationship between man [sic] and his environment. He [sic] is a participant in the creation of all things. (Pirsig, 1974: 368)

The ecological worldview as a participatory worldview

The scientific method, with its emphasis on reductionism, objectivity and quantification, has served society well in terms of technical development, including medical science, but has also given rise to many social, health and environmental problems. By giving primacy to only one way of thinking about the world, much has been lost. As participatory practitioners we need to be aware that the solutions to many problems will not be found in current scientific approaches, but that does not mean 'throwing out the baby with the bathwater'. It can be complemented by ecological, holistic, systemic or integrative thinking, focusing on relationships between objects, the connections between the objects rather than the objects themselves. By integrating different ways of seeing the world, we can get a much broader view and therefore identify better solutions to problems. Einstein himself argued:

> A human being is part of a whole, called by us the Universe, a part limited in time and space. He [sic] experiences himself, his thoughts and feelings as something separate from the rest, a kind of optical delusion of his consciousness. (Einstein, 1950, cited in Calaprice, 2005: 206)

This type of thinking accepts the complexity of the social and physical world. When it looks at the relationships between phenomena rather than the parts, the network rather than the machine offers a better metaphor. Restoring health, for example, is not about fixing a specific body part but about restoring the balance between the physical, mental, emotional, spiritual and social dimensions of a person's life. The ecological paradigm fits with the notion, previously referred to, that the mind is not separate from the world; rather that reality is always in subjective–objective relation. According to Maturana and Varela (1987), cognition is not a representation of an independently existing world, but a continual bringing forth of the world through the process of living. Gregory Bateson (1979), anthropologist, biologist and founder of cybernetics, is one of the philosophers who started to explore these ideas in the 1960s and 1970s. Integrative ways of thinking were subsequently developed by a whole range of writers from many of the life and social sciences in fields such as psychology (Heron, 2005), management science (Reason, 1998; Marshall, 2004; Shotter, 2005), sociology (Habermas, 1984/87; Giddens, 1987), physics, biology, chemistry (Bortoft, 1996; Tiller, 1997; Pert, 1999; Capra, 2003), information technology, and form the basis of complexity science (Stacey, 1996). Bateson's key influence was that he was pivotal in encouraging us to move our focus from seeing 'things' to seeing patterns, that we are part of any field we study and, to understand the field, we must also reflect on ourselves as part of that world, what Capra calls the 'web of life'.

In his book of the same name, Capra (1996) describes some of the salient characteristics of the organisation of ecosystems that, he argues, are necessary to understand in order to develop sustainable human communities. The first characteristic is that of *interdependence*, namely, the fundamental nature of ecological relationships is that the behaviour of one member of the community depends on the behaviour of many others. Thus, the success of the whole community depends on the success of its individual members, while the success of the individual members depends on the community as a whole. To nourish a community means that you need to nourish relationships that create this interdependence. However, those relationships are not straightforward or linear. A small change introduced into an ecosystem can have a major effect. Small changes can spread out and be widened through ever-increasing, interdependent feedback loops, which may in time obscure the original source of the disturbance.

The second characteristic of ecological processes is that they are *cyclical*. One organism's waste becomes another organism's food. Nothing is wasted and this cyclical process ensures the system is kept in balance, and is therefore sustainable. Again, the feedback loops in an ecosystem are important in the provision of information to ensure that the system keeps in long-term balance. We can see now, within human communities, that sustainable patterns of consumption and production need to be cyclical too. Most businesses are not cyclical as they create enormous amounts of waste. However, in the current free market, the social and environmental costs of such production are treated as external variables in current accounting. Thus, not only is the environment treated as a free good, but so are the webs of social relations external to the companies concerned. The market, as a result, feeds back partial information concerning impact on the system as a whole, and this failure to add in the real external costs of pollution and exploitation of labour gives rise to the current crises of climate change and widening social divisions.

These cyclical exchanges of energy and resources in the ecosystem are sustained by the third set of characteristics of ecosystems defined by Capra, *cooperation, partnership and co-evolution*. Such notions appear somewhat at odds with the ideas contained in the neo-Darwinism focus on the survival of the fittest, where the emphasis is on competition and profit that underpins the free market forces of globalisation. By contrast, *cooperation, partnership and co-evolution* involve processes of integration and connection necessary for a flourishing world.

These processes are further sustained by the characteristics of *diversity and flexibility* that enable ecosystems and communities to survive and adapt to change. Ecosystems are always in constant flux but there are certain limits to change beyond which the whole system will collapse. The aim is to reduce the long-term stress in the system: maximising a single variable will eventually lead to the destruction of the system as a whole; optimising all variables will create a dynamic balance between order and freedom, stability and change. This means accepting that contradictions within communities are signs of diversity and viability. However, this can exist only where there are strong and complex patterns of interconnections. A healthy community needs members who are aware of the need for interconnectedness, so that information and ideas flow freely through the networks to create a flourishing whole. Rather than a naïve notion of social capital that assumes homogeneity in community, it calls for an understanding that communities are contested spaces that flourish when practical strategies knit them together as part of a diverse, cooperative, interconnected whole.

These ideas are captured in a story which I (Jane) heard at a conference on urban health in Antwerp in 1997. A group of community leaders from Bangladesh visited Glasgow as part of an urban development project focusing on health issues supported by the World Health Organization (WHO). The material well-being (such as access to running water, light, heat and affordable food) of some of the poorest estates in Glasgow was substantially higher than conditions found in their home country. However, in dialogue with local people, the visitors expressed their horror at the way older people were marginalised, the lack of a spiritual connection and the lack of a cohesive extended family, seeing this as of equal, if not more, importance for human well-being. This was poverty in their eyes.

An ecological worldview leads to different ways of viewing our relationship with the natural world. Take, for example, the decline of fish in the North Sea, and the policy solution of quotas to encourage the fishing industry not to over-fish so that stocks can be replenished. This comes from a non-participatory worldview. Increasingly, ecologists are seeing the ocean and the fishing communities whose livelihoods have depended on them as a whole. From the ocean's perspective, there is a need not only to reduce the level of fishing, but also to increase its biodiversity. It is the reduction of diversity that makes the ecosystem of the ocean more vulnerable, and through a process of negative entropy, reach a decline to the point of no return. For the community dependent on fishing, there is also a lack of diversity, since over-dependence on a declining industry will create potential long-term problems. But, like the fish, the short-term imperative is survival. Most arguments underpinning the development of European Union (EU) policy on fishing relate to measurement of fish numbers and whether such statistics reflect the true facts, unaware of the connections with the wider ecosystem and its destruction. An ecological approach is first to identify and see the connections between ocean diversity and community, and for policy makers to work with communities to generate a wider set of solutions based on diversity and balance.

The consequences of seeing the world in systems terms can be illustrated by the Foresight Report (2007) on obesity, which demonstrated that the common perception that people eating less and exercising more would solve the problem of obesity is an oversimplification of a complex issue. For the first time we have a report that takes a multifaceted approach to the relationships between individual biology, eating behaviours and physical activity, and those of the social, cultural and environmental context. Systems mapping was used to capture this complexity in order to demonstrate the relationships and constraints that may influence the future behaviour of a system at a particular moment in time. By looking at the whole in terms of issues of energy balance, Foresight's obesity systems map arguably represents the most comprehensive 'whole systems' view of the determinants of energy balance that exists. The map was then used to identify key determinants and relationships in order to visualise future scenarios that offered options for policy responses. Such systems mapping undertaken as part of a participatory process is potentially a powerful tool for changing the way we look at things. There are many examples of how this can be done in a variety of contexts in Burns' (2007) *Systemic action research*. However, it is important to remember that such a map is only a tool, albeit a powerful one if a community or group are involved in producing it. There is a danger that systems thinking becomes as deterministic as other ways of viewing the social and natural worlds. It is the core idea of the dynamic of relationships and process that is the essence of the approach.

Obesity is about more than just weight and lack of exercise. From a holistic perspective, it is about our relationship with our bodies and our relationship with the earth. Examples of action based on this understanding are provided by Sustain, an alliance of organisations dedicated to sustainable development. One such example is the Peabody Trust Active 8 Project. In 2007, this charitable housing trust and registered housing project broadened people's understanding of nutrition, with a week of events and workshops that addressed common health problems. Of particular interest are five projects that aim to get Peabody residents involved in food growing. These include the Gardening School, a project based at a school near to a Peabody estate in East London, where residents are involved in cultivating the land and planting vegetables and fruit with the support of a community gardener. There are sessions on how best to prepare the produce for marketing, and the income generated will be used to purchase new seeds, plants, compost and so on.

There are other concepts and metaphors that have arisen around systems thinking that have relevance to working with communities that throw a whole new light on notions of regeneration. A sustainable community is seen as one that makes a positive contribution to the well-being and health of its individuals (Hancock, 1993; Labonte, 1993, 1993a; Dwelly, 2001; Cave et al, 2004). According to Bird (2003), communities can be regenerative or degenerative. Regenerative communities are communities where individuals have a sense of involvement, commitment, learning and change. They actively encourage joyfulness, creativity, love and a sense of belonging, an understanding of the totality and a sense of wholeness. A core element is a sense of and the creation of meaning. Degenerative communities are those in which members experience lack of satisfaction, frustration, hatred and sorrow. Such degeneration is reinforced by actions within society that focus on instrumentality and consumption and where emotions and feelings are not allowed to be expressed, resulting in stagnation and even decline. For complex systems to retain regenerative aspects there needs to be some form of friction and an input of new energy which causes a sense of disorder, otherwise it will reach a state of equilibrium and die (Prigogine, 1997). However, too much change can cause chaos. So what is required is a combination of stability and change: development occurs in complex adaptive systems, like communities, on the edge of chaos (Pascale et al, 2000). This requires what is called corrective feedback: actions that constitute planned results aimed at fulfilling predetermined objectives. This is the common practice in public sector project management and evaluation. Indeed, this underpins the Achieving Better Community Development (ABCD) model (Barr and Hashagen, 2000). But it also requires something else: reinforced feedback. This type of feedback is unpredictable and will contain new information. Thus, healthy communities constantly operate through a set of contradictions and paradoxes that construct new information via two apparently opposing types of feedback, both necessary for maintaining dynamism. When we start to look at the world in a systems way, through a lens that sees the world in relation to ourselves, new understandings and actions are generated.

Arlene Goldbard (2006) recalls a friend, Gary Stewart, who led workshops for teenagers at ADFED, the educational wing of the popular music group Asian Dub Foundation (www.adfed.co.uk). Each participant learnt to compose and produce their own music using fairly primitive electronic sampling technology. Gary describes ADFED's philosophy as "conscious party mode", seamlessly joining pleasure and learning:

> "Some of these young people are under cultural attack, and they're not actually allowed to go and do extra activities. Their parents or guardians have to be convinced that a safe place for them can be provided so that they can interact with other people without being at risk. It's worked out as a 10-week block, and so there are specific technical headings that enable them to learn the specifics of music making. But in addition to that, other issues around racism and anti-deportation campaigns are discussed – they also bring up issues themselves, obviously. There are opportunities for them to talk about issues that affect them personally…. Basically, the music is used as a kind of metaphor. The workshops themselves are about exploring the rhythms of different sounds and exposing participants to connections. It's a bit like an extended metaphor for the connections between people, economics and history." (Cited in Goldbard, 2006: 131)

The need to look at the world as an interconnected system will be illustrated in the following section by exploring the way health and well-being have traditionally been addressed, separating 'health' from the broader whole.

Health and healthy communities from a participatory perspective: the dominant story

Nowhere is the dominant worldview so strong as in the area of health, or should we say illness, and the practice of medicine. Although, there is some fraying round the edges, dominating most people's view of health in western societies is that of fixing the body, and the person who does that is the doctor. Many studies over the years have been undertaken contrasting how people in different parts of the world talk about their health, and they consistently show how this view is not shared by every culture. In many indigenous communities and non-western societies, a much more holistic view is taken of health and ill health, resulting in very different approaches to health creation. So pervasive is the medical view of health in western society that it underpins a number of assumptions held by different professional groups, their responsibilities, how they behave towards one another and their expectations. This came into stark relief for me (Jane) two years ago when, during one of our faculty's many reorganisations, I ended up sharing an office with a colleague from social work. I knew we had a common interest in evaluation, but during our discussions it became clear that because I was from a healthcare context it was assumed I knew everything about illness, what the Swedes call a *sjukvård* (literally, sick care) perspective. Similarly, while working in community settings, it has often been a real uphill struggle to persuade those working in a community that health is more than medical care, and just as central to community development as the so-called 'health' sector. Similarly, it is difficult to persuade health professionals that they do not hold the remit for all health work. If we are to build healthy communities, we have to drop our masks and see the health and well-being of an individual and a community from a much broader perspective. By health, we mean an organism, whether an individual or community, in which all its aspects are fully integrated and functioning at individual and collective potential. It is functioning optimally when 'its capacity for interaction with its world is actualised and practised' (Murphy, 1999: 43).

So, to be clear, in this book we are taking a broader view of the notion of 'health', namely, health as well-being or wholeness (Labonte, 1994):

* feeling vital, full of energy
* having good social relationships
* experiencing a sense of control over one's life and one's living conditions
* having a sense of purpose
* being able to do things one enjoys
* experiencing a sense of connectedness.

Within the health promotion community of practice, there is much written about healthy communities and cities, and the ecological model of health that underpins the rhetoric (Dooris, 2006). Yet, as a community of practice, we find ourselves paying lip service to this participatory view of the world, subsumed under medical hegemony (Scott-Samuel and Springett, 2007). It pervades all government documents, research and project funding. Until recently, projects directed at promoting health and well-being have had to demonstrate that they were directed at heart disease, diabetes, specific cancers or suicide; the focus currently, however, is individual lifestyles, teenage pregnancy, drug or alcohol abuse, smoking, physical activity or weight control, or lifestyle diseases such as obesity or alcoholism. Where well-being is considered, it is differentiated as mental health promotion, tying it closely to mental illness. The dominant approach to health promotion still does not pay real attention to the complexity inherent in how people negotiate their everyday lives. It continues to objectify people into categories such as class, socio-economic, gender or ethnic group, labelling them as target groups, ignoring the relational aspects of their lives and therefore decontextualising so-called 'health-related behaviours'. Yet practices that create health and well-being are embedded in a co-creation process involving both the individual and the collective. This is often revealed in people's 'knowledgeable narratives' (Popay et al, 2003).

The policy solution to contemporary health promotion is to recruit 'lay' health workers or 'peer' health educators as a means of working with what are called 'excluded' and 'hard-to-reach' groups, in other words, those who have been marginalised or discriminated against (Baker et al, 1997; Altpeter et al, 1999; Cuijpers, 2002). Despite the use of techniques, such as participatory rapid appraisal in needs assessment (Cornwall and Jewkes, 1995; Collins, 2005), on the whole, such 'lay expertise' is seen as a means by which health promotion interventions are contextualised as the delivery point for pre-formulated health packages by 'external experts'. Local knowledge is not given any value as a source of experiential practical knowledge for developing the interventions themselves (Lacey et al, 1991). External interventions reflect the approach to practice that pervades health systems, and which privileges expert or scientific, generalisable knowledge as the only source for deciding what to do. Thus, knowledge creation is inherently top-down, emphasising experimental knowledge, that is, that which is tested through engaging in a rational experiment and then disseminated through systematic review to a largely health professional audience in keeping with a medical episteme. A culture in which professionals do not accord value to the skills and experience of community members is thus enhanced (Green and Mercer, 2001; Ansari et al, 2002).

Knowledge continues to be decontextualised from everyday reality. The different elements of lifestyle are separated out rather than seen as real issues that face people in their lives, with physical health as part of a larger whole of well-being and community, and ordinary people as thinking, feeling beings. The downgrading of the emotive, value-based aspects of thinking processes is perpetuated by privileging the rational and ignoring the meaning systems people share as a result of sharing the same social world (Bolam et al, 2003). In fact, the failure to understand and value different knowledge systems and cultures in a broader context has led to the differential impact of public health interventions, increasing the very health inequalities that they are trying to address. Indeed, if you take the issue of smoking cessation, you find that most smoking cessation initiatives have historically tended to reinforce health inequalities, since quit rates are most frequent among the most affluent (Jarvis and Wardle, 1999). The resistance of those in poverty to anti-smoking advice remains high, even in areas where resources for smoking cessation services have been substantive (Chesterman et al, 2002). Lawlor et al (2003) have argued that smoking can be deemed a rational response to everyday reality, involving a clear assessment of risk in relation to life chances as well as being a health promotion mechanism in itself. So-called hard-to-reach groups are more likely to relate to the advice of those living in similar circumstances rather than a health professional perceived as an authority figure with different cultural norms and experience (Richards et al, 2003, Springett et al, 2007).

At this point, I (Margaret) am mindful of Martha's story, as a single mother of two young children and community activist:

"I know I should really give up smoking. I can't afford it and it's no good for me. But, you know, when I can't stand any more and the kids get too much for me, I go upstairs and light up. I know about passive smoking, and don't want to damage their health, so I pace up and down puffing away, until I feel better. At least this way, I calm down and they don't get battered!"

We are using health promotion as an illustration, but similar examples could be used in any other area, such as transport, housing and regeneration, where a particular perspective dominates and where the part is not seen as connected to the whole. What we hope to demonstrate here is the way that external interventions come from a reductionist view of the world. If you want to change something, it makes sense from a systems perspective to focus on the part of the system that you believe is likely to generate the most change. In doing so, it is necessary to be aware of the interconnections between that part of the system with other parts, as any change will impact on the system as a whole as it rebalances, accommodates or moves to a new form or state in response to the change. However, an intervention is not normally considered in this way. It is treated as an isolated phenomenon, acting on an isolated individual, operating in vacuum. Moreover, when 'evidence' is being collected to measure its impact, data collection is restricted to the isolated phenomenon. If there are consequences beyond the immediate intervention, these are rarely picked up.

If we conceptualise interventions in a different way, and see them rather as an interruption to an existing dynamic flow, activity or pattern, they take on a different feel, particularly when internally rather than externally determined. Through reflection and then action on those reflections, the social norms that have been taken for granted can be interrupted and diverted by actions at a community level. So, when we talk about social action in system terms, we are talking about what can be called 'appropriately deliberate interruptions' as colleagues from the Master's degree in Community Work at Bergen University College call them. These are much more likely to introduce new energy or change existing energy flows to the benefit of the whole.

Thinking ecologically about health

In the past 20 years, there has been a push, both directly or indirectly, for an alternative more ecological perspective in the West. It is underpinned by a salutogenic approach to health (Antonovsky, 1996), that is, what makes you well rather than what makes you sick, and the concept of balance. This has come from two quarters: one, the alternative/complementary healthcare movement, particularly Chinese and Ayuverdic medicine, which are systems of understanding with regard to health that have been practiced for thousands of years; the other, the professional field of health promotion itself. Over 20 years ago, WHO supported the Ottawa Charter on Health Promotion. In the years following, Hancock and Perkins (1985) developed a model, emphasising the interrelationships that characterise health, the 'mandala of health'. The model incorporated the notions of health found in many native cultures around the world, that of body, mind and spirit, but also notions of ecology – human beings' relationships with their environment, including community and society. Hancock (1993) further developed the model, characterising a healthy community as one that balances health, environment and the economy in a way that is viable, equitable and sustainable. A holistic and socio-ecological view of health also meant a commitment to issues of equity and social justice. If health is a matter of balance or wholeness, as characterised by the Anglo-Saxon root of the word 'health', then inequality in social and economic terms represents a lack of balance, not only in inequalities in health, but in the health of humanity as a whole. In this way, one could see unemployment as a lack of balance in the distribution of work, current economic difficulties as a lack of balance between short-term profit and long-term gain, or between wealth and poverty, the market and the common good, or between the global market and the local economy. The solution is a focus on the whole system, beginning with the balance of a healthy city or community. This implies the involvement of both the community and other non-health sectors in decision making, particularly local authorities, who have a key role in creating health (Blackman, 2006) through their decisions concerning employment, education, housing, water and air pollution and poverty. Internationally, this thinking led to the development of the Healthy City and Community movement, mentioned in the introduction to this book.

The choice of the word 'mandala' for the model is significant. Wood (2007) describes a mandala as a universal symbol of the self. It is thought to express the totality of the psyche in all its aspects, including the relationship between the self and the whole of nature. The mandala, Wood argues, always points to the ultimate wholeness of life, and the overwhelming majority of mandala symbols are characterised by the circle, the ultimate symbol of wholeness. To Jung, the universal occurrence of the mandala structure in the mythical motifs of different world cultures signified that it represented the collective component in the human psyche, which he called an archetype. The symbol occurs in rock engravings, in sun worship, in modern religion, in myths and dreams, in the ground plan of cities and churches and in Navajo sand paintings to restore health. Its use in explaining the meaning and significance of existence, Storr (1974) suggests, shapes an underlying attitude to the world. The contemplation of a mandala is meant to bring inner peace, a feeling that life has again found its meaning and order, even in people who know nothing about it (Wood, 2007). Story, too, is about the power of the circle:

> "We prompt community music and story circles so the participants can
> begin to hear and appreciate their own voices. We pick a theme for
> the circles, maybe some compelling incident in their local history or
> current event, and community members start telling and listening to

each others' stories and songs. This becomes compelling, like fresh news, because participants often hear new information about a common experience. From the circles, a complex sense of a particular place begins to emerge. The songs and stories, which are often recorded, become the basic ingredients of community celebrations that end the second phase [of a Roadside residency]. We often have these celebrations around potluck suppers. People get up and play music, sing, and tell the stories that they've by now somewhat crafted. Through big, structured celebrations, the community voice proclaims itself in public."
(D. Coorke, Artistic Director of Roadside Theater, Appalachia)

Yet although these notions of a mandala of health speak in different ways to many people, the practical reality of changing the way people act in relation to specific issues in the health establishment, and those institutions that contribute to health, has not fundamentally changed. People were attracted to the idea of creating healthy communities and cities, but found it difficult to implement in practice due to strong institutional barriers and constraints (Berkeley and Springett, 2006). It constitutes participatory thinking, but not participatory practice. Why? Because the majority of us think in a dualist and non-participatory way, and because the whole concept challenges existing power structures which are themselves the consequence of thinking dualistically. Take, for example, the notion of health inequality. This is now at the forefront of contemporary public health practice, yet what does that practice entail? In the UK at least there is the continued mapping of the problem, with the expectation that those responsible for commissioning health services to measure their practice in terms of equity will eventually recognise sticking plaster solutions. In essence, this is treatment of the symptoms of inequality, not the causes. As we said in Chapter 2, we have seen the hegemonic appropriation of the language of participation and community development, but little to convince us that this has anything to do with equality.

The conflict between a holistic model and the Cartesian world of health can be seen most clearly in the area of community arts. In this field most participants and practitioners involved share a common, holistic view of health (Angus, 2002). Health is seen as encompassing more than the absence of disease, and is, rather, a positive concept, including issues such as personal and social identity, human worth, autonomy, responsibility, self-direction and control, participation in making political decisions, cultural and spiritual needs and celebration. While the social determinants of health are acknowledged, what distinguishes the way the concept is used by community arts is its very emphasis on wholeness and relationship rather than individual parts, on essence, rather than the measurable and material. Practitioners of arts projects thus hold a much more expansive and ecological view of health than the many public health practitioners, who still assume a concept of individual or population physical health as understood by conventional medicine. The holistic view is reinforced by the language of the arts that tends to deal with the whole rather than parts for expression, and these are known to engage the brain through the senses in a non–linear way. As is often said, a picture paints a thousand words. This engagement with the whole is also reflected in ways of working, particularly in those community arts projects that purposefully address issues of power in society. Some writers have argued that the very use of the arts in health will actually be instrumental in creating the major shift in worldviews that this chapter is talking about. Angus (2002) argues that arts activity may be contributing to shifting and expanding cultural and institutional understanding of 'health', putting into practice in new ways the values underpinning the health promotion process: participation, enablement and empowerment, equity and social justice. Arts–based health projects have progressed the notion of holism further by revealing and exploring issues around health and well-being that have been ignored by medicine, including the emotional and spiritual as well as the physical, mental and social. Yet funding support for such projects remains insecure and vulnerable.

Beth Alberg of Uppsala University told us the following story:

"We have been working in my home country Kenya for some years trying to change attitudes to HIV/AIDS and the sexual practices that encourage its transfer. We went to one village and they said we are not interested in working with you on that issue, but we do need help planting trees. We are trying to replant an area and animals keep coming and eating the new shoots, so we need help with building fences to protect them. We also need help watering them. Together we came up with the idea of an adopt a tree campaign whereby each child in the area would look after a tree, and we brought in some water engineers we knew to help with tapping the local water. The trees also became a meeting place for the children, and we were able to talk to them in informal ways about the issues we were concerned about. This drew the parents in, and they started seeing the benefits in education, and some even started questioning the local practice of female genital mutilation, an issue we had dared not introduce. As the trees flourished, it attracted many birds and the local people are now talking with nature conservancy people about protecting the area for nature. All this started with a child and a tree."

Co-creating reality, consciousness and healthy communities

Among the developments that have been part of new scientific thought in physics, ecology and neurobiology, and which have been taken up and developed in transpersonal psychology, deep ecology and soft mathematics but not openly in health promotion, has been a reinterpretation of the nature of consciousness and its relationship to the material world. These ideas find resonance with the work of Dewey (1925), Merleau-Ponty (1962) and others, referred to at the beginning of this chapter. Consciousness, it is argued, creates physical reality. So, although there is a widely held belief that there is a separation between inner and outer worlds, there is a growing body of thought that sees both as part of an underlying, unseen energy system, what Bohm (1980) has called the 'implicate order'. When we start to think in these terms, we see how important patterns of thinking are in creating the world around us, and vice versa. It also puts a new slant on the feminist adage, that the personal is political. Within this view, any of us working with or in communities are co-creating realities through our thoughts and beliefs, conscious and unconscious. It requires us to be critically conscious, that is, not only to be self-aware, but also to realise that in any transformation process we are part of that transformation and that it needs to proceed both within our selves and in the outer world. Everyone thinks about changing humanity out there, but few think about changing themselves (Murphy, 1999). This is a view that dislodges power and status, with everyone including the facilitator as both teacher and learner, engaged in an act of developing consciousness and in generating meaning. Furthermore, if we see this relationship between the inner and outer worlds as a complex energy system and therefore connected to the wider ecosystem, then we can see how the same characteristics of complex adaptive systems that we talked about in the discussion of healthy communities start to provide us with useful metaphors for understanding transformation and change.

In seeking to understand reality, the mind actively transforms reality. We are sentient beings, however, and thinking is only one of the many threads with which the tapestry of our sensitivities is woven. All the senses and the emotions are part of the process. Things become what our consciousness makes them. Our mind participates in the creation of our world and the nature of that process is important in determining outcomes. We make sense of reality by filtering it through our minds and our emotions, constantly processing and transforming what we experience, and in doing so, co-creating our reality. Skolimowski (1994) argues that our western traditions have locked us into language, perception and thinking that creates a bias towards being rather than becoming. However, to understand the world is to understand this process of change, for every act of reality making is an act of change, part of the process of transformation. Hence our emphasis on learning to question as a route to critical consciousness: by so doing, we create an upward spiral of understanding. Just as in complex adaptive systems, this encourages regeneration within the system; in other words, learning and new information introduces a new energy. In this way we expand consciousness and our world. Skolimowski (1994) talks about the need for a yoga of transformation. He uses the word in the sense of a set of strategies and principles that one needs to follow to develop a new mind set. He argues that this is part of the methodology of participation. The gift of transformation is one you give yourself at the end of the long and difficult journey that these principles imply. He identifies 10 principles:

1. Become aware of your conditioning.
2. Become aware of deep assumptions which you are subconsciously upholding.
3. Become aware of the most important values that underlie the basic structure of your being and your thinking.
4. Become aware of how these assumptions and values guide and manipulate your behaviour, action and thinking.
5. Become aware of which of your assumptions and values are undesirable because they dwarf your horizons or arrest your growth. Each of these assumptions may be held at a subconscious level and from there may be controlling you.
6. Watch and observe instances of your actions and behaviour while they are manipulated by undesirable assumptions and values. Identify the causes and defects.
7. Articulate the alternative assumptions and values by which you would like to be guided and inspired.
8. Imagine the forms of behaviour, actions and thinking that would follow from these assumptions and values.
9. Deliberately try to bring about the forms of behaviour, thinking and action expressing the new assumptions. Implement in everyday life and watch the process. Repeat the process because practice is important.
10. Restructure your being in the image of these assumptions and thereby restructure your spiral of understanding.

At first glance this would appear to be an individualistic process. In a participatory world, however, the old dualism between structure and agency, between self and society, no longer pertains. Community integration is as much about the integration of the self, as of the self with other. In order for the self to be integrated, you have to participate in the wider whole. As different perspectives on reality are shared through this process, then a wider reality is co-created. Plato tells the story of a cave where prisoners only see themselves as shadows thrown up by a fire. Similarly, a scientific theory provides only a shadow outline of 'reality'. Different ways of knowing create different ways of understanding a particular phenomenon. For someone in the position of being outside the cave, it does not make sense for the prisoners to fight over which view is the best one. We need to put the whole together to get the best picture.

Some of what we have talked about in this chapter may appear to readers far removed from the practical reality of working with communities. Perhaps what has been said seems largely metaphorical or even metaphysical. Yes, in practice, it is difficult to hold a vision of connection in the way described here and to act on that, at the same time as being in a dualistic world where the norm is to think and act in a separated way. Constant critical self-reflection is called for on the long journey to the active embodiment of participatory thinking, that is, its incorporation into the cells of our bodies so that it becomes as natural as eating and breathing. However, it does not require a total shift away from systematic and scientific thought or from sociological and political theory. Just as a mind without emotions is unbalanced and can lead to irrational acts (Dimasio, 1994), the alternative is also true. It is all a matter of balance; that point at the edge of chaos where stability exists alongside change, where people's stories exist alongside statistics and where emotions form part of any analysis. This is the point of paradox encapsulated so well by the symbol of the Tao, the yin and yang.

Nature and our relationship with it cannot be left out of the equation. Poverty and sustainability, the key themes in this book, cannot be treated as issues in isolation from nature. We are not just talking about relations between ourselves, but with the universe. This means working with nature rather than on it, just as a participatory approach works *with* people rather than *on* them.

Notions of energy and of meaning, of working with nature as well as a sense of the collective have strong links to non-western views of spirituality. By spirituality we do not necessarily mean religion; rather the sense of the non-material, of essence. In a dualist mind set, matter is separated from spirit. But in many parts of the world, the separation of the secular from the spiritual is anathema. Peat (2008) talks of what he calls indigenous science. He argues that indigenous knowing, shared by many indigenous communities across the world, from North America to Australia and New Zealand, is a vision of the world that encompasses heart and head, the soul and the spirit. Knowledge in these societies is acquired through a coming to knowing. This requires us to stand back from a surface reality to engage with a much deeper knowing in a search for underlying connections at different levels, including consciousness. In the same way, Chinese characters favour a sense of a fuller meaning, deeper than the literal (Ong, 1997), quite unlike the symbolism of the western alphabet. This is what Heidegger (1963) calls being in the world, where the world around us is experienced as so much part of us that it is not viewed as an object. This consciousness is at the heart of indigenous knowing based on a world in common, which questions western notions of personal ownership of land, sea and sky. As Grace, my (Margaret's) seven-year-old granddaughter said thoughtfully, "Why do people put fences around their gardens? Why can't we take them down and have a big, happy space where everyone can be together, and talk and laugh and play?".

This coming to knowing is also what Chia (2003) discusses when exploring East Asian approaches to creating and acting in the world. In East Asian cultures, the individual is only a secondary effect of social relations, and not a basic unit of society, as in the West. The self is a by-product of perpetually shifting constellations of relations and experience. Thus knowledge is not acquired through the written word, but rather through direct observation and action, and through a process of de-cluttering previously acquired thoughts and knowledge. From Peat's (1986) exploration of how Native Americans in Canada think and act in the world, a useful set of comparisons of these two ways of thinking can be derived in a typically linear western way, demonstrated in Table 3.1.

Table 3.1: Different ways of seeing the world

Western science	Indigenous science
Linear thought	Being, experiencing
Logic and structure	Relationship
Fragmentation	Connectedness
Dualism	
Material and concrete	Spirit and emergence
Fixed laws	Flux, change and transformation
Knowledge as something to be processed and accumulated	Coming to knowing through experience, watching and listening, ceremonies and songs and entering the silence
Individual rights and justice	Obligations, dialogue and balance
Abstraction	Stuff of life

We learn from this that new ways of acting and thinking can be absorbed, almost by osmosis, through constant, direct observation and through constant practice. If communities and those in power are to see and act in the world in different ways, they have to constantly experience other possibilities. This is not dissimilar to the practice in China during the Cultural Revolution, that of intellectuals being sent to work with farming communities, although we are not advocating forced labour, or what could be called radical empiricism. On a practical level, it is those mind-stretching exchange visits that take place between communities that help us see ourselves through the eyes of others, internationally and nationally, like the Chinese contingent that visited Scholes Community Garden in Wigan, or the women of Hattersley Credit Union who supported and trained others in Toxteth, Wigan and elsewhere. Simple human contact across difference alters consciousness.

The challenge of thinking participatively

The ideas presented in this chapter are at their heart very simple. Everything is connected. We have suggested that western science provides a useful but limited tool for understanding reality and needs to be integrated with embodied and other forms of knowledge to help us make good deliberative interruptions that can change the world. Thinking in a participatory way is a different way of knowing; it alters our view of the world and leads to ways of being that are based on cooperation and a world in common. Ecological ways of knowing lie at the core of this worldview, and we can take metaphors from the natural world to understand communities and their relationships in a more dynamic way. Wilber et al (2008) provide a useful model to help us understand with our limited western minds the different interrelated elements that we need to address at one and the same time in the process of expanding consciousness, illustrated in Table 3.2.

Table 3.2: Elements of integrative practice

	Interior	Exterior
Individual	What I experience *Psychology*	What I do *Behaviour*
Collective	What we experience *Culture*	What we do *Systems*

Source: Adapted from Wilber et al (2008)

Our current modes of thinking are not moving society towards a better world; they are taking us further and further away. The troubled times we live in require us to look at the world and our part in it in new ways. The challenge is to work within our selves and with communities in new ways, based on new possibilities. The old ways of thinking are no longer adequate, and have left us with a world that is emotionally hollow, aesthetically meaningless and spiritually empty (Goodwin, 2007). In the next chapter we explore examples of where, despite this context, people are increasingly engaging in participatory practice in a non-participatory world, but are finding resistance to change.

FOUR

Participatory practice in a non-participatory world

> The world everyone sees is not THE world but a world which we are bringing forth with others. (Maturana and Varela, 1987: 245)

Entering the term 'participatory practice' into Google™ generates over a million hits. Workbooks and workshops abound offering processes and tips of how to engage in participatory practice. Many of these owe their origins to the knowledge and understanding of people living in non-western societies. However, as most people know, a workshop here or there is unlikely to change behaviour and practice overnight. These are moments of engagement with participation which may, over a period of time, enable communities and organisations to develop both the skills and trust in the process, and only then if they can see some value accruing to that engagement (Cornwall and Coelho, 2007). Sometimes these moments are transformative; more often it requires the consistent application of a set of values and principles and many of these moments to reach a point where people change the way they think about the world. It has to become embodied. We can know something intellectually, but need to feel it and believe it in order to live it. There are tools that aid this process, giving people a taste of a different way of being, and many such tools are interwoven into the chapters of this book, all founded on participatory values and principles. But each context calls for a different process, and so there is no step-by-step guide. It calls for an evolving praxis, where these tools are part of theory in action.

Equally, we have to be mindful of claims to participatory practice that are superficial, giving lip service by using the language of participation but not following the process through according to the underlying principles discussed in this book. Taking a partial perspective is dangerous, and can reinforce the very system that it seeks to change, creating what Cooke and Kothari (2001) call the 'new tyranny of participation'. The path to participation is a fine line to tread: it is the line that marks the interface of liberation and domination. Dangers arise when transformative concepts are not fully understood and embodied in theory and practice. Those who are currently working in the range of institutions that contribute to the well-being of a local community need opportunities to explore, theorise and experience working in a participatory way in order for radical change to take place (Popay, 2006). That, in turn, is the beginning of a force that will change institutions and the nature of democracy. It calls for an increase in 'invited spaces for participatory democracy' to overcome the inherited cultural and institutional practices that are embedded in our worldview, reinforcing the existing order and resilient to change (Cornwall and Coelho, 2007). We emphasise the dangers that both Hague and Jenkins (2005) present: without a critical understanding of participatory processes there is a risk that anything participatory is seen as a good thing in its own right, regardless of outcomes. Being aware of the broader structural processes in operation is therefore crucial, and questioning every stage is crucial to ensuring that participation retains its integrity.

As we saw in Chapter 3, an awareness of the interconnectedness of life generates a different starting point in how we operate in the world. This can be profoundly challenging to existing power structures and institutions where hierarchy and the need to control reinforce non-participatory practices. If participatory approaches to practice, where they are emerging, are either partially absorbed into existing practices or remain piecemeal, the transformative potential of this approach will be deflected. This chapter explores some of the stories of participatory practice in different contexts, but it is by no means comprehensive; for every example selected there will be other examples, both similar and different, to match them. We draw on examples from four areas: the arts, health promotion, participatory development and local urban government. In exploring these experiences we look at how different attempts at participation have engaged with the worldview described in Chapters 2 and 3. There are challenges in engaging in participatory practice in a non-participatory world that are not always made evident in the published research literature, in unpublished reports and on websites. The uphill struggle as the optimistic participatory practitioner collides with the hierarchical non-participatory world is captured in Figure 4.1.

Quite recently, I (Jane) was involved in the development of a research centre that was directed at supporting health systems change in another European country. Academia and the healthcare sector are not the most conducive environments in which to engage in participatory practice, and this was made even more challenging by the context, a country in which I did not speak the language. Over

Figure 4.1: Participatory practice meets the non-participatory world

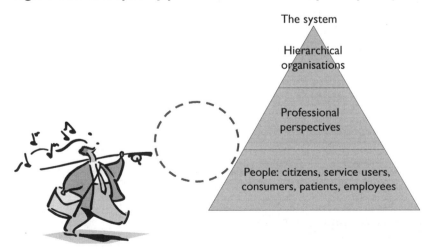

two years I tried to facilitate the development of a team and a way of working around a set of agreed principles founded on participatory practice, what Wenger (1998) calls 'a community of practice'. Wenger sees communities of practice as mutual engagement around a shared practice in which we share our insights and gain new knowledge, engaged in learning and creating new meanings together. This was community development, but among privileged academics who had little previous experience of participatory action research, but who had agreed to work in this way with colleagues in the health sector. Successful community development in any context has to start where people are at. No less so in this one. I had no choice over who should be involved, but each academic had chosen, for a range of personal often undisclosed reasons, to be involved. We struggled to maintain a sense of the collective. Individual egos and the failure to fully commit took its toll; staff left the project. But those that remained continued to engage with the interconnectedness needed to make this approach participatory. They each struggled in their own way alongside colleagues in the health and social care services. Now, four years on, they have reached a point where they say they cannot work in any other way. My colleagues intellectually bought into the concept of participation, but the process of absorbing it into our hearts was a long journey to a very different way of thinking and being; one of inherent criticality and personal as well as collective transformation. We were often buffeted from our intentions by the practices of the wider community and culture of which we were part, not least the processes of change in the structure of the organisation. This unbalanced us, challenging our commitment to the collective whole, exposing the insidious nature of academic, cultural norms.

Participatory practice in community arts

We will start to demonstrate differences in the interpretations of participation in practice by using some examples from the world of art, since art by its nature is holistic. Our exploration of what constitutes participatory practice will start in the area of community arts. Subsequently, we will explore what happens when these approaches are used as tools for promoting health.

Vienna–based writer Christian Kravagna (1998) differentiates between four different types of approaches to contemporary community art:

• working with others
• interactive activities
• collective action
• participatory practice.

In *Modelle partizipatorischer Praxis* (*A model of participatory practice*), Kravagna gives some examples of each type of approach. These different approaches can be transferred to any community context.

The first category, *working with others*, he dismisses as merely fashionable 'socio-chic'. Art curators, for example, may work with other organisations, but only in a superficial sense. It may include artists outsourcing the production of a piece of artwork, but they get all the reward and recognition and have designed the piece of work in the first place. There are many examples of such public art in sculpture parks and town centres throughout Europe.

The second category, *interactive activities*, permits one or more reactions that can influence the appearance of the work without deeply affecting the structure developed by an individual artist. Examples include the 'push-the button' works in so-called 'new media' exhibitions. The interaction is usually momentary, reversible and repeatable. The third category, *collective practice*, refers to the conception, production and implementation of works or actions by multiple people with no principal distinction among them in terms of status. *Participatory practice*, on the other hand, is initially based on a distinction between producers and recipients, is geared towards the participation of the latter and turns over a substantial portion of the work to them, either at the point of conception or in the further course of the work. Whereas interactive situations usually involve the individual and their own art, participatory art is usually realised in group and everyday spatial situations. The aim is to work in different ways with people in their immediate environs in order to create shifts in how we think about and relate to each other. As a result there is much more of a dynamic of reciprocity. It is not just the aesthetic experience that is participatory, but the transfer of power enabling participants to take control of the process, not simply to comment on something produced by others. In this sense, participatory art is a medium for *conscientisation*, a route to becoming critical in a Freirean sense.

Kravagna presents some examples of such participatory practice. The first is the Open Public Library, described as a:

> library without librarians and without surveillance, the stock of which
> is determined by the users themselves through a system of exchange,
> according to which every borrowed book is to be replaced by another
> chosen at will by the user. As an institution, a library of this kind could
> contribute to the self-definition of a community ... and would thus
> be a kind of portrait of the community. (Kravagna, 1998: 7)

When this initiative was implemented in Hamburg, it was accompanied by a sociological study to gauge the impact of the participation process. In three demographically different districts, the circuit boxes of an electrical company were equipped with shelves and glass doors and turned into public, freely accessible libraries. Prior to the project, local residents were informed about the concept and asked for donations of books. Only one minimal rule for using the library was given in writing at the location: 'Please take the books of your choice and bring them back within an appropriate period of time. Additions to the stock of books are welcome'. The lack of further regulations and instances of surveillance transferred the responsibility for how the 'installation' worked and its fate to its users. The research that accompanied the project indicated a high degree of participation, manifested in the almost complete renewal of the library stock in the course of the project, and the generally positive reaction to the whole idea. Reasons given for the attractiveness of the project referred primarily to the display of trust, the possibilities for communication that it opened up and the increase in solidarity arising from the exchange relationships. Even though participation in the project varied from one district to another, and results were varied, ranging from vandalism to support from grassroots initiatives, the outcomes based on communication and relationships indicated an impact that imbued the 'utopian dimension of a radically democratic institution with a real foundation' (Kravagna, 1998: 9). However, we must not get too carried away here because the project was most successful among the population at the highest end of economic and educational status, albeit in an overall population in which the divisions were much less than we experience currently in the UK.

Kravagna also cites the work of Stephen Willats (1976). Since the early 1960s, Willats had been producing kinetic objects and plastic constructions that lend themselves to interactivity with the audience. Critical reflections on the elitist character of the museum and the consequent structure of the art system, however, led him to develop new working methods which built on the 'communicative' properties of the early objects, but which shifted the emphasis in the relationship between people and objects to that of social relationships. 'I consider that the audience of the work of art is as important as the artist, and that the active involvement of people in the origination of art work is an essential part of the process of generating interventions in the social process of culture' (Willats, 2004: 58). In the new approach, the audience became involved in the creation of the artwork, and so the art became of the real world, of the everyday life of the participants. The aim was now to change the circumstances of life through the art: 'From the outset it became obvious that a model of practice would be required that would bind it to the context in embodying the priorities, languages, social norms, behaviours of the audience as well as the institutional constraints of modern living conditions' (Irish, 2004: 63).

Willats felt that the embodiment of repressive structures was to be found most often in the blocks of flats, built largely in the 1960s. As homes, they had a profound impact on the mental and social life of their inhabitants, creating a 'community of the isolated'. So the projects that Willats developed with the residents were intended to set processes of perception in motion, which might lead to critical analysis and change in both individuals' relationships with the environment and social relationships with one another. He believed that there was a latently present 'counter-consciousness' expressed through the subversive re-coding of signs and symbols, from graffiti to vandalism, to inappropriate use of public spaces. His aim was to enable the articulation of different forms of counter-consciousness by connecting from an individual to a collective level.

Willats' model of participatory practice can be illustrated with a project such as 'vertical living' (1976). The chosen place was a typical council housing block of flats, Skeffington Court in West London. Initial contacts with the caretaker and a friend's mother who lived there gradually introduced the idea of a participatory project with some of the residents. Initially, Willats conducted individual conversations over the course of three months, investigating the relationship between the building and daily living habits, leisure time and social contacts. The collected conversations helped him identify collective issues, which provided the focus for further discussion. Finally, picture panels were prepared, each by one resident in cooperation with the artist, addressing a particular issue with photographs and texts. The panels were displayed in the entrance hallway next to the lift, and in the same position two floors up. Other residents were invited to fill in response pages offering suggestions for solutions, and these became incorporated into the public presentation. Aside from necessitating physical movement within the building, the project created a flow of communication that resulted in a network of social relationships. These were found to be so productive that the residents continued beyond the end of the artist's involvement.

Even though Willats started from a concept of art as a socially relevant practice, his purpose was not predetermined: based on his perceptions of the impact of buildings on people's lives, he developed an interruption, a participatory intervention that encouraged critical reflection on reality. This opened up a new framework of action that led to sustainable changes. The emphasis was on people's participation in the issues that were affecting their own lives, and through a process of critical consciousness reaching a collective awareness of the ability to act together to bring about change. There are parallels here with the critical pedagogy of Paulo Freire.

The four types of public art Kravagna identified, with their different interpretations of participatory practice, have at least one thing in common: they emerge from a background of institutional criticism of the exclusionary character of art as culture, and they counter this with inclusionary practices. This would have been dear to the heart of John Ruskin, Victorian artist and philosopher, who campaigned for free public access to art galleries and museums when he witnessed the marginalisation of the urban poor created by industrialisation. However, participation, as a transformative concept, involves much more than widening access. It is about power and consciousness, the participants themselves becoming more fully human players in their own lives.

Community arts in health

> Health is usually described in medical language, but it also needs the
> language of everyday and of poetry, visual imagery, metaphor, myth,
> music, celebration and dreams. (Wilson, 1975: 5)

In the examples above, art is used to engage people in new ways of seeing their
world that lead to new ways of being in the world. However, community arts
are often used to draw people into other agendas. This can be seen in the use of
community arts to engage people in health issues. This has expanded in recent
years, particularly in the area of mental health. For example, in 2003 alone, an audit
of such projects in one largely rural area of the UK, that of Cumbria (population:
500,000), 78 such initiatives were identified (Allen, 2003). In 2007, the National
Strategy for the Arts, Health and Well-being, supported by the Arts Council
and the Department of Health, announced itself as a legitimate arm of public
health policy. However, despite general enthusiasm for the arts in health, many
such projects struggle with short-term funding and small budgets, as well as the
need to demonstrate concrete outcomes in the form of improved health-related
targets. In these ways, potentially liberating forms of practice are absorbed into
mainstream agendas that diffuse transformative potential, just as we are finding
with the mainstreaming of community development. The popularity of arts for
health initiatives lies in the power of their engagement with the way that people
'see' their world. This is the very power that can be either transformative or
domesticating in Freirean terms. For public health funders, it is seen as a way of
accessing people to solve a particular predefined health or social problem, such
as obesity, drug abuse or lack of physical activity. Many such arts interventions,
therefore, find themselves with their foot in two camps. Public health imperatives
demand projects focusing on single issues, while an arts-based approach tends
to focus on the personal and collective well-being of the whole. In negotiating
these two realities, such arts projects potentially provide a vehicle through which
people renegotiate their notions of self, identity and how they feel to a point
where they are able to adopt the healthy lifestyle sought for them by health
educators. But implicit in most public health practice is the notion that medicine,
or at least public health epidemiology, knows best and that a healthy choice in
terms of behaviour is that identified by the external expert. Indeed, it could be
argued that adopting a community arts approach to health is merely enabling the
establishment to absorb radical ideas without disrupting the status quo of medical
hegemony and positivism. As a result, some argue that community arts will become
manacled by the beast, and will lose the creative fire that is its strength and, along
with other participatory practices, become the new tyranny. More fundamentally,
detaching the basis of creative arts from its essence means that the essential human
flourishing that creativity encourages separates that person from that which makes
them whole (Springett, 2009).

The arts have certainly been widely embraced into health education and promotion, particularly in developing countries, as a medium to engage people with key health messages around HIV/AIDS. Elsewhere, the arts have been used to deliver health promotion messages around teenage pregnancy, obesity, heart disease and breast cancer. For example, in the Vital Youth project, which worked with young people of African and Caribbean ethnicity in a part of inner London, participants were recruited through local radio and were involved in workshops with the core staff supported by specialists in script writing, dance and technical issues, such as stage lighting, to develop a play about health and well-being issues at the centre of young people's concerns (Douglas et al, 2000). This was a health education initiative that was relevant to the lives of young people, and encouraged them to become interactive participants in the process, rather than passive recipients of health interventions. By contrast, El Teatro Lucha grew out of a community outreach education programme on toxicology started by the University of Texas Environmental Health Department. Based on forum and image theatre, grounded in Boal's *Theater of the oppressed* (2008) and inspired by Freire's *Pedagogy of the oppressed* (1972), it engaged citizens, public policy makers and scientists across different minority ethnic communities in local collaborative environmental health improvement projects. Based on a dialogical approach to theatre, it generated a large-scale, community-based approach to asthma and lead poisoning across a wide number of communities, funded by the National Institutes for Health as well as the National Institute for Environmental Health for four years, from 2003. It used theatre to both identify the issues, to assess and develop community knowledge of them, as well as to deliver the messages and influence public health policy in the area. The outcome has been personal and community change that has extended beyond the original area (Sullivan, 2005).

It becomes clear that the type of arts medium and initiative depends very much on the local context, the nature of the facilitation and the enabling contextual factors. Creative arts need to be introduced sensitively to people who have spent the majority of their lives marginalised and who see art as elitist and not for them. A formulaic approach does not work as this tends to undermine that central feature of art, creativity, where separation from the world ceases. Its impact is particularly strongly felt where people are involved in a creative act for the first time in their lives, once that initial reluctance is overcome. Of itself, this creates a sense of power and control out of powerlessness, and the impact ripples out, like a raindrop in a pool, to impact on other areas of their lives: improved self-esteem, expression and sociability (Angus and White, 2003). We can see immediately how this mirrors the network and system impacts that we referred to when talking about healthy communities and ecosystems in Chapter 3. Not only does the individual feel change and a sense of connection to the whole, but since the act of creation is also a social act, it encourages further social connections.

This opening out and connecting seems to be a feature of many arts for health projects. For example, in Bradford, UK, as part of the Health Action Zone initiative, an Asian arts organisation developed three different projects delivered in four localities. One involved music and movement sessions in childcare settings involving children and parents in storytelling, playing musical instruments, listening, exploring textures and dancing. A second was a drama workshop for young people of Asian ethnicity with their teachers around the issue of marriage. The third was aimed at involving young people in their local community centre, with four artists, and involved graffiti art, dance and mosaics. A formal evaluation of the initiative found that the impact included local ownership of the project with increased partnership working, resulting in improved contact with local people, an increased sense of well-being and improved relationships. Similarly, in the Tyne and Wear Health Action Zone in North East England, Common Knowledge coordinated a major programme of experimental work using arts-based approaches to examine health. Like the Bradford project, it brought together different perspectives through a multilayered network to increase capacity for arts-based approaches to health by engaging artists, health professionals of all kinds, teachers, local government and the voluntary sector to devise and deliver imaginative health interventions. The resulting network grew out of Gateshead's pioneering three-fold approach to arts in health in the 1990s. This had a strategic layer that worked through a governance group, including representatives from local authorities, the arts, education and health, and a constituency layer of representatives (that is, people who have participated in events). Organically, over 50 projects were developed through building alliances, with regularly held 'revelation days' to explore new ways of working.

The organic nature of such work, when given the right environment, is further illustrated by Looking Well, a rural initiative that grew out of a community consultation in 1995 that revealed high levels of depression, loneliness and isolation among the farming community. Established as a charity by local artists living in the area, the project was run on a shoestring from a rented shop in the local village of Higher Bentham in North Yorkshire, UK. It was found that conversations about sensitive issues, such as depression, were able to take place more easily when the participants' eyes were focused on a creative activity. The art was displayed and distributed in local locations, including a health centre. In seven years, this arts-based activity regenerated a community, with over one third of the population involved in its activities. One of the original mothers, who had been experiencing depression, along with five others, are now employed, and the local GP has been able to identify positive health outcomes in individual patients.

These examples tell us very little about what went on inside the official story and how the act of co-creation, through, for instance, a lantern festival, a mosaic, a quilt, a play, the creation of a community garden or the building of a community centre, really felt. Was it participatory practice in the truest sense? What we see from the outside is the 'expert' in one aspect of life reaching out to the 'other' with the agenda, the mode of art, and the boundary of the participatory process predetermined. The world is clouded by the imbalance of power in favour of the expert. In true participatory practice there is an animator, a co-facilitator, who is sharing in the process of transformation. That does not take away what is a consistent theme in these examples of community arts for health, that it is the very act of 'doing art', and particularly of doing art collectively, that changes people's lives by engaging with underlying elements of personal empowerment that, in turn, connects individuals with a wider collective empowerment. As the community arts example has shown, participatory practice is more than community involvement or health promotion; it is a practice that engages people in areas of life that may not be the focus of the original activity. On the other hand, many accounts of such practices report bringing excluded people into areas of control, reducing spaces for dissent by reinforcing the status quo (Barnes, 2007). For participatory experiences to lead to sustainable change, attitudes of the powerful as well as the marginalised need to be brought into a process of thinking differently and acting differently. We need to examine the way decisions are made, identify who makes the decisions on whose behalf, and explore different interests within the process itself. This means a socially responsible approach that not only enables involvement, but also acknowledges people's equality of worth, provides freedom from oppressive, debilitating conditions and enables the expression of people's full potential (Stringer, 2007). It requires practitioners not only to become more critical, but to develop the skills of a sensitive facilitator and conflict manager.

Participatory practice in local government

Participatory practice both requires and supports the development of participatory democracy and deliberative governance, and these are inextricably linked. Engaging in participatory practice requires an acknowledgement of how the rules by which decision making operates in contemporary society contributes to and reinforces dominant power relations that assume superiority. It also requires an understanding of how the micropolitics of engagement can subvert even the best institutional designs (Gaventa, 2006). Paying attention to and changing the rules and processes by which decisions are made helps encourage and support participatory practice (Gaventa, 2004). For example, much is taken for granted in the way meetings are conducted in existing bureaucracies. How a room is set out, how the agenda is set, who records the discussion, whose voices are heard, what is talked about and how decisions are reached contain the very essence of liberation/domination. In such contexts, even the most simple changes, like renaming chairs as facilitators, change the dynamics. Incrementally changing such practices within the existing non-participatory world can start a cultural change. It is such 'spaces for change' (Cornwall and Coelho, 2007) that are the small steps to the creation of new democratic arenas. It is in the area of local government that new experiments have started, and these experiments are instructive in how the rules of engagement enable participatory practices.

In a world where the material dominates, at least in western societies, power over decisions on budgets is real power, and it is to these we now turn to explore efforts that are being made to engage in participatory budgeting in local government, where the conditions have been created for people at grassroots level to have a genuine decision-making role. The origins of participatory budgeting, as with many participatory practices, lie in Brazil, where it was linked with the expansion in citizen-based community associations and civil society as a practical way to put people's priorities at the forefront of public investment. Ordinary citizens of Brazil have consistently backed politicians offering participatory budgeting within their manifestos. It was pioneered by the Workers' Party and in 2002, Luis Inácio Lula da Silva of the Workers' Party (Partido des Trabalhadores [PT]) won the Brazilian national elections to become President. This has further encouraged the take-up of participatory budgeting in Brazil and beyond (Rodgers, 2007). Originating in Porto Alegre in Brazil in the late 1980s, there have been some recent experiments in the UK. One such example is the Manchester-based Community Pride Initiative (CPI), where the motivation was the creation of good decision-making systems to assist those distributing public resources so that they would not be wasted inappropriately. (Community Pride Initiative and Oxfam, 2005) The experience in Manchester found that the quality of participative decision making depended on clear communication and lines of accountability, a common understanding of the direction in which to go, transparent rules on how dialogue was concluded and how actions were begun, as well as relevant and understandable information on which to base decisions. They also found that the style of participation should match the expectations and experiences of participants, and that it depended on the trust generated in the processes used. They should be inclusive, easily understood and applied consistently over time. Indeed, in Porto Alegre, a key document was the set of rules for the process, amended and updated each year by a representative group of participants. This need for rules of process ties up with the findings of those who have explored complexity and systems (see Chapter 3). As Capra (1982: 268) says, 'the process of a machine is determined by its structure, but an organism is determined by its process'.

Participation can only grow if it is seen to make a difference. This means action, not just listening to what participants have to say. They must be able to track where their ideas have gone, the extent to which they have been acted on, and why. Thus, the participatory budgeting report that lists all the proposals for action is another key document in Brazilian models. Finally, to create that trust and make it really work, those with power must accept the results. If the local authority does not implement the outcomes, however low the apparent quality of participation, it cannot expect to maintain and build participation in future years. This is where fundamental power shifts towards communities affected by participatory budgeting start to take shape. The evidence from Porto Alegre suggests that their success is pulling more and more people into the process because people see change happening and want to be part of it. Democracy has become re-oxygenated. This is not just to do with the number of people participating. The process builds confidence and skills, for instance, talking effectively and empathetically with and between political leaders, specialists in agencies, and fellow citizens from many different backgrounds. The transparency of the process involves much more than accountability; it has become an important factor in widening the scope and acceptance of participatory budgeting.

Porto Alegre operates through public forums in 16 regions of the city. Members of the public meet together in their neighbourhood each year, in April, to discuss key issues, and to agree their priorities for investment. This could be a range of issues, but past ideas have included pavements, sewage facilities, evening classes and children's play areas. The findings of these neighbourhood meetings then feed into regional plenaries, which are held in May. Community groups from across the region come together to choose their top three priorities for local investment. School gyms, often the context for these plenaries, start to fill up from early evening, and in many areas over a thousand people attend. Schoolchildren entertain early arrivals with samba performances on the stage, while participants queue up to register. Large screens are displayed at the front and the participatory budgeting process is explained to participants by staff from the Community Relations Council. This is a key department at the City Hall responsible for facilitating the participatory budget. A number of speakers are then given three minutes each on the microphone. Anyone can choose to speak, if they put their name down when they register. They put forward their main priorities for investment and campaign for others to vote for the same issues. The mayor then addresses the meeting to discuss key city-wide issues for people to consider that year. S/he reminds people that participatory budgeting is a good opportunity for local communities, and that they must think carefully before choosing their priorities. The meeting ends with two votes. In the first, people choose three priorities for investment according to 15 themes. These include education, youth services and transport. Councillors for the Participatory Budget Council (one of a number at the City Hall) are chosen through a second ballot.

This example of participatory democracy illustrates some of the challenges and the rewards that such an approach produces for sustainable social and environmental development and places a different lens through which to view democratic governance from that currently in use in the West. Melucci and Avritzer (2000) argue that such approaches are more able to reflect and deal with the complexity and cultural diversity that exists today. The democratic elitism of representative democracy means complex environmental and social problems are reduced to bureaucratic technical fixes and simplistic, inflexible and potentially harmful solutions, rather than engaging with a rich variety of background and life experience. But, as a lesson for participatory practice in a non-participatory world, this example of participatory budgeting shows how transparent, formal rules and accountability procedures are oiling the wheels of true participatory practice.

Participatory practice does not imply structureless practice, but involves structures that enable participation and the development of critical connections with others in ever-widening networks, as, for example, in the Tyne and Wear Arts for Health initiative. A critique of much existing participatory practice, particularly that which invokes service user involvement or consumer choice language, sees participatory practice as narrowed to the tokenistic end of Arnstein's (1969) oft-quoted *ladder of participation*, particularly by management and bureaucrats. Such issues have been explored in fields as wide apart as architectural design, tackling environmental problems, information systems development and organisational development, and it has been found that some participants have been disadvantaged in terms of power. This is why it is essential to have an analysis of the way that power works, not only structurally, but in the micro-contexts of everyday life. Conflict and contradiction need to be the focus of any participatory process, not just consensus seeking, otherwise power relations negate the process and participatory practice becomes instrumental or a socio-technical fix. This calls for a downgrading of the technical, formal, abstract scientific approaches and a wider recognition of contextual, subjective and non-material dimensions of human experience (Chambers, 1997).

Participatory research

Participatory research aims to apply the concept of participation to research. It is popular with development agencies, such as Save the Children and Action Aid, and it has attached to it a number of specific techniques and tools often talked about under the umbrella term of 'participatory rapid appraisal' now variously called participatory reflection and action or participatory rural appraisal (PRA) (Chambers, 1997). The key issue for us here is the nature of the relationships between researchers and research participants. As White and Pettit (2004) say, the social life of any research project, its principles, conduct and the relationships established, is central not only in terms of ethics but also in the quality of the information and learning that takes place. As participatory research is scaled up, there is a danger that it moves away from delivering the views of the people, becoming 'tone deaf to subtle characteristics of the lifeworld in ways of seeing and experiencing' (White and Pettit, 2004: 32).

What is participatory research in its purest form? The idea is that researchers, acting as facilitators and guarding against their own biases, seek to minimise any power differentials between them and the researched. The research design, therefore, is flexible, able to respond to changing contexts and emergent findings as they arise. Methods are often visual and interactive to allow participants with all backgrounds to participate in both generating and analysing the data. In its purest form, power over the process is shared and the research question and design is controlled by all those involved. When the analysis is complete, participants share ideas on how to act on the findings as well as how to evaluate any action taken. This means that those who participate have their knowledge respected, have control over the research process and influence over the way the results are used. Training is offered and support given as appropriate. This ranges from helping people feel confident to develop at their own pace, enabling people to come together to share and discuss progress, to ensuring that people who cannot continue still have their voice included in the research in some way. At its best, participatory research can be both challenging and rewarding as it respects the views and rights of those involved, counteracting the reaction that many communities give: "We've heard it all before and nothing ever happens!".

Many examples of how this works in practice can be found in Minkler and Wallerstein's (2008) *Community-based participatory research for health*. One of the most exciting areas where such approaches are being used is in work with young people helping to identify issues and problems that they see as pertinent to their everyday lives. Such approaches have also been used extensively in the area of environmental justice and workers' rights. Quantitative data is often needed in participatory research to indicate wider trends or risks. In this respect, Minkler and Hancock (2008) draw on an example of research done by the grassroots organisation, Concerned Citizens of Tillery, based in North Carolina in the US. This group was concerned about the impact of industrial pig farming practices on the local environment, in terms of environmental degradation, poor health and in terms of the livelihood of local people. Their perception was that the industrial pig farming units were located in poor and disadvantaged areas because the owners believed there would be less opposition to their practices. In 1996, a partnership between the local community and researchers from the local university received money to quantify the problem using the expertise of an epidemiologist alongside the community members, who evaluated the data quality using their local knowledge. The research questions originated from the communities and decisions on the research process were made with the community members. The results were put together in a press release that was mutually compiled, and the group were eventually invited to present their findings to the Agricultural Committee. In this case, the data collection was undertaken by the university researchers, but in many other examples local people themselves collect information, having been supported in developing the necessary skills. Many years ago, this was the case in a project in a poor area of Glasgow. Dissatisfied with a survey relating to health undertaken by a local university, the local community was supported by a health visitor in doing their own survey, asking questions in relation to health and well-being that related to local understanding. Eventually the whole process led to the building of a locally managed health and community centre. The entire process was recorded and documented in the form of a collage created by the residents. That same collage was eventually copied in a mosaic and formed the floor of the entrance to the centre (Bruce et al, 1995).

These approaches to research, as with other participatory practices, have been brought to the North from the South. In the South they have proved useful and effective in addressing the previous failure of the development industry to consult local people, resulting in a plethora of high-cost and inappropriate technologies and ineffective actions. However, they have also been much criticised for becoming a new form of colonialism whereby western perspectives and priorities are imposed on oppressed groups (Jackson and Kassam, 1998). In countries stripped of the institutions of western bureaucracy, with cultural traditions that support collective action, albeit not always founded on values of difference and diversity, such participatory research approaches have provided great potential for working participatively in a culturally sensitive way. Such an example is Kyrgyzstan, where participatory research is being used to develop rural healthcare. Originally, from a small project in the poor rural area of Jungal in Naryn Oblast, a model was developed that has been extended to the whole of rural Kyrgyzstan using a 'training the trainers' approach. Naryn Oblast is the poorest region in a country that is now among the poorest of the former Soviet states. The population survives primarily on sheep farming and horses. Tiny villages, at altitudes of 1,500m (4,900ft) and more above sea level, each with just a few hundred people, are spread out across a wide area. The terrain is harsh and difficult. The collapse of the Soviet Union and the abrupt end of funds from Moscow led to an almost complete collapse of the health system. The Swiss Red Cross (funded by the Swiss and Swedish governments) has been implementing a project to improve primary healthcare using participatory research.

The process starts with an analysis of the health situation in each village, with the people using a tool specifically designed for this purpose based on principles of PRA (see earlier). The project staff train a local primary care staff member, usually one per village, to facilitate people's analysis by using this tool. The analysis is done in small groups of about 10 people called together from neighbouring households for a session that lasts an average of one or two hours. As many group sessions as needed are undertaken to provide most households with a chance to participate. Following the training, project staff, many of whom are part of a developing health promotion workforce, supervise the staff member for one or two weeks in order to ensure the quality of their facilitation, since it is crucial to guide people through the process without influencing the outcome.

The tool centres on the question, 'What do you need to stay healthy, to live a healthy life?'. This focuses the discussion on the determinants of health rather than on the treatment of diseases. The people list these determinants on a sheet of paper. When they have finished the facilitator shows them a list of the main elements of primary healthcare, as outlined in WHO's Declaration of Alma-Ata, and asks the group to compare it with their own list. Invariably, the people have named all or most of the same elements in their own list: healthy nutrition, clean drinking water, education, hygiene and sanitation, special services for mothers and children including pregnancy care, vaccinations and family planning, provision of essential drugs and basic treatment. Often they have named more than these, such as sport, clean air, and so on. The facilitator asks the group to list the most common and important diseases in the area. The group then ranks them and identifies the five diseases that are most burdensome for people in the village.

The determinants of health and the most important local diseases are then listed along the side of a big sheet of paper. Two lines are drawn to mark a system of coordinates, the vertical axis indicating the degree, between 0% and 100%, to which a given determinant or disease is present in the village. The group discusses and assigns a percentage value to each issue. At the end a line is drawn connecting the individual estimates. The result is a graph profiling the village's health situation as seen by this group of people, and includes the key elements of the Declaration of Alma-Ata on primary healthcare. Such an analysis is done up to 100 times per village taking up to a month, depending on its size, in average involving members of about 70–80% of households. Sessions with only women and only young people are also carried out. The results of the analysis are compiled on village, rayon (district) and oblast (region) levels in two categories: determinants of health and burdensome diseases. The village health committees (VHCs) that have been created then act on those diseases that emerge as priorities on the oblast levels. The VHC is elected through representatives of neighbourhood blocks, and forms action groups for each campaign issue which plan, implement and monitor the activities. There is careful documentation and record keeping, all of which is kept in a room at a relevant local centre, usually the first aid post. VHC members' intimate knowledge of the neighbourhoods means that they can help people with specific problems that have gone undetected by the primary care team, as well as being a vehicle for spreading health promotion messages about good practices, for example, hygiene. Continuous organisational capacity building for the VHCs is provided by the donor agency, with the aim of developing sustainable organisations that can become a permanent partner of the health system for health promotion, and which also include other health issues in their agenda, such as access to sports facilities for young people and tree planting where appropriate. An organisational structure has been developed that avoids overburdening the board of the VHCs and brings many people into the activities, including local schools.

Observations I (Jane) made on a recent visit there indicate that the approach has had a substantial impact on the development of skills within rural communities, albeit from the base of a high level of literacy. However, as the process has developed, agencies and government departments and the medical profession with their own agendas have tried to coerce communities into addressing needs that reflect their interests or perceptions. The project leaders have had to work to ensure that community-identified needs are not subsumed under these external agendas, and support local people to strike a balance between their own priorities and the opportunities for resources from such agencies. This is common everywhere. And it has to be said that, while much monitoring takes place, the process is not used to generate critical reflection and debate, bearing in mind that critical reflection is a crucial element in transformative change. Nevertheless, the remarkable success of the initiative lies in engaging people in a rural health and healthcare development process at grassroots level, and then integrating it into a developing medical system, suggesting that when the medical system was stripped of its resources it was also stripped of the institutional constraints on participation. Interestingly, the process has been less successful in urban areas where the issues are more complex and the population more unstable and shifting.

Participatory research projects need to be critiqued according to their underlying principles. I (Jane) can remember attending a health promotion research conference in Edinburgh where a research project was described as participatory, but when scrutinised the 'participation' referred to the training of local people in questionnaire administration. This produced, I am glad to say, a very vocal critique from the audience. For those striving to remain true to the principles, many complain of insufficient space and time to break down barriers and prejudices, and insufficient resources for identifying safe spaces of trust to create the optimum environment for participation. This was achieved in the Commission of Inquiry on Poverty, Participation and Power and with the ATD Fourth World Project to pool knowledge on poverty initiatives. But on the whole, in the UK, funding for social and health research is marginal compared with the huge resources devoted to yet another epidemiological survey. There is still a long way to go. Canada and the US are much further ahead in formally supporting such participatory approaches to research, and linking them directly with development.

Extensive examples of the power of participatory practice in research are hidden in the many Masters and PhD theses that go unreported. One powerful example we found is reported in Forester (1999), of a Master's project undertaken by Cornell researcher activist Mary Jo Dudley, who worked with a group of domestic workers. It started as a video training project in which the workers exchanged stories of sexual harassment and abuse that they had never told before. They decided to get the views of the general public, and chose to interview men and women about their perceptions of domestic workers' situations. The solidarity and trust they had developed in telling each other stories encouraged them to research other views, and share their experiences with a wider audience. The reciprocity of telling their stories to each other, and then researching others' views, meant that they not only worked through their own trauma, but also understood those experiences in a broader context. The final outcome was not the video presenting their analysis of their situation, which had been the original aim, but the development of political awareness and the confidence to argue their case in other settings.

Participatory research has a profound impact on all involved, participants and original researchers alike. This can range from the realisation that survey instruments often ask the wrong questions about the wrong things, to an emotional and political awakening about the purpose of the research. It calls for an openness to transforming ourselves, our relationships with others, and ultimately our world.

Reflecting on participatory practice in a non-participatory world

Horton (1998: 228) argues that, 'if you believe you have a goal which you can reach in your lifetime, then it is the wrong goal'. The examples given above are merely a selection of attempts to engage in participatory practice. We argue in this book that participatory practice involves a set of values over which there is no compromise. It is by placing those values at the centre of our practice and by the pursuit and operation of these principles that we seek to transform existing conditions, and avoid the appropriation of the notion of participation as a new tyranny (Cooke and Kothari, 2001). Those principles are common to all good participatory practice, whether at the level of a workshop or a bigger experiment in new forms of democracy. Ute Bühler (2004) argues that we should take our cue from the Zapatistas in Mexico. Central to their practice is the principle of dignity that they argue is not something to be studied but something to live or die for, something that does not walk with the head but with the heart. Bühler quotes the words of the EZLN (Ejército Zapatista de Liberación Nacional [Zapatista Army of National Liberation]), used during a 'March of Dignity'. It reads like a poem.

Dignity is a bridge.
It needs two sides that, being different, distinct and distant become one in the bridge
    without ceasing to be different and distinct, but ceasing already to be distant.
When the bridge of dignity is being made,
    the us that we are speaks and the other that we are not speaks.
On the bridge that is dignity there is the one and the other.
And the one is not more or better than the other, nor is the other more or better than
    the one.
Dignity demands that we are ourselves.
But dignity is not just being ourselves.
For there to be dignity the other is necessary.
Because we are ourselves always in relation to the other.
And the other is other in relation to us....
Dignity, then, is recognition and respect.
Recognition of what we are and respect for what we are, yes,
    but also recognition of what the other is and respect for that which is the other....
So dignity is the tomorrow.
But the tomorrow cannot be if it is not for all, for those who we are and for those who
    are other....
So dignity should be the world, a world where many worlds fit.
Dignity, then, is not yet.
So dignity is yet to be.
Dignity, then, is struggling [to] eventually be the world.
A world where all worlds fit.

Source: Words of the EZLN during the 'March of Dignity', Puebla, 27 February 2001, quoted in Bühler (2004: 6)

Bühler takes this further, and argues that dignity and respect mean becoming a participant in a dialogue in which neither speaking nor listening is one-sided. We have to take into account the life histories of people, not ignore the informal everyday processes of people's lives. It commits to learning from both failure and success, and gives the opportunity for those involved to choose particular approaches. Acknowledging and respecting the dignity of people is key. It demands commitment to a genuine search for solutions that respect the 'other' as well as the 'self'. And the starting point is the honouring of the contextual, subjective and non–material dimensions of human experience.

If we take the central principles of dignity, respect and social justice, we see that there are institutional barriers and constraints on such practice. These barriers act to prevent the creation of spaces for this type of engagement to take place, often shrinking the opportunity for critical reflection, dialogue and understanding of difference. Much of the writing in the research literature on participatory practice whether in research, evaluation, education, democracy or community health talks of 'imagining the flowers but working the rich and heavy clay' (Jacobs, 2006: 578).

However, as we explore that practice which purports to be participatory, we find certain themes emerging, particularly in the intransient area of the health sector, that reveal how institutional practices create the conditions for non–participation, closing spaces for ecological knowing, both in the public and private sectors of our lives. First, there is the dependence on grants and short–term funding – the health sector and urban regeneration is replete with projectism. Competitive tendering not only takes a great deal of energy, but sets up poor communities against each other in a bidding war. Second, governmental institutions tend to focus on target groups and indicators determined by top–down processes. Third, the silo nature of governmental institutions divides life into separate entities; environment is separated from economy, and economic development from social and spiritual well–being. Fourth, in some domains certain forms of knowledge are revered at the expense of other forms, with 'scientific knowledge' perceived as superior. This is particularly rife in the health sector where the clinical gaze and its associated practices create opportunities for those with the need to have power and control to act in ways that reduce participation, increase bullying, and where hierarchy, not critical questioning, is the norm. This is also increasingly rife in other public sectors, such as universities. There is a creeping disease of evidence–based practice, prioritising only positivist–derived research at the expense of other ways of knowing (Schwandt, 2005). This, in turn, buys into the neoliberal agenda and audit culture of new public sector management with its project management tools (for example PRINCE2), where linear processes reduce the opportunities for dialogue and critical reflection and where accountability is to the top, and not to the people. People are pursuing a route up the greasy pole of career advancement, a pole created by the inevitable stretching of salary scales, in a world defined by individualism. Fifth, much of so-called participatory practice is tied up with service delivery, and purloined by consumer speak and notions of customer satisfaction. Finally, participation implies power sharing, a high level of trust and giving up the need to control. Psychologically this calls for a sense of internal security in those involved. Despite the rhetoric of collaboration between agencies, professions and the people whose lives they seek to influence that has been a feature of the modern state for at least the past 40 years, agencies still struggle with the silo thinking that dominates public sector organisations.

A preoccupation with working together still involves a struggle with anything more than a perfunctory engagement with the people they seek to serve. Agencies which previously thought their primary responsibility was the technical issues of housing or transport, now find themselves required to engage in partnerships with local people. It calls for high exposure without the security of ivory towers. I (Margaret) have often seen 'powerful' men sweat when, dislocated from the protection of their ivory towers, they have been faced with a community group on its home ground.

Foucault (1980) asserts that in challenging power and oppression, we should not focus merely on state apparatus and ideologies but, rather, on domination and the localised techniques and tactics for domination, including those officials and functionaries who carry out the exercise of power (the material operators of power) as well as the specific manifestations of that power: the forms of subjection, the infection of localised systems and the strategic apparatus. Those of us who are currently immersed in these structures, as people who provide or receive services, have to begin this task. We need to penetrate the barriers identified in this chapter, make a few holes, and then make them bigger by engaging in the act of co-creating other possibilities through cultures of organisational learning, dialogue, integrative thinking and systematic problem solving, thus expanding the critical spaces in existing practice. In what follows we explore those ways of working that are necessary to enable this to happen.

Section Two
Participatory praxis

FIVE

The use of story

> Now that we have no eternal truth we realise that our life is entirely made up of stories ... truth is made up of stories. So we can rehabilitate myth ... myths are the stories people live by, the stories that shape people's perception of life. (Cupitt, 2005)

The relevance of story to participatory practice

The transformative process begins in the stories people tell about their everyday lives. Freire's (1972) comment on naming the world in order to change it gives us a clue that stories of everyday life not only transmit culture and maintain the status quo, but by telling our stories, retelling them, then rewriting them we find we can create counternarratives that steer a course to transformation. Our first encounters in community as practitioners begin with the way we listen, respectfully, to the stories of life as it is experienced. This is the foundation of critical dialogue, the point at which trusting mutual relations are formed. In a process of dialogue and reflection, we learn to question the stories we tell, and by examining them a little more critically we find they contain the key to oppressions.

> Stories create the way we see our place in society and the way we perceive it as moulded around us: telling us what to expect of each other and ourselves. They shape and make sense of our world by reiterating the social and political order. Soap opera, Verdi, strip cartoons, and Shakespeare tell us what is good and what bad, what likely to succeed and what fail. (Bolton, 2005: 108)

Story surrounds us. Human beings are storytellers by nature, and we are drawn to them for many reasons. The four dimensions of the self – our feeling, our intellectual, our physical and our spiritual selves – are all part of an interactive, internal whole; in turn, this interacts with political and cultural contexts, to change and be changed by our place in the bigger, external whole of humanity. We use narrative to express our experience and understanding of all these dimensions of being. 'Narratives express the values of the narrator; they also develop and create values in the telling' (Bolton, 2005: 104). It is this powerful potential of story to capture life experience in order to understand it, and then to use story to create counternarratives of change that we are interested in. McAdams et al (2006: 31) suggest that stories also 'mend us when we are broken, heal us when we are sick, and even move us toward psychological fulfilment and maturity'. There is also a counter side to stories: they embed myths into society, embracing aspects of culture about particular groups of people, selling them as fundamental truths which may not necessarily be in the interests of the people they portray. At this point, we could link the theory of Antonio Gramsci and the notion of hegemony as *common sense* in relation to myths and legends. 'Myths incorporate archetypal symbols that remain viable today if our imaginations are active enough to make us conscious of, and curious about, our origins and our destiny. Myths capture a given society's basic psychological, sociological, cosmological, and metaphysical truths' (McAdams et al, 2006: 34), but the interests of the whole are not necessarily mutually represented. Stories can be dominating or liberating depending on whether they are absorbed as truth or whether they are questioned. We have talked about dissent as a vital component in the process of change, and in this chapter we are investigating the use of story as transgressional. In using story to question why things are as they are, we transgress the false consciousness that the world is a fixed experience, that it cannot be changed. Story then becomes part of the toolkit of transformative practice.

When questioned, stories can be interruptions in our everyday lives that lead to new ways of seeing the world. The process of telling and being heard results in self-esteem when we experience that what we have to say is relevant and of value. If we are not heard with respect, our voices are silenced, and we feel demeaned. But the simple act of listening to people's stories, respectfully giving one's full attention, is the beginning of the process of personal empowerment. The stories we tell about who we are and how we make sense of the world around us can be told and retold as we learn to question given truths. For instance, women's stories have exposed relations between knowledge and power, revealing that positivism's quest for a single truth was an expression of dominant male interests. The notion of beginning in experience reveals multiple truths and different ways of knowing. We begin to rewrite our stories with new insight – Black feminist thought emerged from the particular realities of Black women's lives and the interlocking, intersecting inequalities that get reproduced as a complex web of oppressions related to 'race', class and gender that result in marginalisation from knowledge production (Ramazanoglu and Holland, 2002: 70). Black and female truths become eliminated from a dominant truth, subordinated by racism and patriarchy. Feminist pedagogy has focused on narratives of lived experience as a participatory strategy with groups of women to identify the social and historical forces that have shaped these narratives. I (Margaret) was introduced to the work of Sistren, a theatre group formed by Kingston women, by my friend and colleague, Paula Asgill, of Jamaican heritage herself. Weiler (1994: 31) describes Sistren as a 'collaborative theatre group made up of working-class Jamaican women who create and write plays based upon a collaborative exploration of their own experiences'. The collective sharing of experience is the key to the knowledge of our socially and politically given identities. It is the process by which we discover our power as subjects in active, creative engagement in our world. The Combahee River Collective, a Black lesbian feminist organisation active in Boston in the 1970s, were instrumental in developing the concept of identity politics.

They argue that 'the most radical politics come directly out of our own identity, as opposed to working to end someone else's oppression' (Weiler, 1994: 32). In fact, we would argue that understanding our own identity, and the history that constructed it, is key to becoming self-critical, and therefore the basis of engaging critically within what we loosely term 'identity groups'. This, in turn, becomes the basis for transcending boundaries of 'race', class, gender, culture, nationhood, in mutual, autonomous alliance. In these ways, personal stories become collective narratives and move towards a transformative potential. A more critical gaze on power relations reveals that White western patriarchal privilege is structured into the stories we tell, positioning us in 'raced', classed and gendered relationships with each other.

'We are all storytellers, and we are the stories we tell' (McAdams et al, 2006: 3). We tell and retell our stories according to the way we make meaning of our lives, exploring ourselves in our world. As Mo Griffiths says, '... the self is never unencumbered ...a self is always in the process of being constructed in and by particular circumstances' (Griffiths, 2003: 388). On an inner, reflexive level, the stories we tell about ourselves grow in complexity, as our childhood develops and emerges in young adulthood, as a search for identity: Who am I? How do I fit into the world? (McAdams et al, 2006). Here is a retrospective story written by Barack Obama, an inner reflection of his own sense of identity and his awareness of racism in a White-dominated world. It was triggered by the unexpected discovery of an article in *Life* magazine, and in that moment his life changed. Previously, his White mother had told him that 'to be black was to be the beneficiary of a great inheritance, a special destiny, glorious burdens that only we were strong enough to bear. Burdens we were to carry with style...' (Obama, 2007: 29). Then, one day, as he waited for her in her workplace library, he became fascinated by the books around him:

> Most of the books held little interest for a nine-year-old boy [but] eventually I came across a photograph of an older man in dark glasses and a raincoat walking down an empty road. I couldn't guess what this picture was about; there seemed nothing unusual about the subject. On the next page was another photograph, this one a close-up of the same man's hands. They had a strange, unnatural pallor, as if blood had been drawn from the flesh. Turning back to the first picture, I now saw that the man's crinkly hair, his heavy lips and broad, fleshy nose, all had this same, uneven, ghostly hue. He must be terribly sick, I thought. A radiation victim, maybe.... Except when I read the words that went with the picture, that wasn't it at all. The man had received a chemical treatment, the article explained, to lighten his complexion.... There were thousands of people like him, black men and women back in America who'd undergone the same treatment in response to advertisements that promised happiness as a white person. I felt my

face and neck get hot. My stomach knotted; the type began to blur on the page. Did my mother know about this?...

I went into the bathroom and stood in front of the mirror with all my senses and limbs seemingly intact, looking as I had always looked, and wondered if something was wrong with me. The alternative seemed no less frightening – that the adults around me lived in the midst of madness. (Obama, 2007: 29, 52)

Consciousness, as Obama illustrates, is an inner narration of experience. This begins in the second year of life when 'I' becomes distinct from 'me', and we start to become narrators of our own experience. By young adulthood our narrative identities are the stories we live by (McAdams et al, 2006). But identities are not fixed; they change with age, experience and changing consciousness. Participatory practice engages in the process of transformative change by working with story as a transformative tool. Out of our personal stories emerges a deeper understanding of the way that our lives have been socially situated by structures of power, and we begin to see the personal as political. Together, we discover that we can change the world by changing the way we make sense of our experience of the world.

Stories of everyday life, then, begin the process of transformative change at the point of personal empowerment. 'In the process of telling the story, people realize they have acquired a tacit knowledge about things that previously they would not have been able to articulate' (Bray et al, 2000: 95). As Carolyn Steedman (2000: 72) says, 'The past is re-used through the agency of social information, and that interpretation of it can only be made with what people know of a social world and their place within it'. The boundaries between truth and fiction are blurred: we tell and retell the stories of our lives differently according to our audience, our recollection and our insight, thus stories become shaped by time and space and understanding. A more critical consciousness emerges when we start to question our stories, and learning to question is provoked by external interventions in the form of people, thoughts, ideas, insights that we brush up against, critical encounters in the everyday. These encounters create interruptions in our acceptance of what is, opening up 'the places where we rework what has already happened to give current events meaning' (Steedman, 2000: 5). And it all begins in the understanding that 'any sense of the extraordinary is grounded first of all in ordinary experience' (Quinney, 1998: xiii).

Story as the telling of everyday experience

My story defines who I am. And if I want to know myself, to gain insight into the meaning of my own life, then I ... must come to know my own story. (McAdams, 1993: 11)

Coming to know our own stories is the beginning of becoming critical. Participatory practitioners listen to and share everyday stories as the respectful opening of a mutual partnership. It is a relationship founded on the fundamental belief in people to be autonomous subjects in their world. Our stories embody the way we have come to see our world and make sense of our place in it. This process begins so early in our lives that our identities are shaped by what is reflected back to us about who we are, and we tend to accept these messages with all their flawed contradictions unquestioningly. Therefore, our stories contain the values and attitudes of the status quo that rank us in order of perceived importance in society. If these have been internalised as *common sense*, and written into our stories of life as we experience it, then this also gives us a starting place for questioning our assumptions. In this way, the process builds self-respect and mutual respect through trust, dignity, conviviality – silenced voices become heard.

In a process that gradually becomes more critical and more collective, little stories link voice to narrative 'by taking the particular perspective of an individual seriously; that is, the individual as situated in particular circumstances in all their complexity [and linking this] to grander concerns like education, social justice and power' (Griffiths, 2003: 81). For Freire, this is not a handing over of personal stories, but the claiming of our stories as the route to our identities, claiming our right to be autonomous beings.

> Moving from silence into speech is for the oppressed, the colonized, the exploited, and those who stand and struggle side by side a gesture of defiance that heals, that makes life and new growth possible. It is that act of speech, of 'talking back', that is no mere gesture of empty words, that is the expression of our movement from object to subject – the liberated voice. (hooks, 1989: 9)

An analysis of power helps us to understand how the deeply personal is profoundly political, and personal stories become liberated voices. This idea is relevant to research I (Margaret) did with Paula Asgill, which linked the failure to sustain critical alliances for social justice between Black and White women to a sense of identity as the basis of autonomy. Without personal autonomy, we lack the self-confidence to reach out across difference; alliances break down in the face of anger, insecurity and a host of other behaviours that arise out of unequal power relations (Ledwith and Asgill, 2000, 2007). Doyal and Gough (1991) take this even further, suggesting that autonomy of agency is a basic human need that leads to critical autonomy, and that this is the prerequisite of critical participation in society, the basis of collective action. In this respect, they consider the denial of participation – marginalisation, social exclusion – to be a dehumanising act. In these ways we can see how the use of story can lead to a more critical sense of the ways in which our identities have been shaped. A sense of who we are in the world gives us the confidence to claim our identities with pride, to reach out as equals and act collectively for a common good, and the beginning of this process of change lies in the personal story. We begin to see that dignity leads to confidence, and confidence leads to self-esteem in a process of critical consciousness, thus self-esteem becomes a political not personal concept (Griffiths, 2003). Story is a deeply reflexive process which leads to altered consciousness, weaving critical connections between personal lives and the structures of society that differently shape those lives. This is the basis of a movement from passive object to critical subject, a process of humanisation (Freire, 1972).

We are natural storytellers. Through story we discover new ways of knowing. Not only is this retrospective, even beyond our lifetime, beyond death, but it is empathetic, it enables us to identify with other lives, and so story offers us a collective possibility. In dialogue, we seek a connection, we suspend our own truth to explore other people's truths, and in doing so move towards a collective narrative, a collective knowing, a consensus on experience lived that embraces a diversity of voices. In these ways, story offers us a form of search and research that generates theory in action and action through theory. It is an imaginal and presentational form of knowing – stories, non-verbal presentations, artwork, poetry, metaphor, myth (Heron, 2001: 338). Beginning in our everyday stories, we become teller and re-teller of our world. We expose the assumptions, contradictions and paradoxes of everyday life, and through a deeper knowing we re-vision what is possible, we reposition ourselves in relation to reality. We see the world in different ways, and we act in different ways. Our stories become a mediating force between narrative and non-narrative, between experience and making sense of the experience, and so theory in process is an evolving narrative of the everyday. This way of seeing story as everyday and extraordinary, fictional and factual, defined and refined is captured by Lori Lansens in the novel, *The girls*:

> Aunt Lovey had so many stories to tell. When we were children, they were made-up stories about Ruby and me, but as we grew older the stories became memories, extrapolated upon and polished, and they began to stretch beyond Ruby and me to Aunt Lovey and Uncle Stash, their courtship and their youth, then further back to stories about her mother, and hers. After a while, I sense that Aunt Lovey was not telling me the stories so much as entrusting them to me. It was Aunt Lovey's belief that all ordinary people led extraordinary lives, but just didn't notice. (Lansens, 2007: 102)

This understanding gives a greater power to the role of story as a transformative medium. Collective narratives become oppositional responses to dominant narratives, they become counternarratives that critique the metanarratives we have inherited as part of the Enlightenment's quest for a single, dominant truth. Personal stories challenge hegemonic narratives,

> those legitimating stories propagated for specific political purposes to manipulate public consciousness by heralding a national set of

common cultural ideals. The notion of counternarratives in this sense carries with it Foucault's 'counter-memory' and the idea of counter-practices, but in a specific and local sense. Such counternarratives are, as Lyotard explains, quintessentially 'little stories' – the little stories of those individuals and groups whose knowledges and histories have been marginalized, excluded, subjugated or forgotten in the telling of official narratives. (Peters and Lankshear, 1996: 2)

Story and critical theory

... if we understand the world narratively, as we do, then it makes sense to study the world narratively. For us, life – as we come to it and as it comes to others – is filled with narrative fragments enacted in storied moments of time and space, and reflected upon and understood in terms of narrative unities and discontinuities. (Clandinin and Connelly, 2000: 17)

The concept of theory often conjures up the notion of a self-contained body of scientific knowledge, a real truth that makes sense of the world and can be applied in practice. This interpretation of theory is so entrenched in a western worldview that it is often taken for granted and accepted as the only way of seeing the world. Participatory practitioners believe that theories are provisional ideas that are organic in relation to the ways in which we see and experience our changing world. In this sense, theory and practice form a symbiotic unity, a living praxis, knowledge in action and action as knowledge (Reason, 2002). When we question the role of traditional approaches to making sense of the world, we begin to see that 'theory generation is far from neutral, but is a deeply politicized practice' (Whitehead and McNiff, 2006: 28).

Cavanagh (2007) says that it was only with the advent of postmodern thought that we began to fully question the nature of theories that define people's lives from a dominant, authoritative position and asked whose interests were represented, what assumptions were being made and who was hidden, distorted or silenced from the frame. If, as practitioners, we fail to engage in theory generation, and so leave policies to be formed on theoretical assumptions that contradict our practice, we are leaving ourselves open to a constant struggle in which theory and practice are at variance. Theory is a knowledge claim that contains an explanation of why things are the way they are. But there are many different ways of making sense of the world and many different experiences of life in the world. Any practice which claims to be predicated on equality and social justice has to heed these diverse ways of knowing and being in the world, and engage critically with both theory and practice. Theory generation is political, so to be uncritical is to entrench the dominant order of things unwittingly. In these times of frenetic activity, where the pressure to act overrides the time to think, we need to pay attention to creating critical spaces where we can reflect and have dialogue about our ideas, experience and practice.

Let us link this with Freirean thought. Freire stresses that transformative theory begins in lived reality, in the stories of the people, in relations of trust, mutuality, respect, and that dialogue is the basis of this praxis. Cavanagh talks of his earliest readings of Paulo Freire as learning about 'faith, hope, humility, love and critical mindedness' (Cavanagh, 2007: 43), and that a quarter of a century later he still finds this set of values powerful as a frame for reflection and learning. Similarly, in that same period of time in Scotland, I (Margaret) was introduced to Freirean pedagogy, and it touched me at a profound level, enriching the scope of my practice to a quality beyond the influence of any other ideas. Peter Mayo (2004: 10) suggests that the 'fusion of reason and emotion' contained in Freire touches people in a holistic way that reaches beyond the limitations of the intellect. Emotions and intellect in symbiotic relation offer a power that reaches beyond any consideration of skills. Cavanagh, for instance, talks about love as an essential component of compassion and solidarity that gives us the capacity to imagine a better world for all humanity. Freire talks about his work as a pedagogy of love, a love that is similar to the participatory worldview re-visioned by Gandhi when he told the unemployed millworkers of Lancashire that he loved all children of the world *as his own*. It is the deepest level of compassion which leads to our belief in people's infinite potential, it is the quality that sustains the process of change, it is the basis of becoming self-critical and self-accepting, without which we are benevolent, tokenistic or altruistic – none of which are transformative qualities.

The idea that personal narratives reveal the political nature of our lives is fundamental to Freirean pedagogy (Freire, 1972). In dialogue with each other, we are often introduced to critical insights that slice through entrenched taken-for-granted attitudes about everyday reality, and in a process of reflection we redefine ourselves, reposition ourselves in relation to reality. As Foucault says, the self can be authored by us, and we can produce our lives as works of art in which we become self-determining agents that resist and challenge power structures (Danaher et al, 2000: 150). As teller and re-teller of our life experience we create knowledge in action that repositions us in relation to the past and present with a more critical awareness. Stories are rewritten in the light of dialogue and reflection on dialogue, repositioning us in relation to knowledge; in ongoing dialogue, as readers of our own stories and those of others, we generate new ideas, new perspectives, new theories.

Reflection on experience engages us in what Freire saw as a process of 'denunciation and annunciation': the 'act of analyzing a dehumanizing reality, [and to] denounce it while announcing its transformation' (Freire, 1985: 57). This narrative approach also engages with feminist pedagogy, locating the personal as political by linking voice to narrative through the myriad of little stories that lend themselves to collective narratives for change.

Gramsci helped me (Margaret) to see how dominant ideas permeate the very surface of our skins, persuading us to accept as 'common sense' the contradictions of everyday life and to act in ways that are often not in our best interests. This is the basis of anti-discriminatory analysis. Gramsci emphasised the role of myths and legends in perpetuating domination, and saw critical education, history and culture as the key to knowing who we are and what has shaped our reality on a multiplicity of dimensions in order to act together for change. A transformative reach, from personal empowerment to collective global action, is vital to any critical analysis. 'The starting point of critical elaboration is knowing what one really is ... as a product of the historical process to date which has deposited in you an infinity of traces, without leaving an inventory' (Gramsci, 1971: 324).

Story in the process of becoming critical

Story starts in the personal, an 'exploring inwards':

> ... but if fiction is to be the basis for a process of reflection that is to be sustained, we need a format where questioning and exploring beyond one's initial set of ideas is made explicit and is built into the writing process itself, as well as into the discussion of the writing.... In order to sustain the reflective process, a format is needed which is flexible enough to allow different ways of writing to be combined, a format which allows the writer to move easily between description, imagination, creation and analytical commentary. (Winter et al, 1999: 65)

Darder tells of the way she encourages students 'to reach into themselves and back to their histories' (2002: 233). This offers an important past–present–future dynamic, 'moving between present and past with a view to contributing towards a transformed future' (Mayo, 1999: 147). Story, in this way, becomes a tool to explore memory and history, helping us make connections with the way that our past created our present. Darder supports her students to analyse these stories from theoretical perspectives. *Problematising* 'reading', she begins by asking them to reflect on their earliest memories of stories they were told by those who love them; this is extended to include stories they learnt to read within school. Analysing these stories about stories, she works with them to discover what has shaped them in their world, revealing insights that may not emerge in any other way.

These deeply personal stories become the vehicles of critical consciousness. By problematising aspects of our stories, we tease out the political connections with the structural forces that have shaped our experience and contributed to the identities we have assumed. Stories are fragments of the multiple contexts that created them (Treleaven, 2001). By exploring the political nature of everyday encounters, we move towards the critical consciousness necessary to demystify the dominant hegemony, revealing life with all the stark contradictions that we live by.

Stories offer potential for change by working on this past–present–future dimension:

> Of particular importance to an action research project concerned with radical change in everyday life, stories facilitate connections between a story teller's past and imagined futures, creating potential for new ways of being and acting in the world. (Treleaven, 2001: 267)

Treleaven (2001: 264) used this approach in three stages:

1. Spontaneous, unstructured storytelling of critical incidents from everyday life developing listening as part of the dialogical process, '"wondering, questioning, doubting" (Brunner, 1995, cited in Treleaven, 2001), in critical reflection with self and others, seeking to embrace tensions in ways that lead to multiple paths of exploration' (2001: 268). 'One story evoked another, creatively releasing the memory of others. Understanding these stories was not hurried by applying analytic processes in the early stage. We initially told our stories as a way of building relationships ...' (2001: 264).
2. A more structured approach to bringing some of those stories back into the group for collaborative reflection, understanding and action. Collaboratively identifying the dominant narratives as well as counternarratives threading through the stories, subject positions, power relations and binary thinking.
3. The reconstruction of old stories in new forms to connect in strategic alliance beyond the immediate group in action research cycles that spiralled outwards.

You can begin to trace the pattern of story as a reaching inwards to explore the self under the microscope of a self-reflexive narrative, to discover the ways in which 'the social is embedded in ... skin and bones' (Berger and Quinney, 2005: 265). Denzin (1999, cited in Berger and Quinney, 2001) suggests that a storied approach should seek meaning in the stories themselves, as through storytelling the powerless become powerful. During apartheid in South Africa, everyday stories were heard by listeners as dissenting voices: 'Like the Coyote myths of the Lakota Sioux, Aunt Nancy stories of the African slaves, and Jakata tales from the Buddhist tradition(s), these ancient stories provide vital tools that continue to engage listeners, teach values, *and* challenge social norms' (Berger and Quinney, 2005: 199).

Journalling is a way of recording stories of everyday life on a regular basis. I (Margaret) find it particularly useful to write my stories in the quiet of the early morning as I reflect on the previous day. I use the right-hand page to tell the story and the left-hand page to record insights, questions, doubts, critical connections, reflections and action. This reliving of everyday stories helps us to develop a more inquiring engagement with life as well as an openness to engaging with others. To hear stories about other lives, and not to judge against a truth but to be open to many ways of knowing helps us to listen from the heart and to be open to a connected knowing (Belenky et al, 1997). Connected knowing is the link between the introspective engagement and the empathetic knowing that we need to form collective alliances across difference. 'Without intimate knowledge of one's self one cannot enter into intimacy with another, that one "who is essentially a stranger to himself [sic] is unlikely to forge an affective connection to someone else"' (Kohn, 1990, cited in Goldberger et al, 1996: 230). Without self-knowledge we cannot be open to similarities and empathies between self and other, so necessary in the process of transformation. Wendy Derbyshire, community activist in Hattersley, uses reflection on the use of story with the Hattersley Women Writers, a group that led to Hattersley Women for Change. Her reflections on practice help us to identify how powerful her use of story was with a group of women who had never had the confidence nor the inclination to write about their lives.

> "I loved my involvement in that group; it was often the high point of my week. It's such a powerful way of seeing how human beings can learn to connect with each other, I think. What did we have in common, apart from gender? Well, we'd all arrived in Hattersley as part of some social engineering by the power brokers of the early 60s, but I don't think those two things could entirely explain the bond that was created between us. We were all ages, and had not experienced life the same way, but something very powerful was at work in that little band of women, most definitely.
>
> "Everyone started out nervously at first, and were hesitant at sharing what they'd produced. I could really identify with the things they said about scribbling away in secret at home, and trying to find either the space to do it or the time. Fear of a partner or family member picking it up and saying 'What's all this then? Catherine Cookson better look out!' or some other kind of a jibe, was common. But they did write, they did carry on, despite the butterflies in the pit of the stomach before they shared their most recent offering.
>
> "Nobody ever needed reminding to give respectful silence to a member who was reading their work aloud, possibly for the first time. Neither could the enthusiasm and appreciation of a participant's offering be constructed as anything other than sheer pride and admiration, truly felt. We learnt such a lot from and about each other and it was so exciting to see the women's confidence increasing week by week.
>
> "The feelings of surprise and wonder that were generated among us as we realised that we were very capable of investigating what was important and meaningful to us about our lives, became replaced by trust and the real desire to have some very frank exchanges about just what constituted our own particular worldview, and how it felt to live it. I liked the silence in the group at those times. It was a time

for listening, digesting and reflecting on what we had heard, and just as importantly, respecting the owner of the hand that propelled an ordinary pen to write such extraordinary things.

"Through Mary's vivid description of learning to live life differently due to sight loss, *our* eyes were opened. When she spoke of her pride at living in Hattersley, a place that hasn't got the most positive image outside of its boundaries, then *our* chests became inflated by the air of affirmation radiating from her passionate statement. I was proud to stand with her a few months later, on International Women's Day, in a packed theatre, as we both read our poetry to a lively audience of people who just loved to hear the stories of other people's lives.

"For me, I learnt about the power of listening, not only to the spoken word, but to the spaces in between. I began to understand that there are times when each gap doesn't need to be filled up just for the sake of it. Sometimes though, that left unsaid was the most profound – I began to think of what kind of question would begin to unlock it." (Wendy Derbyshire, 10 April 2008)

Listening from the heart

Wendy's reflections on the practice of story help to identify how the significance of trust and respectful listening in storytelling can lead to the personal and collective autonomy for change. Starting in personal stories, a group of women who had never had the confidence to write, let alone share their writing with others, were able to move from deeply personal stories of lived reality to exploring the political relevance of their lives, and then collectively act together for change, both in the community and beyond the community, in such a short space of time.

Wendy offers us some fine insights into separated and connected knowing: separated knowing more distanced, critical and questioning; connected knowing empathetic, open, attempting to understand from deep inside by entering the place of the other person or idea in order to understand it. Both need critical feedback to take the process forward (Goldberger et al, 1996; Belenky et al,1997). This also links Giroux's notion of border crossing to the use of story, a way of being open to different ways of knowing and being by seeing life from across a border. 'Connected knowing [is] a rigorous, deliberate, and demanding *procedure*, a way of knowing that requires *work*' (Goldberger et al, 1996: 209), and as such needs to be structured into our practice. Finding expression to describe what has been silenced and subordinated calls for integrating the inner voice and encouraging new forms of dialogue to reach a collective consensus on new ways of knowing that lead to new ways of acting – we believe that story offers one such approach. Uncertainty and openness are pre-requisites of this connected approach, and in suspending our own truth, we open ourselves to the possibility of empathy as a way of making sense of collective experiences in order to act collectively for change. As Maxine Greene, respected educational philosopher, has often stressed, a commitment to bringing multiple voices into the conversation about teaching and knowing as a way to break through the old to create the new calls for passionate commitment (Goldberger et al, 1996). In telling our stories and our histories, we heal fractures and create new possibilities – with insight, hindsight and foresight, we reach into the past in order to understand the present and create the future.

Story as participatory action research

> A participative worldview draws our attention to the qualities of the participative-relational practices in our work. Issues of interdependence, politics, power and empowerment must be addressed at both micro- and macro-levels, that is, in inquiring relationships in face-to-face and small group interaction, about how the research is situated in its wider political context. (Reason and Bradbury, 2001: 448)

We stress that participatory action research is an integral part of participatory practice in a constant process of search and re-search (Freire, 1972), and in this section we take a more focused look at its role. Story, as we continue to emphasise, is the beginning of dialogue. Equally, story can encompass first-person research/practice (personal level), second-person research/practice (interpersonal or relational level) and third–person research/practice (collective/organisational level) – all mutually generating and reinforcing one another (Torbert, 2001: 256). This is a vital concept in relation to collective action for transformative change, and does not happen unless we rigorously structure it into our practice. Here we see the connection between being critical and collective action – both of which are sticking points in participatory practice. As Torbert notes, 'not only are we individuals unpractised and unpolished in the domain of inquiry in the midst of our daily lives, but so are our intimate relationships, our organizations, and social science itself ... we rarely experience ourselves as present in a wondering, inquiring, "mindful" way to our own action' (Torbert, 2001: 250). If we are serious about our commitment to transformative change our practice needs to become self-critical and critical in its engagement with face-to-face groups, communities and organisations, as well as in the larger collective formations that are necessary for transformation.

In relation to the idea of personal autonomy leading to collective action, Doyal and Gough (1991) locate this confidence and sense of identity in story. They suggest that autonomy of agency is a basic human need that leads to critical autonomy, and they see this as the prerequisite to critical participation in society, the basis of collective action. These theoretical insights link the practical strategy of reflection as story with a political discovery of who we are in the world. The problem of identities shaped as 'oppositional', defining the self as what one is not, has given rise to knowledge claims of difference from a diversity of singular perspectives based on 'race', gender, religion, ethnicity, age, sexual orientation, 'dis'ability, but this still fails to get to grips with the multiplicity of oppressions that affect great numbers of people, for example, the issues faced by poor, older Black women. It also raises issues of knower and known. Whose voice is telling the story, and who is making sense of it? The passion evoked by the discovery of voice by those whose voices have been shut up and shut out releases the energy to act on new-found confidence from places where large numbers remain *unknown* and researchers remain *unknowing* (Bing and Trotman Reid, 1996). In this respect, Mo Griffiths (2003: 21) emphasises the theory and practice of acting with and for others by paying 'continuing attention to practicalities and specificities, while the theorizing continues, and a continuing attention to careful, rigorous, theory and reflection while presenting practicalities and specificities'. She calls it a philosophy that engages with the conditions of all people, 'others' and 'us', thinking and acting, with and for.

In community-based action research we pay particular attention to 'listening carefully and respectfully to indigenous voices [by] learning to create spaces for the mutual exchange of wisdom' (Pyrch and Castillo, 2001: 379). This is specifically designed to counter the fractured parts of our knowing that have been subjugated by the rationality of the scientific revolution by opening dialogue across difference that connects to 'soulful voices within ourselves' (Pyrch and Castillo, 2001: 379). Thinking in these ways, we can begin to create active projects to locate locally based wisdom as resistance to the neoliberal global project that attempts to standardise us all within an economic imperative. Engaging across difference of gender, culture, 'race', ethnicity, North and South, these co-researchers have used story to develop knowing beyond the intellect, 'to hear those quiet sounds of foam, created by Ganma, we need to listen with our hearts, to be aware of the "experiencing", and not just the experiences that happen to us', and in doing so 'we give, we receive, we unite, and we create something new' (Pyrch and Castillo, 2001: 380-1). We cannot force new knowledge: as my (Margaret's) little granddaughter Grace demonstrated to me the other day, when we try to capture foam in our hands it evaporates into nothing. It is only through the simple act of gently opening our hands to connect with the foam that it will linger, revealing itself to us; so it is with new knowledge, 'if we approach its diversity and complexity with an open spirit of humility, a willingness to be permeated, that the new knowledge also reveals itself to us. Humility helps us to grow, to listen, to share, and to know how to give and how to receive. It teaches us how to create a knowledge that is "ours" not "yours" or "mine" – to create not only a "you" or "me", but a "we"' (Pyrch and Castillo, 2001: 381). A world held in common is one in which we are able to reach across all aspects of difference to act together on issues which are wrong. In these ways, an altered way of 'knowing' the world (epistemology) results in changed ways of 'being' in the world (ontology). Stories offer the potential for radical change when they are understood as 'more than just a story' by investigating 'the ways they are produced, the ways they are read, the work they perform in the wider social order, how they change, and their role in the political process' (Plummer, 1995, cited in Treleaven, 2001: 267). The basis of transformation is 'In critical reflection with self and others, seeking to embrace tensions in ways that lead to multiple paths of exploration' (Treleaven, 2001: 268).

Story is a route to engaging community in self-inquiry and self-knowledge: 'the telling of a story slows the mind down and lets the story sink underneath the skin to reveal something of the spirit' (Hustedde and King, 2002: 342). Stories are important rituals in community, 'part of the search for who we are and the search for meaning as a community ... community rituals can provide stability and continuity and can promote a sense of solidarity and cohesion' (Hustedde and King, 2002: 343). The process takes communities forward as co-creators of their own futures. For instance, the Native American tradition of acknowledging seven generations of community takes the past–present–future dimension from solid historic connections through to marking change and planning directions for the future. Stories can also be used as community healing rituals in reconciliation and dialogue. Hustedde and King (2002) give an example of the way that a unity candle was used in a public meeting in a community torn apart by land disputes and coal mining. The meeting opened with community leaders and coal mine operators symbolically lighting candles to indicate their willingness to talk, and then lighting one unity candle together to symbolise their desire to find a common resolution to their differences. This set the tone for cooperation as valuable in healing divisions and building solidarity.

Story in practice

Let us take a look at some ideas of how to use story in practice. I had the good fortune to meet Chris Cavanagh in Portland, Maine a few years ago when he facilitated a planning retreat for the board of the Pedagogy and Theater of the Oppressed organisation. It was here that I (Margaret) learnt about the work of the Catalyst Centre in Toronto, which is where Chris is based. The centre provides courses to develop techniques with popular educators from a wide variety of contexts, from working with domestic violence and street violence to unemployment and literacy. One of the techniques Chris has developed is storytelling in the practice of social justice, which he approaches in the spirit of us all being born storytellers. He uses a seven-stage structure for developing these skills (Cavanagh, 2004: 13).

Cavanagh's seven-stage structure for storytelling

1. Listen:
Learn to listen. Listen to yourself tell your friends about your day. Listen to others. Listen for the ways in which they tell a story. Listen to the choice of metaphors, adjectives, punch-lines, character. Listen to their body-language. Listen to your body-language. Listen to the things unsaid. Listen to the moods. Listen to how you don't listen.

2. Choose:
Choose stories that mean something to you.

3. Structure and Pattern:
All stories have structure and pattern. It begins with: beginning-middle-end AND, some stories are: accumulative; 3s, 4s, 5s, 7s…; circular; journey and return; descent and ascent; circles within circles; set-up and punch-line.

4. Visualize:
See the story – run it like a film. Map it out on paper. Story-board it. Memorized words and phrases are easier to forget than images.

5. Tell:
Rehearse. Tell it to a mirror. Bug your friends. Sub-vocalize, ie mutter. Tell it perfectly 100 times. Tell it to kids – they are kind and unforgiving critics. Tell it 1,001 Friday Nights of Storytelling. Tell it to the stars. Don't forget about eye-contact.

6. Reflect:
ASK for feedback. ASK for negatives. ASK for positives. LISTEN to them both and avoid defensiveness. An opinion about your telling is merely advice that can be taken or ignored or taken in part. Listen to yourself tell. What did you leave out? What did you like? How do you feel when you're finished telling?

7. Research:
Look for other versions of the story you told. Hold a story in your head as you go through the day and look around to see where else that story exists. Read books about storytelling and narrative and myth. Write your thoughts. Talk to your friends about your thoughts.

In these ways, we can develop structured skills in the use of storytelling as a vital component in the toolkit for transformative practice.

Stories do not inevitably depend on language. When working with Vietnamese refugees who had arrived in Scotland traumatised by their experiences, with little or no English, I (Margaret) developed a way of using photographs and drawings to stimulate the acting out of feelings and experience, which in turn would generate language to capture the concept involved. In these ways, stories provide healing, literacy, cross-cultural understanding, political awareness, empathy, fun and much more.

Fiction writing is a useful stimulus for reflection. Fantasy, folk tale, poetry and song can all be used as genres to distance the experience and create a more objective element in the telling of personal experiences. Bolton (2005) talks about the use of parody, in this respect, and one person's use of A.A. Milne's *Winnie the Pooh* characters, Tigger and Eeyore, to represent people and relationships in the story of a life.

Storytelling is also theatre. Popular theatre is used for reflection and learning. It takes many different forms, from public performances to acting out intimate vignettes on oppressive experiences, in order to understand how to bring about change. If we combine street theatre with the idea of critical public spaces as places for creating critical dissent dialogue, we can come up with some exciting ideas for using the contested spaces of public squares and market places to begin the process of questioning. In early modern times, these were not places of silence, but brought together diverse social groups, and often the carnivalesque was a source of questioning and subverting the existing social order. The taken-for-grantedness of everyday life can be turned inside out, 'all that jolts us out of our normal expectations and epistemological complacency' (Gardiner, 2000: 65). We should not be afraid to claim back these sites 'for oppositional activity, playful deviance, and educative exposure to the full range of people and values that make up a society' (Dixon et al, 2006: 191). This is the way we begin the process of questioning.

Probably the most transformative cultural artistic form of popular theatre is the Theater of the Oppressed, developed by Augusto Boal in the 1970s. He devised a range of techniques, including forum theatre, which I (Margaret) experienced in a Boal workshop at a Pedagogy and Theater of the Oppressed conference. Since the birth of this organisation in 1995, the vision of Doug Paterson from the University of Nebraska at Omaha, Augusto Boal has run workshops attached to the conference, more lately with his son Julian. He was profoundly influenced by Paulo Freire, yet the only time the two friends appeared together in public was when they were presented with honorary doctorates at the third Pedagogy and Theater of the Oppressed conference in Omaha, Nebraska in 1996. Little did we realise as we were inspired by these gargantuan influences on world-wide community-based practice that Paulo Freire would die quite suddenly in 1997, and that this would be followed by the equally sudden death of Augusto Boal, significantly on International Workers' Day, 1 May 2009.

Using the public square and the carnivalesque to turn life inside out!

Photo: Jack Taverner

Boal's forum theatre is an interactive theatre form that is developed from a lived experience of discrimination. This may be an experience of racism or violence, or anything else that has felt marginalising. After this first showing, there may be a brief discussion among the audience, facilitated by a character known as the Joker. The play is restarted, but this time, whenever a member of the audience, a 'spect–actor', has an idea that might change the experience for the protagonist, the person who is the victim of oppression, the play is frozen and without dialogue the spect–actor takes the protagonist's place. The scene is re-enacted with the changes and so re-experienced, with the other characters reacting intuitively in role. The audience is able to see the impact of these changes on the entire experience. This continues, with interventions from other spect–actors, until it feels appropriate to have a debate about the learning generated by the changes to the original experience. Empathy and empowerment are generated, as well as ideas about how to bring about change.

The Lawnmowers Independent Theatre Company, founded in 1986, based in Gateshead, North East England, is run by and for people with learning difficulties (www.thelawnmowers.co.uk). It must be one of the most creative companies working in the cultural sector, with many facets to their programme including filming, performances, touring, training, workshops, television, trade unions, policy analysis, research, environmental work, schools and very much more, on national and international levels. Here I (Margaret) want to focus on their theatre work that is based on Augusto Boal's forum theatre. Starting in social reality, a theme emerges from their own personal stories, and out of this they create an interactive play. This is developed and taken into public places, creating a critical space for consciousness and change in the real world. I want to talk about my own life-changing experience with Lawnmowers, when I was fortunate enough to become a participant in one of their workshops. For a day, we were swept up in the interface of fantasy and reality, uplifting music and outrageous costumes captivated us, but threaded through it was the power of real lived experience. Those without learning difficulties were presented with an altered worldview. The Joker helped us to change in with the actors as spect–actors, altering the oppressive experience, seeking interventions that could bring about a world of equality and respect. The actors joined us in small group dialogue to share ideas and experience, creating empathy and trust as mutual participants in the drama of life. In these ways, all our little stories became part of a much bigger collective humanity, and we left changed, having been drawn into the power of story, dramatised, fictionalised, set to music and then re-situated in life.

The learning that comes from this is far more powerful that reading an abstract account. Bolton (2005: 104), talking about 'our storied nature', reminds us that 'information is retained in the human mind as narrative. We do not go to a particular section within a file within a drawer within a cabinet in our memories, we go to a particular place in a narrative: an association of events, faces, voices, place, foods, and sense of roughness or softness.' In these ways, I learnt more from Lawnmowers about the lived experience of having learning difficulties than from any book. I lived the experience, fusing my life, in all its difference, with lives that are different in other ways, and came out with a 'connected knowing' (Belenky et al, 1997).

Lyndsey Wilson, a freelance drama and dance practitioner, talks about the potential of Boal in her work. Degrees in both Contemporary Performing Arts and Audience Participation introduced her to the theory and practice of Augusto Boal, which she applies in her work with Prescap, a community arts organisation. Prescap provides a platform and catalyst for people to explore, realise and value their full potential through creativity:

> "My most recent work was a 36-week project entitled 'My Friends, My Family', with a group of participants with learning disabilities and/or physical disabilities. The group meets every Monday and Friday for an arts and crafts class, and I was asked to facilitate some drama and music-making sessions which might open up new opportunities for the group to explore their creativity with different media. The project aim was to explore the feelings of the participants about the support they receive from their friends and family. The project also included participation from support workers, staff, family and friends. The output of the project was to develop a short film or performance initiated and performed by the group that could be shared with family and friends.

"I arranged a series of one-hour workshops which could introduce the group to drama and movement, developing skills in improvisation, vocal techniques and choreography. Simple games such as 'name and gesture' and 'tangles and knots' worked well for me as a new member of the group – offering me an opportunity to learn names quickly – and for the group as a way of using their imagination to develop gestures which applied, or did not apply to their character. The importance of repetition of these games as a warm-up exercise allowed the group to expand on previous gestures and try out new movements, new characters who said things they shouldn't say and did things they couldn't possibly do in 'real life'. The progression of these games into focus and trust exercises such as hypnotic hands, rhythmic work as a group and partner games such as follow the leader, again built on the group dynamic.

"During this time we also experimented with some writing workshops – producing short monologues about our feelings, collating our life stories and getting things off your chest, so to speak. For some of the group it was the first opportunity to really give quality time to thinking about where we came from and the experiences of our lives, and in this respect it was quite an emotional experience. Using these monologues as scripts for short scenes and improvisations allowed the group a sense of ownership of the work we were creating; it wasn't about me providing a script from a book, these were real words and real people. It was in the drama games and workshops that I saw the development of teamwork as the group began to build a trust in one another and they started to use the workshops as an opportunity to voice their opinions:

> 'My friend lives next door to me in the home and to be honest I was happier before he moved in. It's hard work to live like this and that makes me feel a bit upset.'

> 'The thing that really annoys me is when people talk to my girlfriend but they talk to me instead, as if she can't understand and she needs me to translate. She can understand, she nods her head to say yes and shakes her head to say no and if they ask questions then they should ask them to her and not me. If she wants me to answer them for her she will tell me. So do her a favour, and ask her a question.'

"Further exercises on improvisation with the group such as freeze frame stories (actors begin an improvised scene and audience can freeze it and step into a role) were our next challenge and at times worked very well, dependent on the group of participants. I can't say in any terms that this was an easy process; I would say that a small handful of the group really engaged with the exercises and the majority went along for the ride but for that handful the experience was an empowering one.

"We began discussing what we wanted to put in our film and it was here that I offered a selection of workshops about storyboards and the process of editing and changing what we see and do to create a story we want to tell. For a number of the group, explaining the process of how a film is put together was very important as they didn't have that understanding to begin with. We worked on a form of forum theatre, I asked a small group to act out a story: a new member of the group arrives at the class for the first time and is ignored by everyone. The rest of the group watched and were asked to comment at the end. We then asked the audience if they would do it differently. Different members of the audience then acted out the story in different ways until we were all agreed on what should happen. We then used this story and a Polaroid camera to create a storyboard which we could edit, taking photographs of each scene, close-ups of faces, a cup flying through the air etc so that the editing process was tangible for all members.

"The result of the 36-week process was a short performance piece using drama and movement. The group produced the music for the performance, the costumes, the set and the storyboard as well as the choreography. Alongside this we produced a documentary about the work of the staff at the centre and the participants; this was on show at the exhibition to accompany the writings of the group and their artwork.

"More importantly for the group was the opportunity to try something new and see themselves as artists in their own right; quite a daunting task for some of them. By employing professional artists to work with the group, we had the chance to impart new skills and use new technology in a supportive environment. For example, the majority of the group had never had the chance to use a laptop, and when we worked together to type up our stories, everyone was given the opportunity to type their own dialogue.

"The work produced helped to raise awareness of disability issues with the intention of reducing stigma and discrimination, and for this group the chance to build up the confidence to speak out about their feelings was a pivotal moment in the project. To watch the group at the exhibition when they saw themselves on screen for the first time was captivating. That moment of recognition when they realised what they had made and experienced, and the smiles on their faces as they watched the performance really conveyed the pride and sense of ownership this group had about their artwork. The fact that they all stood up and took a bow at the end of the first showing was testament to that sense of pride.

"The exhibition gave a voice to the group, an opportunity to emphasise to others what a valuable contribution they could make to society. While strengthening their sense of community identity this project helped to encourage the group to see themselves not only as a team of talented artists but as a group of friends who supported each other."

My (Margaret's) story about the Lawnmowers and Lyndsey's story about the influence of Boal on her work are both powerful examples of using forum theatre and related techniques to liberate the marginalised voices of learning 'dis'abled people. The process is one of using popular theatre as a tool for both critical self-consciousness and a critical engagement with the world.

Chris Cavanagh talks about the way in which story is so much a part of our lives that we overlook its significance and power:

> Stories define societies, cultures, communities. They act as social-cultural glue. Our histories are all, of course, stories and there has been much scholarship in the last twenty years that looks critically and sceptically at who wrote the various canonical histories and for whom and in what interests they were written. Postmodernism (in its progressive aspects) and post-structuralism have injected a healthy scepticism about the grand narratives to which we grant normative power. Popular education is a practice that structures and applies this post-structural scepticism in a democratic and rigorous fashion to enable people to tell new and better stories – recovering personal and community histories that have disappeared or were subjugated and subordinated to the dominant (or hegemonic) narratives. It also develops our collective capacities to imagine different stories about where we might be going in the decades we might yet have to live – assuming we survive the imminent crises of peak oil, global warming, extreme neoliberalism and the ever-present militarization of our beleaguered world. (Cavanagh, 2007: 45)

Cavanagh captures a significant number of extremely important points for us. Our histories have been written for us, but whose version of our history gets told depends on the identity of the narrator and in whose interests the stories are told. Postmodernism and post-structuralism have identified difference and critiqued metanarratives as silencing voices. Popular education or participatory practice works with silenced voices that have been 'hidden from history' (Rowbotham, 1977), telling and retelling stories that reclaim hidden identities and in the telling identify dominant power relations that subordinate. In these ways, personal stories become collective narratives which, set within our political times, have the power to make interventions which transform unequal relations and move towards a cooperative 'world worthy of human aspiration' (Reason and Bradbury, 2001: 1), one which acknowledges difference and diversity in all its richness and strength.

Moving forward with the story

> Narratives of liberation are always tied to people's stories, and what
> stories we decide to tell, and the way in which we decide to tell them,
> form the provisional basis of what a critical pedagogy of the future
> might mean. (Freire, 1993a: xii)

Story is woven through our practice in many forms: in dialogue over the most
practical of projects, such as credit unions, or more overtly in community groups
that focus specifically on story writing and telling, or in the development of
community profiles where the stories of how the community evolved are central
to its culture and identity. As well as in oral and written traditions, story can be
expressed in a diversity of ways: in music, poetry, drama, mural and many other
art forms that encourage ways of knowing beyond the word. In the West, the
search for a single truth has elevated 'binary thinking ... which reduces the
languages of analysis to white, hegemonic forms of clarity' (McLaren, 1995: 225).
In other words, the more indigenous and traditional ways of knowing have been
marginalised in favour of a restricted form based on subject/object, Black/White,
right/wrong, glossing over glaring contradictions, and as Gadamer, drawn to our
attention by O'Donohue below, points out, contradiction is an expression of the
integrity of a society:

> A real narrative is a web of alternating possibilities. The imagination is
> capable of kindness that the mind often lacks because it works naturally
> from the world of Between; it does not engage things in a cold, clear-
> cut way but always searches for the hidden worlds that wait at the edge
> of things.... It does not perceive contradictions as the enemy of truth;
> rather it sees here an interesting intensity. (O'Donohue, 2004: 138)

Freirean and feminist pedagogies begin in everyday stories, placing them at the
heart of the process of critical consciousness. In reflection on experience, we name
dehumanising realities in order to transform them (Freire, 1985). This narrative
approach engages with the personal as political by linking voice to narrative
through 'little stories' (Griffiths, 2003: 81) that make the vital connection between
the deeply personal and the profoundly political. It calls for humility, being open
to the experience of others, being open to other ways of knowing that transcend
knowledge for the economy, to become knowledge for a participatory world
where all life flourishes.

Our stories mark the beginning of the transformative process; they are the basis
of our new stories. Little stories become collective narratives, and in an unfolding
dialectical engagement between dominant narratives and counternarratives, the
dance between theory and action questions what is in order to create what
can be, and in so doing a radical transformation of the everyday unfolds. In
these ways, a deep love for all humanity becomes a collective wisdom for a

healthy, flourishing world. Competition against becomes collaboration with as a participatory worldview begins to dismantle the 'power over' of our western worldview in order to transform it into empowerment of the whole. Exploring and re-exploring our stories, we discover that 'everyday life is the source of social change and transformation' (Quinney, 1998: xiii).

We now move on to consider the importance of dialogue in the process of participatory practice, both in relation to story and to the wider process of social change.

SIX

The role of dialogue

The unity of contraries is the mystery of the inner most core of dialogue. (Buber, 1948: 17)

The power of dialogue

Participation involves a dialogical relationship with the world, both human and physical. Therefore, while story can be seen as an essential starting point on the journey to transformation, dialogue lies at the heart of engaging in participatory practice. It is integral to Paulo Freire's approach to popular education, and is a key component of almost any effective approach to community health. Its crucial role in the development of trust is most clear when absent. Absence of dialogue reinforces a world of conflict, of 'other', of fear. Dialogue is about respectful communication and deliberation. A dialogical approach to change and transformation is as much about listening as talking, and as much about dissent as about consensus; the outcome is always increased understanding and acceptance of difference, and in the best cases leads to mutual action. Thus dialogue is both a process of knowledge production and creation, and a basis of appropriate social action. It is about meaning making and mutual meaning making. Without true dialogue there is no participatory practice.

This centrality is also connected to an ecological understanding of the world, since dialogue is about '*with*-ness' rather than '*on*-ness'. It is an inherent feature of an approach that has connectivity as its underlying worldview. Interwoven with the ecological and the dialogical is the need, as argued in Chapter 1, to create critical spaces in which to question the taken-for-grantedness of everyday life. Therefore, a participatory practitioner seeks to create arenas for dialogue which can be time spaces for critical engagement within existing structures, the creation of new structures, or seizing the opportunity to steer transformative rhetoric back on course by introducing dialogue into emerging debates related to participatory democracy. These communicative public spaces provide an opportunity for not only collective meaning making but also creative opportunities for self-organisation and lateral thinking. Through structured as well as free-flowing dialogue, social learning takes place as ideas and experience are explored together across difference to come to mutual understanding. Through dialogical inquiry we come to different ways of knowing. This chapter will explore the nature of dialogue, how it underpins Freirean approaches, the preconditions for dialogue, and the challenges in creating the context for a dialogue of equals (Arnstein, 1969). As participatory practitioners our role is to expand such opportunities for deliberation. This is both political and ethical work and it needs to be both pragmatic and idealist, what Forester (1999) calls playing the mediating midwife of true dialogue and deliberation.

What is dialogue?

A philosophical, social and spiritual concept, the components of the word give a clue to what we are talking about. *Dia* means *through* and *logos* refers to *meaning*. Dialogue, thus, is *meaning flowing through* us. Isaacs (1999) argues that dialogue is a conversation with a centre, not sides. However, dialogue is more than a conversation; it is at its best an interactive process of learning together whereby mutual value is enhanced through the process of meaning making. It is a relational exchange process that allows interplay between people as whole beings, in a trusting and respectful way, to explore new understandings openly through the language of feelings, ideas, facts, dissent, opinions and plans. It is a connected knowing; one that pays full attention to others by suspending our own truth (Belenky et al, 1986).

Dialogue aims to achieve deeper understanding among participants, moving towards recognising that there are many truths, many ways of experiencing and making sense of the world. This is in contrast to a discussion that is concerned with the exchange of opinions, and can be dominated by assertive voices. Also outside the dialogical inquiry is everyday talk and conversation that has sociability as its purpose, although this type of exchange is an essential component of dialogical encounters. In creating the conditions for dialogue, you are also creating structures and conditions for collective learning, learning which connects people across difference to share a world in common. Thus, during dialogical interaction you become more aware of your regular and often hidden thought patterns by the mutual questioning of assumptions and prejudices to raise latent motives and tacit knowledge to the surface. In other words, becoming more aware of each other's espoused theories (what is said) and theories in action (what is actually done) (Argyris and Schön, 1978). Both Senge (1990) and Bohm (1996) argue that something new is also created. Insights previously hidden are shared collectively, not contained in one individual. In these ways, in dialogue, by paying attention and taking care of the spaces between us, we move from interaction to participating in the creation of common meaning. Yet what is created is also constrained by past mental models that may distort or block insightful perception (Bohm, 1996). The challenge is to move beyond the barriers of thought to a thinking which is more expansive and which will reveal new knowledge. This is what we mean by thinking critically. In well-facilitated dialogue, people become observers of their own thoughts, and more open to new ideas that bring with them new possibilities. This is in juxtaposition to what commonly happens in meeting spaces and conversations where meaning is filtered through a web of entrenched ideas uncritically, and old positions are defended.

Society or culture creates barriers and constraints on the construction of dialogue, as we saw in Chapters 2 and 4, inhibiting people from learning together. Modern economic structures and bureaucracies can establish boundaries that become systems of communicative constraint and control. Hierarchy and dictatorship are the most extreme forms because hierarchy tries to impose a singular view of order that denies the reality of complex relations. Hence the NHS and other public sector organisations struggle with centrally determined targets imposed from top down. Dialogue does not just involve thought; it is a fully human process that engages the emotions. The process can cause anxiety, but emotion also contributes to the richness that is dialogue. That emotion becomes a collective phenomenon, part of the collective meaning that is created. This collective meaning respects difference and diversity from an altered understanding without subsuming it into a collective melting pot. Awareness of the need to maintain a fine balance between encouraging the acceptance and validity of identity and emotions and not allowing it to overwhelm any dialogue is a skill of the animator/co-facilitator. Quite often, in very marginalised communities there is a high level of apathy, resistance and fear. Freire (1972) talks of the use of generative themes, those that are relevant to people's lives and therefore generate emotion. Emotions have an energy that emerges from the inertia of apathy, releasing feeling from atrophy and generating action. They are an essential part of being fully human, so a good dialogical space is one that pays attention to emotional energy, which is often the wellspring of creativity.

Dialogical knowledge is relational knowledge. Relationship-specific knowledge (Abma, 2006) has until recently been ignored by science because it is so difficult to capture, define and measure. It is completely ignored by notions inherent in Cochrane-styled, evidence-based practice that currently dominates the social work, health and education sectors. Relationship-specific knowledge is inherently dynamic, continually refined and co-created by interaction with new experiences. It is continually changing as the context of knowledge continually changes, creating new experiences. Some relationship-specific knowledge will be shared understanding, some of it will be a diversity of interpretations. So a dialogical approach to social change requires a periodic review of hidden assumptions during the process, and continuous cycles of learning together in an ongoing dynamic of creating of new ways of knowing.

Belenky et al (1986) differentiate between separated knowing and connected knowing. Separated knowing is the type of knowing that comes through discussion rather than dialogue and also underpins most academic discourse, whereby a stance of doubting (Elbow, 1998) is adopted. Connected knowing emerges from dialogue from relations of trust and empathy: 'the deliberate imaginative extension of one's understanding into positions that initially feel wrong or remote' (Belenky et al, 1986: 121). As dialogue progresses, out of mutual relations of trust, empathy connects ideas with those of others. It is the power of connection that leads to new ways of knowing: people feel respected, heard, affirmed and validated, and so discard the need to defend their position. We are not suggesting that this is a form of mutual admiration: dissent and disagreement are part of the process, but respectfully 'walking in another person's shoes' helps us to empathise with different experiences that have given rise to different epistemologies, rather than fight our own corner. This creates a relatedness, a connection. In exploring multiple truths, we discover that mutuality maintains our identities within a notion of a common good.

Dialogue: Connected knowing

A number of other writers from very different backgrounds have explored the nature of dialogue and the potential of dialogue for transformation. As well as Paulo Freire, whose ideas we work with later in this chapter, the most influential have been David Bohm, the physicist, Mikhail Bakhtin, the Russian philosopher, Martin Buber, the Jewish philosopher, John Shotter, the communication psychologist, and also organisational theorists, such as Edgar Schein and William Isaacs. Their theoretical ideas have been informed by practice-diverse contexts, many involving conflict. They share the notion that dialogue is fundamental to being human, and to discourage it is to dehumanise. According to Shotter, with-ness thinking and talking is inherently interactive and occurs when we come into 'living interactive contact with another's living being, with their utterances, with their bodily expressions, with their words, with their works' (2006: 587). Drawing on Merleau-Ponty (1962), Shotter uses the metaphor of two skins touching each other, becoming cumulatively responsive to each other's touch, and from this a sense of difference emerges. As this living intertwining takes place, new possibilities of relationship emerge, new experiences and new interconnections, and 'a third form of life' is conceived. 'The interplay involved gives rise to an interpretation (a representation) from our responses that occur spontaneously and directly with our living encounters with another's expressions. Neither is it merely a feeling, for it carries with it as it unfolds a bodily sense of the possibilities for responsive action' (Merleau-Ponty, 1962). In other words, we want to know what comes next; the curiosity moves us forward rather than closes us down. Indeed Shotter and Katz (1998) have been able to demonstrate that this creation of a sense of moving forward is achieved as people co-create meaning through dialogical inquiry, from within their lived experience and the living experience of their shared circumstances. When the collaborative dialogical activities cease, the generative nature of the process also ceases.

Shotter (2000) also demonstrates, as many social psychological studies have done, that in such a process it is not only the participants' shared circumstances that are refined and developed, but also participants' identities change. In other words, it is our spontaneous and embodied ways of seeing and acting in the world that change. Thus, dialogue is not only the means by which we marry the individual and the collective; it explores our identities, giving us a sense of movement and action that locates us as part of a collective whole. This is why creating the conditions for dialogue and critique are so fundamental for social action.

Almost all writers on dialogue pay attention to this personal transformation as fundamental and connected to the collective processes. True dialogue, as we hope you will start to see in this chapter, is the active manifestation of the principles that underpin participatory practice. True dialogue encapsulates the fundamental values of participation and is, therefore, a necessary component of transformation. Processes that encourage dialogue differ significantly from current bureaucratic practice. Moore (2007), in an analysis of the SHARP (Sustainable Health Action Research Project) experience in Wales, demonstrated that two enduring features were increased self-esteem of participants and improved connections between local agencies and communities. In examining sources of exclusion, Moore identified that the response and attitude of public servants towards marginalised people reinforced social exclusion, with the result that relations often broke down. Rejection and humiliation results in reinforcing lack of confidence and low self-esteem, demeaning and dehumanising local people. The same project also found that a more skilled dialogical approach to community development avoided interpersonal conflicts and paved the way towards local people working more equally with local services. In order to address political issues collectively, relationships between people need to be respectful.

Most writers on dialogue refer to an essential humanness and how it counters the dehumanisation that is a consequence of social exclusion. Bakhtin, for example, describes the dialogical nature of human life:

The single adequate form for verbally expressing authentic human existence is the open ended dialogue. Life by its nature is dialogic. To live means to participate in dialogue: to ask questions, to heed, to respond, to agree and so forth. In this dialogue a person participates wholly and throughout his [sic] whole life: with his eyes, lips, hands soul, spirit, with his whole body and deeds. He [sic] invests his entire self in the discourse and this discourse enters into the dialogic fabric of human life.... A person enters into dialogue as an integral voice. He [sic] participates in it not only in his thoughts, but with his fate and with his entire individuality. (Bakhtin, 1984: 293)

This contrast with monologism:

Monologism at its extreme, denies the existence outside itself of another consciousness with equal rights and equal responsibilities, another I with equal rights (thou). With a monologic approach (in its extreme pure form) another person remains wholly and merely an object of consciousness.... Monologue is finalized and deaf to the other's response, does not expect it and does not acknowledge it in any force. Monologue manages without the other and therefore to some degree materializes all reality. (Bakhtin, 1984: 292-3)

This closing down or lack of interactivity is both the cause and the consequence of social injustice. It reduces the potential for action, preventing any forward movement. Let us take an example. Surveys are the most common means used in public health to get a picture of a 'problem', usually a problem previously determined by a health 'expert', and the research literature and public health reports abound with descriptions of 'health' as death and sickness inequalities. Questionnaires are designed to generate categories of data that can be easily manipulated statistically, but because of this requirement cannot allow dialogue or at least dialogue may occur around the asking of questions, but not recorded. From such surveys, often for a brief period, a newspaper headline may report the results, but rarely is a course of action for change decided or, if it is decided, it is on the basis of partial information. If this had been a dialogical encounter, then many possible courses of action would have emerged from the process. To be repeatedly asked questions about the 'problem' has led to the phenomenon described as research fatigue whereby people do not respond to questionnaires, thus creating a further bias in any survey results. It also reinforces the sense of frustration of not being heard. By doing another survey, you are not engaging with the underlying causes of inequality, you are merely objectifying people and alienating them further. As an example of anti-dialogue, I (Margaret) remember Hattersley becoming a case study for the A-level syllabus, with the result that coachloads of teenagers from more privileged backgrounds invaded the community to see social exclusion in action, objectifying local people and entrenching marginalising attitudes.

The absence of dialogue between those in poverty and the agencies that serve them manifests itself in spaces that have been created for involvement. Many years ago, a student of mine (Jane's) was undertaking a participatory action research course and had elected to work with a local health forum in Birkenhead, of which she was a member. The forum was part of a local regeneration initiative, and included both residents and officers from a range of local agencies. She recounted how often the meetings had been held up when one of the residents talked incessantly about an issue, generally disrupting the meeting's business. When she asked people if they would be interested in participating in a collaborative inquiry around an issue of their choice, this particular individual offered to volunteer. Despite her qualms, she went ahead and worked with the forum and the volunteers. There was an overwhelming agreement that the focus should be on communication at forum meetings. As the inquiry unfolded, it emerged that the man who had been the cause of her concern had been so frustrated at not being listened to that he resorted to disruption as a strategy. A number of the residents of the forum shared the same feeling, that they were excluded by professionals, both in terms of the language used and a failure to listen. In the collaborative inquiry group, the experience of working dialogically meant that they were able to express their frustration and decide on action to change the situation.

The role of dialogue in Freirean pedagogy

Freire's concept of *authentic* dialogue in particular has important implications for participatory approaches to practice. It embodies the values of participation, identifying and equalising power in dialogical relationships. By this we mean that we cannot deny that power in society has given privilege to certain groups of people at the same time as disempowering others. But by becoming aware of the way that this works, by ranking people in relations of superiority–inferiority, we can construct relationships that have the intention of building a more equal future.

> Dialogue does not exist in a political vacuum. It is not a 'free space' where you say what you want.... To achieve the goals of transformation, dialogue implies responsibility, directiveness, determination, discipline, objectives. (Freire, in Shor and Freire, 1987: 102)

Whilst the roles of teacher and taught in most situations will be different, and not on an equal footing, Freire was very insistent that we must solve this 'dialectical contradiction of opposites' (Mayo, 2004: 52). By this, he meant that there is an inherent power polarity in the way the relationship is constructed and that this can be dismantled 'by reconciling the poles of the contradiction so that both are simultaneously teachers and students' (Freire, 1993a: 72). This is easier said than done, but with mutual respect as the key ingredient, it is possible for both to be open to a mutual process of discovery in which each teaches and learns.

This is a relationship of equality not superiority, so let us look at how it can be achieved.

Dialogue, according to Freire, is the basis of praxis; without dialogue praxis is not possible. This is an important insight for participatory practitioners; it identifies dialogue not only as tool of democratic communication, but as the basis for the entire process of transformative change. Praxis, a unity of theory and action, is the foundation of a more critical engagement in the world, and it is this generation of knowledge in action that leads to change for a more equal, just and sustainable world. This approach calls for paying attention to life in a critical, self-questioning way, moving between inner and outer arcs of attention, as Judi Marshall calls it, working with a multi-dimensional frame of knowing that connects intellectual, practical, intuitive, sensory and other ways of knowing (Marshall, 2001). This process of becoming both critical and self-critical was discussed in Chapter 1 and will be discussed more fully in Chapter 7. In these ways, authentic dialogue begins in the everyday stories of lived experience, and involves a deeper connection of the heart and mind, the intellect and emotions as we have said, and an acceptance of and trust in the fundamental worth of all human beings. It is this that marks the profound difference between dialogue and any other form of conversation. Dialogue overtly intends to equalise power relations between people, whereas in most conversations the power relations of wider society get acted out in personal encounters. For example, Foucault (1980) identifies the way that power gets acted out in our everyday encounters, reinforcing the dominant order of privilege. By understanding more consciously the way that this works, we see everyday encounters as a point of intervention in this process of reinforcement. In this sense, dialogue creates an interruption in the course of everyday experience, prising open the space for change by engaging people in a respectful experience. Just simply by listening, trusting, valuing people in dialogue we create experiences that are healing, respectful and empowering. Think of situations in which you have experienced feeling silenced or diminished and you will see what we mean.

My (Margaret's) mind goes back to a public meeting that had been called in Old Trafford Library. The person facilitating the meeting with the best will in the world was trying to apply good groupwork practice by getting everyone, as an opening exercise, to go round the circle and state why they had come to the meeting. It was many years ago, but I still remember the woman opposite me whose body language screamed panic – yet the facilitator still did not make an attempt to divert what he had started. By the time it was her turn to speak, the sweat was running down her face in rivulets of distress. The act of speaking became an act of emotional torture, and I knew that, left like this, we would never see her again. This is a typical example of the unconscious dominance, confidence and insensitivity of those with verbal privilege, and runs counter to Freirean dialogue in every sense. Darder (2002) says that educators, in an unwise effort to create voice or equality or critical thinking, interpret dialogue to mean that everyone *must* speak, but this is a false notion of democracy that translates into a form of coercion. That is why when you engage in Native American dialogue using a talking stick people are given permission to pass it on without talking if they so choose. 'In dialogue one has the right to be silent' (Freire, in Shor and Freire, 1987: 102), and the ability to negotiate the dialectical tension between authority and freedom is essential to the development of critical consciousness. This can only come about if we have a preparedness to engage in a process of critical self-reflection to enable us to understand as practitioners the essence of our own authority. So, dialogue calls for both intervention and constraint, so that the verbal confidence of those with privilege does not overwhelm those with whom the dialogue is intended to engage. There is in essence, therefore, a dialectical relationship between freedom and authority. 'For all their competence and authority, teachers [practitioners] must be humble to relearn that which they think they already know from others and to connect, through learning … with their learners' lifeworlds' (Mayo, 2004: 93). So, dialogue is not simple. It calls for us to become self-critical; to examine the attitudes, values and prejudices we have internalised along the way. If we fail to do this, to apply the microscope to all the nooks and crannies inside our being that harbour some of the most unwelcome aspects of us, we unconsciously act these out in our practice, and this means that authentic dialogue is not possible. Non-verbal behaviour, a glance, an expression, a hesitation, a doubt, come over loudly, undermining anything our words might be trying to express!

Dialogue embodies human dignity and respect, encouraging people to relate to each other in ways that are mutual, reciprocal, trusting and cooperative. It is a horizontal communication between people who really believe that they are equal in worth, so it calls for a profound belief in people, a trust that we are all infinitely capable. Without this trust, as practitioners we exude an arrogance that we are superior, and this can never lead to transformative practice. Freirean pedagogy is about *listening* to the narratives of people and engaging in *dialogue*, paying respectful attention to the story being told and taking it seriously. In this way, as practitioners we are able to establish strong relationships based on an understanding of local culture; in turn, local people develop a sense of confidence and trust, in us and in each other. 'Paulo somehow connected his whole being, his reason and emotion, to the whole being of another [in dialogue] about something which he and the other person wanted to know' (Ana Aranjo Freire, cited in P. Mayo, 2004: 80). The opposite of this is *cultural invasion*, or *anti-dialogue*, which involves the imposition of one's assumptions, values and perceptions of the world on others, silencing and disempowering.

Freire sees the essence of dialogue as 'the true word', and the true word is a unity of action and reflection. Therefore to speak a true word is to engage in praxis: to name the world and in doing so to transform the world.

> Human existence cannot be silent, nor can it be nourished by false
> words, but only by true words, with which humans transform the
> world. To exist, humanly, is to name the world, to change it. Once

named, the world in its turn reappears to the namers as a problem and requires of them a new naming.... If it is in speaking their word that humans transform the world by naming it, dialogue imposes itself as the way in which [humans] achieve significance as [humans]. Dialogue is thus an existential necessity. (Freire, 1972: 60–1)

Dialogue, then, lies at the heart of the process of humanisation. It opens the path to critical consciousness. Only dialogue, which requires critical thinking, is also capable of generating critical thinking. 'Without dialogue there is no communication, and without communication there can be no true education' (Freire, 1972: 65). Freire sees dialogue as the act of engaging in praxis: by speaking 'the true word' we name the world, and by naming the world we transform the world. This involves a critical engagement with the world: we question our reality and expose the contradictions we live by.

So, how do we turn the concept of *dialogue* into a skill? Let us explore some of this thinking in relation to practice. Dialogue involves listening from the heart with true compassion rather than simply the act of hearing. It requires paying full attention to others, noticing not reacting. Often in our western world we are taught to be preoccupied about defending ourselves against the words of others, reacting rather than really paying attention to the meaning of the encounter. If we can substitute our need to dominate or defend ourselves, we can adopt a more humble position in relation to others. For instance, if a teacher is trained to think that her role requires her to know the answer to every question, she is likely to adopt a superior/inferior relationship with learners, authoritative rather than mutual. On the other hand, if educators are trained to understand that there are multiple truths, many ways of seeing the world, and that they are there to teach people to question, not to answer questions, their approach is immediately more open, more equal, less arrogant, more humble. It is a mutual quest for understanding, and in this context dialogue becomes an encounter of equals. If in our hearts we believe we are superior or inferior then there is no trust. The power in the relationship becomes understood through trust, mutuality, reciprocity in a common quest for a world founded on greater peace and justice. 'Dialogue requires an intense faith in [others], faith in their power to make and remake, to create and re-create, faith in [their] vocation to be more fully human (which is not the privilege of an elite but the birthright of all)' (Freire, 1972: 63). Freire was firm in his insistence that true dialogue cannot exist without love and humility, and that this is a critical not an emotional positioning.

The Joseph Rowntree Foundation published findings of research into people's perceptions of today's greatest social evils, and top of the list came the decline of community, seen as a consequence of the rise of individualism (www.socialevils. org.uk, accessed on 9 May 2008). We raise this point because we clearly grieve for a sense of connectedness that is encapsulated in the concept of community. But community is a contested space: it is heterogeneous and needs to be informed by dissent. Here we wish to introduce the notion of critical dissent dialogue, in which dialectical encounters across difference lead to new understandings and greater community strength and representation. These power relations give an energy to change, and lead to alliances across difference. If we understand social difference as the basis of multiple truths, we are on the path to acceptance. A dialogical situation presumes the absence of authoritarianism, a dialectical relationship between authority and freedom. Dialogue means a permanent tension in the relationship between authority and liberty. But, in this tension, 'authority vis-à-vis permitting student freedoms which emerge, which grow and mature precisely because authority and freedom learn discipline' (Shor and Freire, 1987: 102).

In summary, dialogue method as discussed by Freire (1972) equalises the power between people and bridges the silencing or controlling of the powerful to the powerless. It begins with *problematising*. This simply means that there is a focus to the initial debate that is relevant to the people involved, and it sends out signals that participation is expected and needed in the process (Shor and Freire, 1987). This often takes the form of a *codification*, or a way of capturing an aspect of life's reality and bringing it into the group in the form of a photograph, story, poem, cartoon, drama or music (for more in-depth discussion of problematising, see Chapter 9). This generates relevance, interest, debate and alternative perspectives as dialogue within the groups deepens and gradually shifts from the codification, assuming a more critical analysis of the issue. Through a process of questioning – *Who? What? Why? When? Where?* – the taken-for-grantedness of everyday life is dismantled, a sense of confidence and self-belief is developed and the determination to act for change emerges.

Developing the skills to connect the personal to the cultural and political context is the basis of dialogue. Without this, personal cases become pathologised by placing emphasis on the inadequacies of the individual rather than the system. Our challenge is to find a strategy for locating 'little stories' in the bigger political picture, and to expose the personal as political. In this way, *dialogue* begins in the stories of the people, and in *problematising* personal/local issues, exposes socially constructed identities which have been silenced:

> in this respect, a postcolonial narratology encourages the oppressed to contest the stories fabricated for them by 'outsiders' and to construct counterstories that give shape and direction to the practice of hope and the struggle for an emancipatory politics of everyday life. It is a pedagogy that attempts to exorcise from the social body the invading pathologies of racism, sexism, and class privilege. (McLaren, 1995: 105)

The collective narratives that emerge from 'little stories' lead to knowledge in action, to knowledge that is 'dynamically produced and emerges out of relationships with one another and the world. Knowledge is a living process – a living historical process that grows and transforms most freely and openly within an environment that is informed by dialogue' (Darder, 2002: 66). This locates dialogue at the heart of praxis: in a process that both generates and is generated by dialogue people can claim their right to 'the power to create and transform' (Freire, 1972: 63). Through dialogue we explore different realities, and in a process of questioning those everyday experiences we make critical connections not only with structures of discrimination that create unequal lives but also with the potential for action.

Challenges of creating conditions for dialogue

Dialogue is a fragile process, and to enter into equal, dialogically structured relations with others is not easy. Many situations inhibit dialogue and favour more confrontational communication forms. There is a space between 'self' and 'other' where 'speaking so that others want to listen, listening so others want to speak' is sensitively and skilfully maintained. We have argued that dialogue only truly takes place where there is mutual regard and trust, leading to an openness to having one's own ideas examined, as well as examining the ideas of others. It calls for an acceptance that the communication will always be in process, fluid and changing, on the borderline between what we can know and what we do not yet know and what we can never know. It is a process that shapes us as much as we shape it. These elements can be profoundly challenging because we have to suspend our learning to unlearn and relearn. This is a far cry from the 'post-political' vision of a world beyond Left and Right, beyond hegemony and beyond antagonism, a world in which all space for dissenting dialogue has been removed, suggested by Giddens (Mouffe, 2005). Giddens' (2000) perspective on 'one-nation politics' as non-conflictual consensus is fundamentally flawed in respect of the role of dialectical engagements that are so crucial to the formation of new ideas. Dialogue, contrary to the notion of non-conflictual consensus, calls for dissent, disagreement, discomfort as ways of dialectically engaging with a thesis-antithesis-synthesis approach to knowing and being. Without this, hegemonic spaces flourish unchallenged.

Many organisations, whether delivering services such as healthcare or those who have regeneration as their focus, find it extremely hard to engage in dialogue because they often want an outcome that favours their view or interests. How often do health promoters engage with communities or individuals with the assumption that the latest health advice about lifestyle is the right one? Similarly, healthcare organisations often engage with Black and minority ethnic communities, encouraging them to help develop responsive and appropriate services when they have already had outcomes set and targets put in place when the community may have other, different priorities. Fundamental to true dialogue is an openness to unanticipated outcomes. Anger is very different from apathy; it has an energy that can be channelled towards action, and should not be feared if it is handled appropriately. However, dialogical approaches can be abused when seen by those in power as a mechanism for appeasement or consensus. Our task as participatory practitioners is to engage vigilantly in a process that treads the line between liberation and domination, to be politically aware of the dangers at the same time as encouraging and expanding opportunities for the silenced to be heard.

Not only do predetermined political agendas stop true dialogue, but so do inherited traditions or resistance to any sort of personal development on the part of the participants. These can take the form of dialogue-blocking behaviour. At this point, I (Margaret) am mindful of a friend who was manager of a mental health/community development project in a building that straddled the boundary between a large Manchester hospital and the local community. This particular vignette is situated in the first 'management committee' meeting involving participants, the local community and health service managers. One of the health service managers arrived, besuited, with copious files and notes under his arm, and looked confused when confronted with the circle of chairs that were filling up. "We don't read from papers, Steve", my friend gently whispered as she leant towards him, "we speak from the heart." This encounter changed Steve's view of the world. He came in 'mufti' to subsequent meetings, and spoke from his heart! Other forms of dialogue blocking include a resistance to experimenting with different forms of communication, such as art and theatre, or the failure of those in power to participate alongside others. Many times have I (Jane) organised whole systems events to include decision makers alongside citizens, only to find on the day such decision makers suddenly disappear halfway through the process. However, there are also many examples of where such dialogue-stopping circumstances are overcome so that those involved suddenly go beyond ordinary conversation and begin to hear, truly understand and engage in authentic expression to reach the point of thinking together that Bohm and others talk about. At this stage, the co-creating of meaning flows freely and is unimpeded. Collective creative thinking emerges from genuine empathetic listening, respect for all participants' safety, relating as equals, suspending judgement, sincerity, courage, curiosity and disclosure of assumptions. A symmetrical form of communication develops. This both requires but also creates trusting relationships and trust in the process. This does not emerge by osmosis, but calls for skilled co-facilitation to ensure the integrity of the process. These co-facilitators act as guardians of participatory democracy, vigilantly ensuring that the core values are upheld in practice. Any attempts to manipulate or direct the process towards a desired outcome kills it. The reward for perseverance is that the achievement of true dialogue is transformative, inspiring unique and creative outcomes, sometimes out of polarised positions.

Dialogue in a multicultural and diverse society involves the deconstruction of the structural constraints that shape both reality and the dialogue itself. Without this, dialogue merely replicates social divisions. This calls for an analysis of the way that power works in society. In order to identify the way that discrimination is embedded at every level we have to have a critical awareness of how we are created unequal. Authentic and effective dialogue is based on the notion that everyone has the capacity to understand the world and to express their view of life as constructed out of experience. This is fundamental to both Gramsci and Freire's thought. Dialogue involves a journey of discovery through racism, sexism, disablism, homophobia and general xenophobia that creates realities other than our own. For example, deeply reflexive understanding of the supremacy of Whiteness can be a consequence of hearing everyday realities out of which Black identities are shaped. Understanding this hegemony is part of effective dialogue. This can often be uncomfortable, which is why it vital to maintain respect – respect for the uniqueness of the individual but also for those cultural activities, practices and ways of viewing the world that are culturally distinct. As Habermas commented, 'A correctly understood theory of rights requires a politics of recognition that protects the integrity of the individual in the life contexts in which his or her identity is formed' (1994: 138).

Dialogue can never work as a top-down process. In Sweden, where the cultural values centre around issues of equality, safety and consensus, dialogue conferences are now being frequently used within both public and private organisations to develop policies and programmes. Sweden is a well-developed representative democracy founded on proportional representation, so the participants of such conferences tend to include local politicians, executives and managers. In Skåne, for example, dialogue conferences were a key element in the development of a local policy document on health and welfare, *Skånsk Livskraft*, which lay out the vision for health and social welfare in the local region. National policy, directional rather than definitive, had developed the concept of *Närsjukvård* as constituting how health and social care should be more locally and citizen-focused, and further dialogue conferences took place to decide what the concept meant in terms of the health and social sector locally. However, local frontline workers and citizens themselves were excluded from the dialogue, with the result that few understood the concept. This eliminated them from deciding the courses of action they needed to take along with others in their daily practice, thus negating the purpose of the dialogical process (Petersson et al, 2009: forthcoming). Successful dialogue requires participation of all stakeholders in a process in full reciprocity of expression, setting aside organisational or professional positions, and other external sources of power.

Most dialogical spaces take place in informal settings. People are encouraged to dress informally, not to use titles or positions on name labels, just given names. This encourages open investigation of participants in a fully human way, with greater freedom in ascertaining collective and mutual interests beyond a role. Open sharing of information and transparency of decision making fosters mutual understanding, and what is created is done so together, transcending pre-existing beliefs and attitudes. Participants reflect a diversity of identities and experience beyond that of a role that leads to fuller democratic outcomes that reflect more fully the interests of society. Conflict and difference in a respectful context becomes a source of creativity.

Creating dialogical/rhetorical/communicative spaces: some examples from practice

In the past two decades a rapidly growing movement for dialogue has been developing. In the US alone the website of the National Coalition for Dialogue & Deliberation (www.thataway.org) serves as a hub for dialogue (and deliberation) for facilitators, conveners and trainers, and houses thousands of resources on these communication methodologies. Given the wealth of experience that can be found in the contemporary literature this represents a rising tide of new approaches to social change. On pages 133–36, you will find some examples of dialogical encounters to help you gain confidence in creating arenas for dialogue in critical public spaces. As these approaches gather momentum, there should be a move towards deliberative democracy becoming commonplace (Cornwall and Coelho, 2007).

As mentioned above, creating the conditions for dialogue requires good facilitation. We have seen how many obstacles inhibit dialogue and favour more confrontational communication forms that come under the title of 'discussion' or 'debate'. Common obstacles, including fear, the display or exercise of power, mistrust, external influences, distractions and poor communication conditions can all prevent dialogue from emerging. Therefore, dialogical methods and tools have certain things in common; they focus on enabling open communication, honest speaking and genuine listening. They allow people to take responsibility for their own learning and ideas. They also create a safe container for people to surface their assumptions, question their previous judgements and worldviews, and change the way they think. Many of the techniques draw their inspiration from indigenous and forgotten ways of being, and also from inspiring leaders, such as Gandhi and Nelson Mandela, who demonstrate acts of forgiveness, suspend judgement and listen to all sides. Most dialogical spaces have clarity of purpose that will engage people but not are not too structured, that is, completely open-ended, and therefore not attached to specific outcomes. There is usually a set of principles that guides the process. In open space technology (see below), developed by Harrison Owen, the principles include: whoever comes are the right people, whenever it starts is the right time, whatever happens is the only thing that could have happened, and when it is over it is over. There also is only one rule: the 'law of two feet', which effectively means people are encouraged to take responsibility for their own learning, and if they feel they are not learning or contributing they can leave and move to another group.

Usually there are some key questions that are being asked in a dialogical session. Most writers would argue that good questions that stimulate thought processes are key to dialogue. Questions that lead people forward into a dynamically driven future are good questions, and in order for this to happen they need to have meaning for participants, igniting the process of learning and change as answers are co-created collaboratively. These questions should come from the hearts and minds of people involved, so considerable thought and discussion have to take place as preparation. Such an approach also comes from a deep belief in the intelligence and wisdom within everyone, not just so-called experts. As Gramsci maintained, everyone has the capacity to be an 'intellectual'. From the start, the process moves from fragmentation to connectedness. So animators/co-facilitators need to be aware of everyone, and talking to everyone who will be involved beforehand helps to inspire confidence that each person is recognised and appreciated. The ultimate level of inclusion is one in which all participants share facilitation.

A dialogical process is like a collective story. There is a structure, a beginning, a middle and an end. Two processes unfold: a divergence process in which all possibility is encouraged, which can be unsettling, so good facilitation is needed to ensure that people feel confident and trusting in the process. Then, periodically, a convergence process is required. At this point, insights are made explicit, perhaps on sheets of paper on walls, in pictures or words. During this phase a new step in the ongoing process is outlined. Most transformative processes give rise to a painful stage of 'storming' or 'confused fog' that brings an overwhelming sense of confusion. Holding that and staying with it is crucial; this is the place where innovation and creativity emerge. Senge et al (2005) argue that this is the point at which participants should stop talking and spend some time in silence; others advocate continual dialogue. Whatever course the process takes, all techniques and tools require co-facilitators who are capable of staying with what is at any moment. The facilitator embodies the values and principles that are the foundation of this approach, maintaining its integrity, but at the same time improvising responsibly and intuitively as the unexpected happens. Confidence, humility and the courage to believe in the process are called for.

Many of the aspects of the processes that have been used in creating such dialogical spaces reflect a return to a world we have lost. In indigenous societies living knowledge through dialogue is embedded into everyday life. Through oral history, storytelling, elder councils and proverbs, the principles and rules of the community are kept alive. Time is not imposed on people's lives; life is adapted to a rhythm of the natural world. This sense of connection is removed by a western worldview that sees humanity as superior to nature. Time restrictions, even in specific dialogical techniques, often reduce the opportunity to suspend judgement, to listen from the heart and to fully engage with others. There are some common elements whether the tradition is indigenous to Africa, the Americas or the Pacific islands, where people and the process of coming together is more important than timing and structure. It starts with the calling of a circle. The circle represents unity, an unbroken whole. This ensures people face each other and everyone matters. Many of the old processes integrate story and dialogue: storytelling as a way of sharing inspired knowledge and dialogue as way of creating a culture of coming together.

I (Margaret) was part of an eclectic gathering of participants from an international conference on community development who were invited to a Mi'kmaq community in Nova Scotia. After travelling for hours, the last one of which involved bouncing down a long track, we were greeted in the stillness by a lone figure smiling, waiting patiently, timelessly. This leader of the local community led us into a wigwam (not a tipi), and invited us to sit in the round. He gently explained that this was their way of connecting with new friends. He lit a sage stick, and talked about the ritual of listening to each person in turn. We shared aspects of our lives and our concerns for the world. He was sensitive to the fears expressed on some faces as the sage stick progressed around the circle, and reminded us all that we also had a right not to talk. The dialogue was continued as we walked the land that is home to the Mi'kmaq people, learning from stories built on metaphor: the trees growing tall and strong in parallel reaching towards the sky, but with their roots entwined together under the ground. We closed our dialogue in the round, expressing altered perspectives that gave rise to new possibilities, all of us thoughtful, united and changed by the experience. There are many such ways of learning from indigenous practices that provide interruptions in the distracted way we lead our lives in the West.

1. Story dialogue

One such attempt at integrating lessons learnt from indigenous cultures and used quite widely in community development approaches to health promotion is the story dialogue process, developed by Ron Labonte and Joan Feather (1996). It holds some similarities to the dialogical process found in Freirean pedagogy. At one level the process is a grounded theory approach to participatory knowledge creation, whereby the participants in the process do the analysis as well as create the data, unlike focus groups where a researcher records the discussion and then analyses it independently. In a way, story dialogue tries to marry science with new paradigm/participatory thinking. It was originally developed as a tool to bridge the gap between theory and practice. In story dialogue individuals are invited to write and tell their stories around a generative theme, a theme that is important to the group and opens up possibility. Sitting in a circle, the storyteller tells their story while others listen; some may be taking notes. After the storyteller has finished, there is a reflection circle whereby each listener in turn shares how the story they heard relates to their own story or experience. Each does this in turn, passing the talking stick while everyone listens. Everyone's voice is heard without interruption. Then a structured dialogue starts, guided by a set of questions: What? (what was the story, that is, what happened, what was going on?) Why? (why did the events in the story happen in the way they did?) Now what? (what does this mean?) and So what? (what are we going to do about it?). To help the process, story reporters keep notes on the dialogue, the participants create insight cards which they group into themes and then produce a statement based on these themes: a theory. One of the interesting things about the process is that participants often find it difficult to move from the reflection circle, where they usually engage with their heart, to the more intellectual process of analysis. Conversely, people used to being in their heads, such as academics, find it difficult to respond emotionally, and in the analysis stage tend to objectify other people's stories rather than empathising from their own experience. Skilled facilitation is required in preventing the first storyteller being questioned and harassed about what they did or should have done in such a situation. Interestingly, in my (Jane's) experience, it is professionals such as nurses who fall into this trap of victim blaming and solution finding. Another danger, found in many circle approaches, is that the first person to speak can have a large influence on what is said and the direction of later dialogue. The best way to handle this is to give sufficient time to reflect and collect their thoughts before others start to speak. More naturally vocal people sometimes find the initial process frustratingly slow; however, those who do not normally speak out in groups appreciate the reflection circle approach. Story dialogue is quite structured although this is not always necessary – it is possible to have a series of dialogues taking place in parallel and then bringing the insights together in a wider group setting. It is also possible for it to be self-facilitated providing sufficient guidance is given on roles and responsibilities.

2. World cafe

One of the challenges of working with groups is the tendency for certain people to dominate the discussion. Social psychological research has shown that the tendency for one voice to dominate is more likely to happen in larger groups. Groups of five or less tend to encourage more equal participation. This depends, of course, on how the dialogue is set up, the context, the informal and formal power structures and the setting. I (Jane) can remember years ago, as part of an evaluation project, visiting a community group to help them to develop an evaluation framework. Having persuaded the project manager to bring all the interested parties together to meet us, we arrived to find the meeting taking place in a room without a window, dominated by a rectangular table. Since this was a community with few resources, it felt inappropriate to demand a different room, although my past experience had shown that this was not a good setting for dialogue. As it emerged, the dialogue became dominated by a White, retired male, who was very articulate. It was not an equal dialogue, and indeed faltered as it effectively turned into a monologue. I decided to take the bull by the horns: "Let's get rid of this table!", I said, and extraordinarily, without comment, everyone got up and helped to get it out of the room. It gave me the opportunity to encourage everyone into small groups, and begin the process of asking the questions again. Dialogue increased dramatically; the one booming voice was not silenced but became an equal participant. Indeed, when we came together to distill what was said, the dominant participant thanked his group and commented on how much he had learnt that day from them.

World cafe is a way of working with large numbers of people but in small dialogical groups in a flexible and expanding way. Examples worldwide include everything from examining Māori forestry claims in New Zealand, to developing the next stage of a health and social care system in Southern Sweden. It makes use of the cafe metaphor by setting up the room in which the dialogue takes place with people in groups of four at different tables for a series of deep participative conversations. Every so often, people are invited to move round. The 'host' is the one person who stays at the table while everyone else moves to a new one. The host summarises the essence of the previous conversation, and the new table members connect to what was talked about and take it forward. Gradually everything is interwoven and networked, a bit like a tapestry, with new ideas and insights creating a collective new set of meanings. The energy that is created in a world cafe dialogue is so profound that many proponents talk of cafe magic. As with similar processes, a good question is one that matters to everyone present. It is important for engaging with passion, moving the process forward. The merits of fostering mutual listening, a spirit of inquiry and curiosity about what is not known are also key elements. This is achieved by talking about cafe etiquette, which includes encouragement to doodle and draw on the tablecloths!

3. Open space technology
Who should participate is an important element of truly democratic dialogue. In open space technology, as in world cafe, the answer is everyone in the whole system. For Harrison Owen, the originator of open space events, who turns up on the day is who is meant to be there. In practice, however, this is often not possible. In the open space processes that I (Jane) have facilitated over the years, it has been important to ensure that at least this operates as a principle so that the number of spaces available for each group of people represents the degree to which they are likely to be affected by the actions that come from the dialogue. Usually this means ensuring community members are involved in significant proportion. In ideal circumstances, there is no question or agenda that structures the day. Rather the agenda is co-created together. The process starts with a circle, however big the group. The facilitator introduces first the main principles of open space, and then the main theme or burning issue that has brought people together. On an empty wall, people are invited to propose sessions and discussions. A period of silence is then provided for people to think, before they are invited to come to the centre and write their idea or question down, read it aloud and post it on the wall. In this marketplace people gradually sign up for groups, or move their paper to connect with others as a way of identifying common interest. Once the groups are formed, the work begins. Someone in each group compiles a report of what is discussed and conclusions and these are posted. There can be many such cycles that mix people up, the policy makers and the recipients of those policies alike. Ideally an open space event ends with everyone coming back together to identify an action group to take decisions forward. Open space or an adaptation of it has been used in many contexts. I (Jane) have personally facilitated such events to create cross-agency indicators of change in an area of Manchester, to develop a mental health promotion strategy in two areas of Merseyside and to develop health promotion in Lithuania and Estonia. Once people have overcome their natural shyness and realise they are equal participants, they enter into the spirit of the process with enthusiasm. The most difficult thing they find is moving from one group to another, to be 'butterflies' or 'bumblebees' in Owen's terminology (1997). As a facilitator, it is important to trust the process. When we used it to work

with key people in the public health system in Lithuania, we had real doubts at the end of day one. People seemed very unenthused and lacklustre, and there was little dialogue going on in the groups. We spent the evening debating what we needed to do to move things along, coming up with many control mechanisms, perceiving that the participants were so imbued with dominant Soviet-style ways of working that they were uncomfortable with taking a lead. In the end, my intuition and my principles would not allow us to intervene. Trust the process, be true to it and do nothing. It proved the right thing to do: things moved on swiftly the following day, enthusiasm rocketed, dialogue increased and the process successfully created some impressive learning and decisions. A participant came up to me and shook my hand vigorously, "Thank you, thank you so much!" she said in broken English. I pointed out through the translator that I had done nothing at all, it was the participants who had done it all.

4. Appreciative inquiry

Negative language is a tool of oppression. Constantly referring to problems can reinforce feelings of low self-esteem and a sense of being a victim. Appreciative inquiry is the antidote to this. For those who are social problem-focused it can feel rather Polyanna-ish. However, as a process it can be very liberating, because instead of focusing on what is wrong the focus is on what is good in order to find ways to enhance it. In appreciative inquiry (Cooperrider et al, 2007) the underlying assumption is that the questions we ask influence the answers we find. There are four overriding principles. First, every system works to some degree to seek out what is positive and lifegiving. Second, knowledge that is generated by the inquiry should be applicable, that is, what is possible. Third, systems are capable of becoming more than they are, and they can learn to guide their own evolution, so consider bold dreams. Finally, the process and outcome of the inquiry are interrelated and inseparable, so make the process a collaborative one. An initial step is taken to define the focus of the inquiry and present it as a positive statement, for example, creating and sustaining high-quality involvement of local people in decision making. This is followed by a collective process called the '4 Ds'. *Discovery* is the process in which there is a system-wide inquiry through conversations and stories, into people's experience of the focus at its best. Then people engage in the *dream* element, building a vision of the future they want, that is, the sense of what the world is calling them to become, a practical utopia. This is followed by *design*, in which people craft those practices, structures, policies that will bring that to life. Finally, through continuously returning to the group, there is *destiny*, defining the plan and putting it into practice. One of the strengths of appreciative inquiry is that it can be done as one summit, or it can be an ongoing process of dialogue. It can be enormously empowering for people to start from strengths. This shares some commonalities with a community assets approach to community, with a focus on resources and capability rather than needs. However, there is the danger is that this can place responsibility to change marginalised lives on local people, avoiding an analysis of power that helps us target the structural sources of inequality on a transformative level.

Dialogue and social change

To address societal problems in his later years, Bohm wrote a proposal for a solution that has become known as 'Bohm dialogue', in which equal status and 'free space' form the most important prerequisites of communication and the appreciation of differing personal beliefs. He suggested that if these dialogue groups were experienced on a sufficiently wide scale, they could help overcome the isolation and fragmentation Bohm observed as inherent in society. Bohm has been criticised for being politically naïve and unrealistically apolitical, however. Indeed, the above selection of dialogical techniques could be said to fall in to the trap of being mere additions to the tyranny of techniques that are called participation (Cooke and Kothari, 2001). They imply, for example, that people have the words to express what they think and feel. It can be argued that even if practitioners utilise local forms of representation such as dance, song and storytelling as a basis for participatory work, the approach would still inevitably constitute a frame in and through which the participants' knowledge becomes formed (see Henkel and Stirrat, 2001). Thus, while participation is usually presented as a means to reveal subjugated knowledge and to access silenced voices, in fact its technologies and social relations actually create new forms of knowledge and ways of knowing.

Herein lies the difference regarding the technologies of dialogue, similar to those outlined above, from those which are critiqued. They serve in the nature of the processes they encourage to interrupt existing social relations, existing repertoires of discourse and dominant power structures. This is because power, rather than being fixed and unchanging, is everywhere; as Foucault argues, it is in fact fluid and changing. Dialogical processes approached as described earlier disconnect customary practice and enable people both to act as reflexive agents in terms of their meaning making, and through deliberation to become aware of the ways in which they are constrained by power dynamics and existing discourses.

The creation of dialogical spaces is increasing. Dialogue is used in classrooms, community centres, businesses, statutory agencies and other settings to enable people, usually in small groups, to share their perspectives and experiences about difficult issues. It has been used to help people resolve long-standing conflicts and to build a deeper understanding of contentious issues, including interfaith differences. This is not surprising since it seems to represent basic common sense in terms of dispelling stereotypes, building trust and enabling people to be open to perspectives that are very different from their own. Dialogue is essential to participatory practice because whether through story, pictures, poetry or dance, there is an act of engagement in a space of mutual respect. It enhances the human spirit in a way that goes beyond our desire for affiliation as human beings. But because we are human beings with all our emotional needs, and because of the existing structures in society, we have to be aware of those very human needs for power and control, of the persistence of old habits and also the cumulative history that acts as a barrier to change. Nonetheless the cumulative engagement in circles of dialogue can generate processes of change towards social justice. In Freirean approaches to adult education the focus is on working in dialogue with oppressed groups. However, the future lies in working in dialogue across whole systems in some of the ways suggested in this chapter. Burns (2007) advocates that we should also work with those who hold the sources of power. It means continuously advocating for such dialogical spaces in a constant critique of taken-for-granted institutional practices such as the way meetings are run, who is invited and what language is used. It also means entering into dialogue with others in such as a way as we ourselves, not just others, are transformed in the process. It is about taking care of those important spaces between, those spaces that are largely neglected in current thinking and practice. In the pressurised public sector, current cultural norms run counter to this. Yet there are stories of public servants who hold those spaces of deliberative practice. Forester's book, *The deliberative practitioner* (1999), is replete with such stories taken from the field of housing and community planning. Using these stories of messy real world practice, he shows how planners have fostered dialogue to create deliberation about citizens' worries, fears, hopes and loyalties, commitments and self-images, and through sensitive listening helped to create pragmatic solutions through public learning in safe spaces.

A colleague of mine (Jane's) in Sweden has been working with a collaborative inquiry group based in a hospital which, alongside colleagues from other parts of the health and social care system, has been exploring how to collaborate better. Despite creating new relationships and understanding the same group came under criticism because it spent a lot of time talking but not doing. The prevailing norm in the health sector was action and doing, so dialogue of this sort was considered a waste of time. This is not restricted to the Swedish healthcare system. At the time of writing the Department of Health (UK) is engaged in an initiative called Pacesetters, which aims to address some of the inequalities in access to services experienced by a range of minority groups such as transsexual people, the deaf, travellers, as well as other specific ethnic and religious groups. The strapline of the initiative is 'look below the surface, change the way we think', and it is supported by an excellent document showing the health sector how to engage with communities, called *A dialogue of equals* (DH, 2008). Those who are involved are genuinely committed; however, at the time of writing many of the Department of Health's traditional practices in meetings, at least, leave no time at all for real dialogue. Indeed, one member of the evaluation team new to working with the NHS remarked, "they seem to talk a lot but there is no action which follows." The pressure to seek early wins to please the minister gives little scope for the space and time to get to the place where there can be a dialogue of equals.

Such examples are not restricted to the health system but they dispel two misconceptions: first, that dialogue does not involve action and, second, that any form of conversation constitutes dialogue. As we have shown in this chapter, dialogue is action for change as it does indeed encourage looking below the surface and changing the way we think. Not only that but true dialogue, not just talking, leads to action. Both are inextricably linked, beyond dualism.

The centrality of learning through dialogue as a key to transformation

It is important to re-emphasise that, when we are talking about transformative change through dialogue, we are seeing dialogue as a core to a social learning process whereby assumptions are changed, there is a questioning of taken-for-granteds and a profound shift in underlying values through changes in ways of seeing the world. Dialogue is linked inextricably to reflection, which we explore in the next chapter. Argyris and Schön (1978) named this process of transformative learning as 'double-loop learning' to distinguish it from the type of learning that takes place from experience, and to emphasise that this is learning from reflection in order to improve the way things are done (see Chapter 8). McGill and Brockbank (2004) argue that something extra is required to move learning into a transformative trajectory and that contained and structured emotion underpins the shift. The containment comes from a structured process that both allows the emotion but also contains it. Facilitated dialogue, that is, structured conversations as described earlier, moves and channels the energy for change. As a process it can unpack hidden and embedded discourses within a community or organisation, challenging what seems natural and exposing unequal power relations.

The examples of creating dialogical spaces are merely examples; they have their strengths and their weaknesses with regards to the extent they can unpick the energies of dialogue to move into double-loop learning. They are all highly dependent on good person-centred facilitation and the willingness for the participants to go with the process as well as their dialogical skills. They are all merely techniques; in other words, they are highly dependent in their outcomes on the participants and in terms of systemic change on the context in which they take place and the actions that are taken. Moreover, the capacity to engage in true dialogue is not one that is encouraged or taught. It requires the ability to communicate authentically and to listen. As Maslow (1969) pointed out, good listening is rare and it is also largely missing from our educational system. Real listening is non-judgemental. It means attending to the other person as a whole person and it means not just listening to their words but also the non-verbal messages, paying attention, not evaluating or commenting internally on what is being said. It also means asking questions that are open rather than closed after restating what you think you have heard. It means giving feedback to what you have heard in an empathetic way. These are all skills that can be developed with practice, but which many find hard.

Most writers on dialogue have come to their understanding of its importance because they share a critique of a world that emphasises only the material and the analytical. These ills of alienation and fragmentation are seen reflected in modernity, devaluing human relationships, encouraging isolation, dehumanising and even devaluing the meaning of existence. The first step to social change is to bring alive to those who act in this way what they are doing, and through dialogue reflect back the values implied by their actions.

We have now explored two of the core interrelated dimensions of participatory practice, story and dialogue. In the next chapter we move on to the third, which, when combined with story and dialogue, has the potential for learning that leads to transformation: critical reflection.

SEVEN

Critical reflection

Reflection upon situationality is reflection about the very condition
of existence (Freire, 1972: 81)

So far we have argued in this book that participatory practice is predicated on the
key principles of social justice and sustainability with embedded values of equality,
peace, harmony and respect. In the last two chapters we have looked in detail at
story and dialogue, which we see as key elements of a participatory practice which
sow the seeds for individual and collective learning for change. Through story and
dialogue we can start to open up spaces for critical engagement. However, to be
truly transformative, reflection is an essential component of the process of change,
and as such it needs to be interwoven with the process of action, alongside story
and dialogue. It is the continual cycling of action and reflection through critical
questioning that forms the basis of transformation and praxis. This interweaving
produces a fabric of critical knowledge and thoughtful action. Reflection cannot
be an added extra; it has to be integral to all we do. This chapter explores the
nature of reflection, in particular critical reflexivity, which involves going ever
deeper into questioning the taken-for-grantedness of life and its pivotal role
in transformative learning. We look at the contribution of Gramsci, alongside
Foucault and Freire, to an analysis of power, and demonstrate how critiquing
the critiques helps develop our understanding. The spaces for reflection and for
creating critical dissent dialogue have been colonised, and we consider the nature
of reclaiming these spaces in current times. In doing so, we return to the roots
of critical pedagogy and ecological consciousness.

Critical human inquiry as an ecological imperative

As discussed in Chapter 3, looking at the world ecologically means looking at
relationships and processes that connect as a whole, rather than focusing on parts.
It is important to understand the inherent dynamic that energises and keeps an
ecosystem in balance, while allowing it to evolve. In systems terms, this means
paying attention to feedback, to cycling the energy within the system to encourage
a mutual, reciprocal process. In Chapter 9 you will see that the model we develop
in relation to the ideas in this book captures not only the idea of wholeness, but
also the importance of feedback. When we engage as practitioners with people
in a process of mutual inquiry, we contribute to the expansion of each other's
knowledge. This is relevant in every context, at every level, not only grassroots
practice, in a process of collectively becoming critical. For example, in Chapter 1
we introduced Pitchford and Henderson's (2008) critique of the way in which

we have allowed government agendas to blur such concepts as community development, community involvement and community engagement into one amorphous feel-good agenda that does no more than lay the responsibility for social justice at the feet of those who are most marginalised. We are concerned that our commitment to deepening democracy is being obscured, that public sector organisation and decision making is more removed from local communities than ever at a time when social divisions are becoming wider than ever.

Rowan's cycle model remains a keystone for understanding where reflection and change fit in the process of transformation. As shown in Figure 7.1, it offers a clear diagrammatic structure for taking an emancipatory action research approach that is central to critical praxis.

Figure 7.1: The cycle model

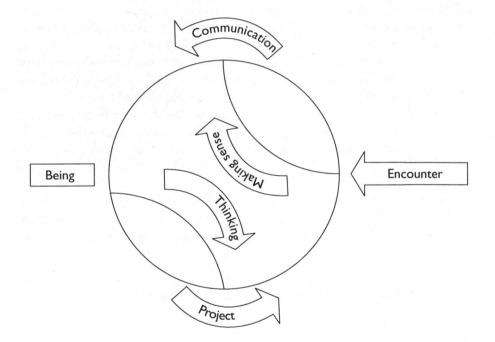

Source: Adapted from Rowan (1981), © John Wiley and Sons Ltd, reproduced with permission.

This cycle model is particularly useful in seeing how to integrate reflection and action in the process of community development. Although it is possible to enter the cycle at any stage, for ease of explanation we will begin at *being*, the stage at which we become aware that our practice needs to change. What we have been doing is no longer relevant to what is happening, and we need to think about things differently. The cycle has an inner and outer flow. As we move into the stage of *thinking*, the arc indicates an inward process of seeking. We reflect, have dialogue with others and gather information until we have some idea about appropriate action. At this stage, we move outwards to *project*, involving more people as the process moves on. A plan of action is formulated based on new thinking, moving the contradiction of the existing situation towards new practice. Continuing the outer movement, we move towards *encounter*, the stage at which we engage in action with the community. The model is flexible and at any stage it is possible to flow back and forth, in and out, according to confirmations and disconfirmations. But there is a point at which analysis and reflection on action is appropriate and we move inwards from *encounter* to a stage of *making sense*. This is the stage at which 'experience turns into meaning and knowledge' (Rowan, 1981: 100), and where a balance between achieving understandable simplicity and complex connections has to be reached. For the process to become useful, there is a need to share the experience. Following the arc outwards to the stage of *communication*, with new understanding emerging from practice, we are generating knowledge in action and need to share it so that others can learn from the experience. In the sharing of new understanding and how this influences practice, experience becomes a collective learning on a much bigger scale. Practitioners, in partnership with the community, need to share this new knowledge by giving talks, publishing, presenting at conferences and meetings, via the Internet, and any other way that communicates the experience. By sharing knowledge we influence policy and practice on a much wider level; in these ways local projects can have global influence., as multiple cycles build on one another.

It is important to keep the cyclic nature of the process intact. If we fall into the trap of seeing the process as linear, evaluation, reflection and planning become seen as optional extras and easily overlooked as the end of an action. Seeing the process as cyclic captures the integrated nature of the process, each aspect of vital consequence to the others in a process of learning and change.

Understanding reflection and its role in learning and change

> Perspective transformation is the process of becoming critically aware of how and why our presuppositions have come to constrain the way we perceive, understand, and feel about our world; of reformulating these assumptions to permit a more inclusive, discriminating, permeable and integrative perspective; and of making decisions or otherwise acting on these new understandings. More inclusive, discriminating, permeable and integrative perspectives are superior perspectives that adults choose if they can because they are motivated to better understand the meaning of their experience. (Mezirow & Associates, 1990: 14)

Reflection is a key element of learning and development, and a crucial dimension in the process of transformation. Writers and philosophers John Dewey and Jürgen Habermas, among others, have contributed to the theoretical foundation of reflection. Practical approaches to understanding the role of reflection in learning have been underpinned by the notion of the adult learning cycle first identified by David Kolb (1984) and the model of reflection developed by Boud et al (1985). Reflection in these approaches is seen as a process of sense or meaning making. For people to change their 'meaning' schemes (specific beliefs, attitudes and emotional reactions), they need to engage in a process of ongoing critical questioning, not just as an intellectual exercise but as an 'intuitive, creative, emotional process' (Grabov, 1997: 90), involving a 'fundamental change in one's personality involving […] the resolution of a personal dilemma and the expansion of consciousness resulting in greater personality integration' (Boyd and Myers, 1988: 280). This process involves three interrelated elements: receptivity, recognition and grieving. A person has to be receptive or open to considering 'alternative expressions of meaning' (Boyd and Myers, 1988: 277) for any learning to take place. Recognition involves a realisation that there is a need for change. Grieving is when the individual takes on a new way of doing things or tries to integrate new ideas into their lives. They must then come to terms with the fact that the steps that they have taken before are no longer relevant to what they are going to have to do in the future. This whole process is a cyclical one of going inwards and outwards. It also moves back and forth between the rational and the imaginative, drawing on the 'realm of interior experience, one constituent being the rational expressed through insights, judgments, and decision; the other being the extra-rational expressed through symbols, images, and feelings' (Boyd and Myers, 1988: 275), moving back and forth between the rational and the intuitive/imaginative/subjective. This is why the use of different forms of art in combination with the rational are powerful tools for transformation. Poetry, art, drama, all engage with these intuitive elements, involving more holistic dimensions of our being beyond the intellectual – emotional, physical, spiritual. The importance of the emotional dimension in reflection is supported by recent brain research regarding the embodiment of knowledge. Memories and emotions are stored in all cells of the body, so transformation, from this perspective, is also a process of embodiment. We need to be aware of this and be prepared for our own internal emotional responses and recognise those in others.

The metaphor of the butterfly emerging out of the cocoon of a caterpillar is often used to describe the process of transformative change. The caterpillar holds within it the elements of the emerging butterfly, but in the chrysalis stage the original caterpillar is broken down and destroyed. Senge et al (2005) grapple with this idea of change and transformation. They come up with what they call the theory of U. For them, while the logical and rational 'head work' can lead you to the point of potential transformation, the shift at the bottom of the U, the stage before you move to change, is difficult to describe or replicate. It is essentially a spiritual experience during which one feels connected to a greater whole. Even if the social and intellectual processes that encourage dialogical and critical reflection can be put in place, it is a more elusive, intangible matter as to whether the change occurs. In an attempt to set up the conditions for change, Jaworski and Scharmer (cited in Senge et al, 2005: 88) developed an approach to collective problem solving, which, while developed in an organisational development context, has many similarities with reflective community practice following an emancipatory research approach. As a dialogical process it involves three elements: *sensing*, *realising* and *presencing*. Sensing involves storytelling and dialogue as described in previous chapters. Realising is the action phase whereby insights are shared and then turned into concrete action. Presencing is considered to be a dimension that has been neglected in social and personal change. They believe that participants need to spend time in silence developing the capacities of letting go and letting come, that is, equivalent to the grieving process referred to earlier. Effectively, they are placing contemplation or meditation at the heart of reflection as a balance to the complexity that the information-sharing nature of the story and dialogue process has generated. This presencing experience is about returning to simplicity, creating emptiness and connecting to what really matters. Through this process of silence, a shared purpose and a deeper connecting is obtained. While the personal health benefits of mindfulness are now well established (Ludwig and Kabat-Zim, 2008), here it is presented as a tool for collective change. This is reflection at its most fundamental. Yes, we need to question our taken-for-granteds, but it is only when we also sit with our unknowing and questioning in silence and be, that transformation takes place. So stillness and silence need to be present as part of reflection because of the multifaceted, holistic integrated nature of the process. It involves asking the question, 'What is going on here?' at the same time as allowing our subconscious to process our thoughts and feelings, helping us integrate them into our whole being. How often have you grappled with a solution to a problem, gone to bed, only to wake up to find the solution has been processed and a new view of the world has emerged? Here we return to the notion that personal consciousness leads to a transformative autonomy, that in turn leads to a collective autonomy, a precursor of transformative collective action (Doyal and Gough, 1991).

Reflection with all its components is often an uncomfortable and challenging process, and so can be consciously and unconsciously resisted. Professionals can find it particularly threatening, despite the popularity of the term 'reflective practitioner', as it can unsettle identities, expose insecurities and challenge our very existence. Often when I (Jane) run workshops on the evaluation process for professionals, especially if they take place over two days, participants who have been undertaking work on the first day report confusion and ambivalence at the end of the first day, but return the following day full of enthusiasm to finish the tasks with surprising speed and relish. On the first day they are asked to explore, with their co-workers, clients or community members, why they are doing what they are doing, and whether and how it will lead to change. The systematic process of questioning that is encouraged sometimes leads to the painful realisation that their project plans will not lead to the change they want, and sometimes the painful awareness that they are at variance with the purpose of the project. This is made more profoundly challenging when they have been funded by a particular organisation to do a specific task or to generate a particular outcome. The notion that they can challenge and change the process is usually seen as impossible. I (Jane) can remember in one such workshop a member of a local council who was engaged in a community initiative around leisure and health and was using the initiative as a case study to develop evaluation skills with people from another project. During the day he became increasingly concerned and depressed, and in the reflection session at the end of the day he expressed profound antagonism to the whole day's work. I doubted if he would turn up the following day, and was concerned about the impact that this would have on the group. The next day, however, he turned up early, full of energy, saying he had rung his boss that evening and had discussed the whole thing, with the result that they had agreed to abandon their original plan and engage stakeholders in developing a more relevant project. His co-participants in the workshop were so motivated by this bold step that they suggested that they work with him on a trial run as the case study for the day. In the end, their enthusiasm generated two days' work in that last day. From this, you can see that despite the initial resistance, resentment and confusion inherent in critical thinking, there is also joy, exhilaration and excitement in the process of transformation, leading to self-confidence and empowerment (Brookfield, 1987).

Being critical

Although the idea of reflective practice, first coined by Schön (1983), has been mainstreamed in contemporary professional higher education and in the notion of learning organisations and action learning, much of the reflection that takes place is severely limited in its potential for transformation. It remains largely what is termed 'single-loop learning'. Schön was highly critical of what he saw as the dominant rational/experimental model of learning, seeing such approaches as severely limited in situations of social change. Such approaches are also profoundly hegemonic, serving the purpose of maintaining the status quo in the interests of the powerful and privileged. Schön argued for a more 'existentially' oriented approach, which, he argued, leads to double-loop learning in which reflection takes place not only on specific actions but on the broader context of the action, that is, why are we doing this in this way and what are the assumptions implicit in it? Hawkins (1992) further argues that we need to take reflection to a third level, where we reflect on and question our values, ecological as well as social and economic. This is what Bateson (1972) calls 'level 3 learning', whereby constricted awareness is released and new frames of references are accessible. This can be related to levels of critical consciousness in Freire's process of *conscientisation* and the recognition element Boyd and Myers (1988) talked about. Bateson and others see this as a discovery of something that is already there: it is consciousness that learns, and consciousness is a collective phenomenon. We would argue that it is through the process of becoming critical and being critically reflexive, combining reflection with action as praxis, that such transformation or changes in consciousness begin to happen.

Gaby Jacobs (2008), drawing on the work of Barnett (1997), shows how the process of reflexivity, as compared to reflection, takes place within the 'doing'. It means combining the ability to reflect inwards towards oneself as an inquirer and towards the understanding that is the result of that (domains of self and knowledge, see Table 7.1 below); and then outward to the cultural, social, historical, linguistic, political and other forces that shape the context of the inquiry (domain of the world). The concept of reflexivity is used to refer to the combining of the inner and outer dimensions. This combination of inner and outer makes it different from the kind of reflective practice that encourages only the inward movement. It refers to the challenging of the taking-for-grantedness of everyday life; digging beneath the surface of what appears as 'real' or 'truth' to arrive at a deeper understanding of an issue or problem and one's part in it. It calls for going within to question one's own assumptions about the world. This *epistemological reflexivity* helps us to see how the way we view the world influences the way we choose to act in it. And at the heart of the process is the empowering insight that the self is involved in knowledge construction (*personal reflexivity*); in other words, we can change the world by changing our understanding of what is possible. This process is a

Table 7.1: Becoming critical in thought and action

Domains			
Levels of criticality	Knowledge	Self	World
4. Transformatory critique	Knowledge critique	Reconstruction of self	Critique in action (collective reconstruction of the world)
3. Refashioning of traditions	Critical thought (malleable traditions of thought)	Development of self within traditions	Mutual understanding and development of traditions
2. Reflexivity	Critical thinking (reflection on one's own understanding)	Self reflection (reflection on one's own projects)	Reflective practice (metacomptence, adaptability, flexibility)
1. Critical skills	Discipline-specific critical thinking skills	Self-monitoring to given standards and norms	Problem solving (means-end instrumentalism)
Forms of criticality	Critical reason	Critical self-reflection	Critical action

Source: Barnett (1997: 103), cited in Jacobs (2008: 223)

result of engaging in critical praxis, that is, combining theory with practice, with action. Only through this interweaving of inner, outer, critique with action can we reach transformation.

Gaby Jacobs provides a compelling account of these ideas in action. She shows how a group of health promotion practitioners transformed as they moved through the levels of reflection and how over time critical thought was accompanied by emancipatory action in the world. Labonte (1994) once called health promotion the 'practice of the disempowered helping the disempowered'. Through coming together in learning circles to explore one of the fundamental tenets of health promotion, empowerment, this group of health promotion practitioners started to question their practice in a wider context, transcending the personal and institutional barriers to change. They started asking, Whose voices are heard? Whose stories are told? What is not said, not seen or acknowledged as relevant? In doing so not only did they transform as people, but this extended to the way they worked with communities, listening more, introducing more expressive ways of working beyond the intellectual, such as Flamenco dancing, the use of arts and body work based on Aikido principles. Importantly, they became confident in explaining the greater potential of their new participatory approaches to practice. Developing such competence in critical reflexivity is a far cry from the utilitarian and instrumental lists of skills and competences that have been developed within public health for health promotion practitioners in recent years in England. As I (Jane) have written elsewhere, this reflects the neoliberal and medical hegemony that still dominates public health practice (Scott-Samuel and Springett, 2007).

Reflecting on power

Participatory approaches to practice call for analyses of power. This is the basis of becoming critical: questioning the ideas that construct everyday life. Ontology, or a theory of being, is the way we see ourselves in relation to the world around us which helps us to make sense of why we live life as we do and how we give meaning and purpose to our lives, the way we act in the world. Epistemology, influenced by our ontological perspective, is a theory of knowledge, or making sense of the world that is informed by particular values. So, if dominant attitudes persuade us to see the world in terms of a natural order of superiority and inferiority, we are likely to make sense of and create our lived reality accordingly. However, if we question the world around us and begin to explore values of equality and connection with the whole of life on earth, this will lead us to different ways of knowing, and in turn, to different ways of being. In these ways, epistemologies and ontologies are part of a living theory, or practical theory that evolves from everyday life in order to transform the way things are for the better. Theory and practice become synthesised into praxis as we create theory as part of life itself. To begin the process of change we need to have theories that help us to understand the rules we live by, how they are agreed by society as a whole and how they become embedded in everyday life; for this we turn to critical theorists.

'Critical theorists begin with the premise that *men and women are essentially unfree and inhabit a world rife with contradictions and asymmetries of power and privilege*' (McLaren, 2009: 61, emphasis in original). As critical educators, we seek theories that are dialectical, that locate the individual as one who both creates and is created by society, to the extent that it is impossible to understand one without the other. In this way, 'critical theory helps us focus *simultaneously on both sides of a social contradiction*' (McLaren, 2009: 61, emphasis in original). By focusing on this idea, you can see that any site of domination is also a site of liberation, and it is by understanding the nature of power that we are able to transform it into empowerment.

It is important to remind you that ideas do not emerge in a vacuum; they emerge in a time and place, and build on ideas and experience that have gone before. In this sense theories are never right or wrong; they contribute to a collective understanding that builds on a past–present–future continuum. As we mention later, bell hooks honours Freire for offering her the conceptual tools to question her life as a Black American woman, and we have already mentioned in Chapter 2 the way in which Ruskin, from another culture and another time, profoundly influenced Gandhi's thought and action. This notion of honouring our intellectual debts leads us, in this brief consideration of power, to place a rough structure around the evolution of ideas of power used in community-based practices over the past four decades.

Antonio Gramsci

At this point, let us examine Gramsci's contribution to our understanding of power. Antonio Gramsci was imprisoned by Mussolini for 10 years until his death in 1937 for nothing more that taking a dissenting position on fascism. Prior to this, he had been a political journalist and activist, and his deep concern about power in western societies was based on this praxis (for a more detailed discussion of Gramsci's life and ideas, see Ledwith, 2005). Gramsci's understanding of the way that power permeates society through our participation in social groups has had a profound influence on community development since *Selections from prison notebooks* was published in English in 1971. This coincided with the publication of Freire's *Pedagogy of the oppressed*, highly influenced by Gramsci's ideas, and together the wide availability of these books transformed the radical potential of community development practice by both offering insights into the nature of domination/subordination and offering ideas for practice interventions. Gramsci was concerned that the historical changes of his time were resulting in social control less reliant on overt force. He developed the concept of *hegemony*, the way that a dominant group asserts control over other social groups, to address not only coercion, the state exercising control through the law, the police and the armed forces, but also *ideological persuasion* as a force that persuades people to consent to the dominant social order exercised through cultural institutions such as schools, the family, mass media and churches. His emphasis was on the subtle and powerful nature of persuasion, reaching inside our minds to convince us to consent to life as it is and so slot into our prescribed place in the social order. Dominant attitudes are sold to us as *common sense*, and we internalise these attitudes, even though they may not act in our interests. He saw this acted out through moral leadership, with teachers and others in positions of influence in our personal lives reinforcing dominant ideas sold as *truth*, as *common sense*. Hegemony, in these ways, asserts control over knowledge and culture, affirming the ideas of the dominant culture and marginalising and silencing others.

You may wish, at this point, to reflect on how you see this in action in your own lives. Wink (1997: 42), for instance, gives an example of a high school in an African-American community in which the principal stormed a classroom and physically removed a student, saying that rap music and break dancing was against the rules: 'we set the rules, and when we do, we mean business'. In this example, the rules and the physical policing by the principal are coercion; the way that the dominant White culture is threaded through the curriculum to the exclusion of Black cultures, and the subtleties of the way it is delivered by teachers results in consent to dominance. This is very similar to my own (Margaret's) experience of classroom teaching, in which the culture of the staff room is one of constantly judging the worth of pupils, filtering some to the centre, others to the margins in a self-fulfilling process. In other words, the messages are so powerful that they are absorbed into the minds of children. Unless teacher education involves an analysis of power and status of the teacher across the difference and diversity of the classroom, schooling inevitably remains hegemonic: a site where the dominant control ideas that maintain their dominance, and the subordinated produce ideas that maintain their subordination (Mayo, 2004). In these ways, the system becomes self-perpetuating, maintaining the status quo with a flexible balance of coercion and consent.

Hegemony is only maintained through the collective will of the people, therefore the development of a counter-hegemony, a different way of making sense of the world, plays an essential part in the process of change. This links to what we were saying earlier about epistemological reflexivity in the process of questioning false consciousness. Gramsci saw the importance of critical education in opening people's minds to the possibility of change releasing the intellectual potential inside each of us, and the role of alliances between diverse social groups in the process of transformative collective action. This cyclic process of reflection and action is the crux of critical education.

Dominant ideas give credence to a 'natural' leadership and status in society, an assumed superiority that maintains hegemonic control over the mass of people. The power of hegemony is in this fine balance between coercion and consent, and its flexibility in absorbing challenge through tokenism, giving an illusion of democracy. Let us illustrate this point. Schooling is essentially hegemonic. As an institution of civil society, it reaches into the being of young people to reinforce dominant ideas of inferiority/superiority through a powerful process of success/failure, to maintain the status quo. The illusion of democracy is maintained by the occasional working–class 'success', while the social group as a whole remains marginalised. By individualising educational failure, the educational determinants of everyday life are overlooked and 'failure' is taken on board as personal inadequacy, resulting in low self–esteem and a lack of confidence. In a similar vein, Freire (1972) refers to *false generosity*, or tokenism. The inherent contradiction that is revealed here is the way that democratic schooling claims to offer routes out of poverty for children, while the reality is that it is a prime site of hegemony.

Probably the best example of the full might of *hegemony* at work in the post–war period in the UK is that of 1984–85 miners' strike, when state coercion took hold of media control and denied the right to freedom of movement to and from mining communities, at the same time as using ideological persuasion to convince the rest of society that the miners were the 'enemy within', effectively alienating the miners from popular public support (Milne, 2004). Community groups were active in supporting the mining communities, but this was not enough to change popular opinion and the outcome is well documented to offer evidence that this had more to do with the government's desire to dismantle the biggest remaining trade union capable of civic disruption than anything to do with diminishing coal supplies. The power of the state when the full force of coercion and consent are used in combination in this way helps us to understand the nature of hegemony.

In these ways, Gramsci provides an essential insight into the power of ideas to colonise our minds, persuading us to accept the dominant order of things unquestioningly as *common sense*. The struggles against oppression around issues of *difference* are located in civil society. This places the participatory practitioner at the heart of the process. The values, attitudes, morality and beliefs which are internalised as *common sense* by the masses but serve the interests of dominant groups have to be challenged at a local as well as an institutional level. In order for this to happen in a sustainable way, Gramsci believed that the *false consciousness* of subordinated groups was the starting point for participation in the process of transformative change.

Gramsci did not think that the process of becoming critical would erupt spontaneously. In line with his belief in the intellectual potential of everyone, he used the term *organic intellectuals* to refer to those who emerge from their culture of origin. Every social group produces individuals who possess 'the capacity to be an organiser of society in general, including all its complex organism of services, right up to the state organism, because of the need to create the conditions most favourable to the expansion of their own class ...' (Forgacs, 1988: 301). *Traditional intellectuals* can be seen as those who have a sympathetic allegiance to social justice that supersedes their commitment to their own class. They are the catalyst in the process of change by creating the context for questioning lived reality. Although he saw this role as vital in setting the wheels of change in motion, he was sceptical that their allegiance would be sustained; if push came to shove, he believed that historical analysis proved that cultural privilege would be asserted, that they would defect in the face of persecution. Nevertheless, having cut the ties to their own class, *traditional intellectuals* have a useful role to perform in unlocking the process of critical consciousness and action for change.

Gramsci emphasised praxis in the process of change. The term he frequently used in his prison notebooks, 'philosophy of praxis', is the concept of a unity of theory and practice. 'For Gramsci the philosophy of praxis is both the theory of the contradictions in society and at the same time people's practical awareness of those contradictions' (Forgacs, 1988: 429). This concept of critical praxis is of great relevance to our current context in which theory and practice have been falsely dichotomised, leading to practice that is dominated by policy agendas that are unquestioningly implemented in grassroots communities. To capture this dilemma, Mae Shaw draws on the imaginative concept coined by Johnston: 'actionless thought' and 'thoughtless action' (Johnston, cited in Shaw, 2004: 26), the antithesis of praxis. The anti-intellectual times we live in add to this by emphasising 'doing', a skills-based approach to practice over 'thinking' and a critical approach to practice. This inevitably renders us vulnerable to the manipulations of the state.

Jürgen Habermas

The Frankfurt School came about at an important historical juncture: the failure of Marxism to bring about social change in western Europe, the rise of Nazism and the Jewish identity of many of those who were drawn to these neo-Marxist developments in critical thought (McLaren, 2009). The Institute for Social Research at the University of Frankfurt was the nexus for this affiliation of thinkers, which included Herbert Marcuse, Theodor Adorno, Max Horkheimer, Erich Fromm and Jürgen Habermas. Formed in 1923, the Institute was forced to leave Nazi Germany for Geneva from 1933 to 1935, after which it was relocated in New York, and from 1941 in California, until returning to the University of Frankfurt in 1953. The Frankfurt School died with Max Horkheimer (Director of the Institute since 1930) in 1973, although the Institute continued. Like Gramsci (1971), Adorno and Horkheimer (1972) were concerned about changes in the nature of domination: 'briefly put, the colonization of the workplace was now supplanted by the colonization of all other cultural spheres' (Giroux, 2009: 38). Habermas is acknowledged for his contribution to critical theory, so we now take a look at his insights into power in everyday relations.

In *The theory of communicative action* Habermas (1984; 1987) explains the way that what is judged to be normative becomes embedded in everyday behaviour in a way that reproduces the existing social order, the status quo. Whitehead and McNiff (2006: 101) talk about the way that certain practices are accepted as given and 'it is not considered necessary to stop and examine the underpinning assumptions that guide such practices or to question where these rules came from or whether they are useful or outdated or even wrong; we are expected to accept things as the way they are and the way they should be'. This gives rise to, for example, the perceived superiority of Whiteness, maleness, able-bodiedness, heterosexuality and Christianity, and results in behaviours that are racist, patriarchal, 'dis'ablist, homophobic and religiously intolerant, to name but a few. We could develop this discussion in relation to the way that these assumptions of superiority give rise to everyday experience from domestic violence to environmental degradation to female genital mutilation, immigration policy, job opportunities and many more. Attitudes become communicated in everyday discourses, accepted as truths, and structurally integrated into the mechanisms of the state and the institutions of civil society. Without a critical approach to practice, practitioners unquestioningly reproduce the existing order of things. This is why we feel so strongly that there should not be a discrepancy between what we say we do in principle and what we actually do in practice. Communicative action, according to Habermas (1984; 1987) aims to reach consensus through mutual understanding based on agreed qualities of truthful, understandable, sincere and appropriate communication between participants. This is directly related to what he saw as the structural components of the lifeworld – culture, society and person – reinforced by interacting processes of cultural reproduction, social integration and socialisation. Thompson's PCS model in Chapter 1 engages with these three processes dialectically by offering insight into how they mutually interact in discriminatory ways, at the same time as identifying each process as a site of intervention, by *interrupting* the reproductive functions at each level.

Michel Foucault

Michel Foucault, the French philosopher and sociologist, is associated with post–structuralism and postmodernism. He, too, is preoccupied with how people become the conscious subjects of history, experiencing themselves as powerful, not powerless, and by such intellectual emancipation are able to free themselves from the chains of *false consciousness*. He talks about how as subjects we can become 'self-determining agents that resist and challenge power structures' (Danaher et al, 2000: 150). In order to do this, we need to understand the way that *truth* is socially constructed through power/knowledge relations. 'For Foucault, power comes from everywhere, from above and from below; it is "always already there" and is inextricably implicated in micro-relations of domination and resistance' (McLaren, 2009: 72). Power relations, according to Foucault, are embedded in discourse, and by this he means not only words but practices – educational, scientific, religious, legal – that embed dominant discourse in their processes. In this way, we begin to see that truth is not absolute but relational. In this sense, we remain eternally challenged: 'Critical educators argue that *praxis* (informed actions) must be guided by *phronesis* (the disposition to act truly and rightly). This means, in critical terms, that actions and knowledge must be directed at eliminating pain, oppression, and inequality, and at promoting justice and freedom'

(McLaren, 2009: 74). As McLaren points out, *empowerment* means not only setting the learning context for participants to understand the world around them, but also to generate the courage to bring about change.

Much as Gramsci directed our attention from power as coercion to include power as ideological persuasion, so Foucault argues that we must direct our attention from a concentration on the role of the state and the institutions of civil society to include the micro-level of society.

> Hegemonic or global forms of power rely in the first instance on those 'infinitesimal' practices, composed of their own particular techniques and tactics, which exist in those institutions on the fringes or at the micro-level of society. (Foucault, 1980: 99)

He was not negating hegemonic forms of power, but suggesting that they rely on all people being vehicles of power in everyday life, acting out the social and cultural practices at every level. In this sense, our attention is more acutely focused on subjects of power rather than sites or holders of power. We have to become more conscious of power everywhere in the here and now, in the self and in the community, in everyday practices. 'All individuals are vehicles of power' (Kothari, 2001: 141). As we begin to stretch our thought capacities from their binary construction which 'reduces the languages of analysis to white, hegemonic forms of clarity' (McLaren, 1995), we begin to touch the edges of 'power […] conceived to be relational … rather than something that is acquired, seized or shared' (Smart, 2002: 79).

> Power must be analyzed as something which circulates, or rather as something which only functions in the form of a chain. It is never localized here or there.… Power is employed and exercised through a net-like organization. (Foucault, 1980: 98)

Foucault maintains that power is not only asserted as social control in sites and location, in policies and practices, but also colonises our being so that our actions and perceptions are embodied in our selves as well as embedded in society. As Berger (1963: 140) says: 'the structures of society become the structures of our own consciousness. Society does not stop at the surface of our skins. Society permeates us as much as it envelops us'. Hence our emphasis on becoming critical as an inner process of deep reflexivity and an outer process of critical connections, in what Judi Marshall terms 'inner and outer arcs of attention' (Marshall, 2001: 44).

Kothari (2001: 142) warns: 'Despite the aims of participatory approaches and the claims made by participatory practitioners, particularly with respect to empowering the disempowered, it is argued here that participative methods of enquiry simplify the nature of power and are thus in danger of encouraging a reassertion of power and social control not only by certain individuals and groups, but also of particular bodies of knowledge'. Her assertion is that while we fail to see knowledge as an accumulation of norms, rituals and practices that are embedded in power relations, we fall back on dichotomies of power which do not reach the ways in which knowledge is produced or the processes by which it becomes normalised. It is useful to consider Gary Craig's comments on the threats to multiculturalism being reduced to 'just drumming and dancing' in this respect (Craig, 2008: 244). An inability to analyse power at policy and personal levels has led to an inability to understand racism and the subsequent denial of the reality of multicultural societies, with the result that issues of social justice, culture and identity continue to be swept under the carpet. Both these arguments are based on us lacking the conceptual tools of analysis to bring about change, but worse than this, the implication is that our practice not only fails in its intention, but reinforces the existing social order.

Moving critique forward

Criticality calls for critiquing the critiques as an ongoing process. In this way, we deepen insights into the nature of power that gives rise to subordination and exploitation. In this respect, feminist and postmodern critiques of metanarratives led to a deeper understanding of power relations. By the 1980s Arnot, for example, was arguing that hegemony needed to have a gendered understanding, that male hegemony consisted of a multiplicity of moments which persuaded women to accept a male-dominated culture and their subordination within it (Kenway, 2001). When we examine this in relation to Foucault, we begin to see how women's lives are constructed in a qualitatively different way from those of men within a patriarchal view of the world. However, our debts to Gramsci are for the interpretation of the traditional Marxist concept of hegemony, opening our consciousness to the public/private divide and the way that domination permeates the most intimate aspects of our being through our interactions in civil society that remain key sites of male domination. The notion of ideological persuasion reveals hegemony as a process, a continuous struggle to maintain dominance, and we begin to see that feminist consciousness is the beginning of questioning the nature of that consent in relation to patriarchy (Ledwith, 2009).

It did not go by unnoticed that the key players in the development of critical theory and critical pedagogy have all been men, apart from Maxine Greene (Darder et al, 2009). Patti Lather is one of the leading feminist scholars to critique critical theory and critical pedagogy's failure to engage with the woman question, that of female experience and knowledge construction. In the mid-1980s, Lather drew on Gramsci's notion of a war of position and the role of the intellectuals in relation to feminist political action. She took Gramsci's emphasis on everyone's innate capacity to be philosophers and related this to the way that second-wave feminism and its groundswell of experience-based knowledge influenced social institutions to the extent that it constituted a war of position: 'many small revolutions ... many small changes in relationships, behaviours, attitudes and experiences' (Kenway, 2001: 59). She placed particular emphasis on the role of women as intellectuals in the tide of developing critical consciousness. The influence of feminist scholars, such as Lather, has steered the evolution of critical pedagogy more firmly towards a knowledge base that is constructed from 'personal biography, narratives, a rethinking of authority, and an explicit engagement with the historical and political location of the knowing subject – all aspects essential to questioning patriarchy and reconstructing the sexual politics that obstruct the participation of women as full and equal contribution members of society' (Darder et al, 2009: 14-15).

In these ways, post-structuralist critiques of class metanarratives from a feminist perspective laid the foundations for postmodernism from the mid-1980s, dislocating Gramsci and Freire in favour of 'mini-narratives rather than metanarratives, multiple identities rather than political identities, positioning rather than repositioning, discourse rather than the politics of discourse, performance rather than poverty, inscription rather than political mobilisation and deconstruction rather than reconstruction' (Kenway, 2001:60). Gramsci and Freire helped to provide the conceptual tools by which new thinking from feminist, anti-racist perspectives emerged. bell hooks, for instance, refers to Freire's 'blind spot' to questions of gender, but acknowledges the ways in which his pedagogy gave her the conceptual tools that offered her insight into the nature of her own oppression as a Black American woman, helping her to see herself as a subject in resistance (hooks, 1993: 150).

Taking this a stride further still, Weiler refers to Gloria Anzaldua's conception of the new mestiza as a postcolonial feminist, warning that feminism can be an invasion of the self, unless patriarchy is critiqued from western conceptions of linear rationality, White privilege and assumptions of universal truths. Antiracist feminists educators have 'stressed that critical and feminist pedagogies, whilst claiming an opposition to oppression, are in danger of taking a kind of imperial and totalizing stance of knowing and "speaking for" those who are to be educated into truth' (Weiler, 2001: 72). When considering our own power as practitioners, it is important to heed Weiler's warning of the dangers when we use our authority to speak for marginalised people without an analysis of difference and diversity. In these ways, critiques of critical theory formed from male and White experience raised questions of 'race' and gender, with feminists levelling the accusation that metanarratives of class hide more than they reveal. As the move into micronarratives progressed with postmodernism, Foucauldian notions of power being everywhere, in every encounter, gave rise to a backlash from critical theorists such as Peter McLaren, Dave Hill, Paula Allman and others who warn that we are being distracted from the centrality of class and the impact of capitalism as globalisation escalates.

From an ecological perspective, critique has centred around the elevation of humanity, freedom and empowerment through the use of dialogue to structure meaning which flies in the face of knowledge from non-western and indigenous truths that are more focused on biodiversity, claiming that critical pedagogy 'fractures knowledge and supports the further alienation of human beings from nature' (Darder et al, 2009: 17). Although we would like to point out that dialogue can be extended beyond the spoken truth to include such action as that of Vandana Shiva and others in the Chipko movement of the 1970s and 1980s, where Indian women used the Gandhian method of satyagraha, a form of non-violent action, to hug trees to connect with the earth ecologically as a dissenting act against economically destructive practices. Engaging with these critiques has led to a much more considered understanding of the relationship between social justice and environmental justice, with the Paulo Freire Institute for Ecopedagogy expressly committing to 'the construction of a planetary citizenship, so that all, with no exception or exclusion, may have healthy conditions, in a planet able to offer life because its own life is being preserved' (Darder et al, 2009: 18). In this way, ecopedagogy embraces all forms of life of earth in diversity and biodiversity as a love for all life. Paulo Freire was working on ecopedagogy when he died, and some of these ideas are included in his posthumous *Pedagogy of indignation* (2005).

Attempts to universalise theories of oppression have obscured the hegemony of White, middle-class males and silenced the voices of others, relegating difference to the margins. The incompleteness of metanarratives in relation to 'race' and gender resulted in many feminists embracing postmodernism with its fragmentation of power relations and rejection of a grand theory of patriarchy, 'without critiquing its serious political dangers' (Bourne, 1999: 139). One illustration of this can be seen in the denial of an essential identity in favour of multiple social identities, yet, as Bourne stresses, 'difference is not a coat you choose to put on. ... Blackness is a social disctinction, not a personal choice' (Bourne, 1999: 139). The dismantling of collective identities inherent in 'postmodern thought does not explain why men still dominate so many areas of political and economic life, why women's empowerment has proved so limited and why feminism's vigorous counter-discourses are so often disempowered' (Ramazanoglu with Holland, 2002: 101). Benhabib argues that as the world becomes more global, we should be cautious of theories that distract our attention to the fragmented and the local (Benhabib, 1992). This is precisely our critique of theories that fragment and overlook the collective, and why we support a Freirean-feminist approach to social change that offers us insight into difference at the same time as framing this within grand narratives of class, 'race' and patriarchy that situate us in collective alliance for a practical utopian approach to change. 'Postmodernism can teach us the theoretical and political traps of why utopias and foundational thinking can go wrong, but it should not lead to a retreat from utopia altogether' (Benhabib, 1992: 230).

As feminists, throughout the 1970s and 1980s we wrestled with trying to understand the nature of knowing and its relation to everyday lived experience, finding it difficult to understand anything more than a ranked order of oppression that we wore on our sleeves like medals of suffering. In our confusion, we gathered together, and gained status from the number of oppressions we could claim: not only female, but Black, or old, or 'dis'abled, or lesbian ... and in our desire to separate male and female, we alienated each other by banning boys from our gatherings, and other such uninformed actions. However, out of this move towards an understanding of difference, we gradually got to grips with the notion of oppressions as a multifaceted, overlapping system of subordination that gave insight into multiple sites of interlocking power relations (for more on this, see Ledwith, 2005).

Not only is power located within a multi-dimensional system of oppressions in which we are all simultaneously oppressors and oppressed, it permeates the surface of our skins. It is essential that we see this as a complex whole that interlinks and reinforces at every level, but it is also important that our thinking is not fragmented by this complexity. Not only did critical theorists critique postmodernism for fragmenting ideas, but there was also a backlash against those who were concerned with the depoliticising aspects of postmodernism when detaching 'race' and 'gender' from their sometimes violent and crushing everyday realities to an elite position in the academy (Bourne, 1999). Bourne (1999: 136) identifies the way in which 'the "personal is political" concurrently shifted the centre of gravity of struggle from the community and society to the individual', thus replacing action ('what has to be done?') with the reflection ('who am I?') of identity politics. The reality is that we need both to happen concurrently: a model in which identity and difference intersect with class.

Foucault, in suggesting that 'power is conceived to be relational ... rather than something that is acquired, seized or shared' (Smart, 2002: 122/79), is, in fact, critiquing theories based only on class, much as feminists did, for obscuring multiple sites of power. Rather than a unilateral perspective, or even a pluralist perspective, Foucault saw power permeating people's relationships in every interaction, influencing attitudes, identities and perceptions (Foucault, 1980). In focusing on power as a possession, Foucault believed that power had become seen as centralised, that 'the Marxist location of power in a class has obscured an entire network of other power relations'. He does not deny the Marxist model of power, but 'merely thinks that it does not capture those forms of power that make centralized, repressive forms of power possible, namely, the myriad of power relations at the microlevel of society' (Sawicki, 1991: 20). Foucault, in other words, focuses on the power relations themselves, rather than on the subjects (bourgeois/proletarian), seeing subjects as formed out of the power relations – our identities are formed from institutional and cultural practices. So he is not rejecting the notion of class, but merely 'expands the domain of the political to include a heterogeneous ensemble of power relations operating at the microlevel of society' and that 'resistance must be carried out in local struggles against the many forms of power exercised at the everyday level of social relations' (Sawicki, 1991: 23). For Foucault, power is everywhere, not only on a mega-level of state and civil society, but permeating the micro-relationships of everyday life. And, as he saw knowledge and power as inseparable, this leads us back again to the role of critical consciousness at the heart of transformative change.

The relationship between postmodernism and Marxism needs to be approached dialectically.

> The issue is not simply *either* Marxism *or* postmodernism. In some instances postmodern theories may be more productive for understanding aspects of social life than current Marxist theories admit … my concern is with arguing against some versions of postmodern theory and their lack of attention to global capitalist social relations and attendant human suffering.… Marxist theory does best [at] analyzing and challenging the very viability of capitalism in human society. (McLaren, 2000: xxv)

Theory in action

The role of the participatory practitioner is to develop theory in action by questioning the lived experience of local people. In this way, critical insight develops in practice in cycles of action and reflection, creating a unity of praxis in which all participants are united in a common effort to understand the world in order to transform it. As McLaren (2009: 63) says, 'knowledge is a social construction deeply rooted in the nexus of power relations', and this results in very different life chances and life experiences for women, for minority ethnic people, those who are poor or 'dis'abled or old, and so forth in a complex interrelationship in which some 'truths' are seen as more dominant, and therefore reinforced. Participatory approaches to practice begin with the idea that people are differently subordinated and privileged in a world that is full of contradicting ideas that lead to unequal access to power and privilege. Critical theory, as McLaren says, 'helps us to focus on both sides of a social contradiction', through a process of dialectical thinking (McLaren, 2009: 61) that Kemmis describes as more interactive than thesis–antithesis–synthesis because it is:

> … an open and questioning form of thinking which demands reflection back and forth between elements like part and whole, knowledge and action, process and product, subject and object, being and becoming, rhetoric and reality, or structure and function. In the process, contradictions may be discovered (as, for example, in a political structure which aspires to give decision-making power to all, but actually functions to deprive some of access to the information with which they could influence crucial decisions about their lives). As contradictions are revealed, new constructive thinking and new constructive action are required to transcend the contradictory state of affairs. (Wilfed Carr and Stephen Kemmis, cited in McLaren, 2009: 60)

In these ways, participatory approaches to practice involve insight into the relationship between power and knowledge.

Moving forward by being critical

For many people the notion of being critical immediately conjures up something negative and confrontational, especially in the pragmatic and instrumental Anglo-American thought-dominated world in which we live. It has connotations of criticism or attack rather than the contemplative deliberation and reflective questioning that defines it in relation to critical pedagogy, a process out of which we gain knowledge on which to base action for a just and sustainable world. Language barriers reinforce this ethnocentrism and cultural narrowness. As Potvin and McQueen (2008) recently demonstrated in the area of health promotion, Spanish- and Portuguese-speaking parts of the Americas are much more comfortable with critical theory, with the result that a very different epistemology has influenced practice. Most critical theorists do not originate from the English-speaking world. Gramsci was Italian, Foucault and Bourdieu French, Freire Brazilian. But we are not just philosophically deprived; that same Anglo-American cultural influence has been reinforced by neoliberal economic and medical practices, moving us away from critical thinking by silencing dissent and colonising the public spaces for it to take place, reducing participation to consultation and creating a culture of fear. In the next chapter we will show how, when we engage in an expansive, loving process of dialogue and reflection far removed from the notion of criticism, the path to transformation through this apparent slough of despond emerges.

EIGHT

Transformative practice

> Dialogue is considered the self-generating praxis that emerges from the relational interaction between reflection, naming of the world, action, and the return to reflection once more. It is a continuous, purposefully motivated, and open exchange that provides participants the space in which, together, to reflect, critique, affirm, challenge, act, and ultimately transform our collective understanding of the world. (Darder, 2002: 82)

Chapter 7 explored the interweaving of the personal and the collective, the inner world and the outer world, and some theories that can be used as a basis for thinking critically and reflexively. But, you may be saying, how do we put this into practice? For concrete ideas on theory into practice, we turn to Freire initially, followed by a consideration of the benefits of becoming a deliberative practitioner through evaluation.

Returning to Freire

It is necessary to put an analysis of power and knowledge together with practical approaches to liberation, participation, empowerment and transformation through community action in order to achieve a unity of praxis. Paulo Freire was described as 'a profound theorist who remains "on the ground" and a passionate activist who gets us "off the ground" – that is, he makes what is abstract concrete without sacrificing subtlety, and he infuses this concrete way of being-in-the-world with a fire that fans and fuels our will to be free' (Cornel West, in McLaren and Leonard, 1993: xiii). He developed a specific approach to critical education that had 'an impact on a political plane that reached higher than protest into the very workings of revolutionary government' (Westerman, 2009: 548). As we explore his critical pedagogy, you will see how the elements of reflection and action, learning and change, dialogue and story that we have talked about so far in this book are interwoven throughout.

  While social activists and critical educators such as Myles Horton, Angela Davis, Martin Luther King, Malcolm X and others were challenging discrimination and oppression in the US, Paulo Freire and Augusto Boal were challenging conditions in Brazil. They were both arrested, tortured and exiled by the military junta that came to power in the 1960s, Boal to Argentina and then to Paris, Freire to Chile, Harvard and then Geneva, returning to Brazil in 1980 following the amnesty of 1979.

It was his [Freire's] presence in the United States during that precise historical moment, along with the translation of *Pedagogy of the Oppressed* into English, that became a watershed for radical educators in schools, communities, and labor organizations, struggling to bring about social change to public health, welfare, and educational institutions across the country. As a consequence, Paulo Freire is considered by many to be the most influential educational philosopher in the development of critical pedagogical thought. (Darder et al, 2009: 5)

Freire's emphasis was on the political nature of education. Education is never neutral: he emphasised the political nature of education as either liberating or domesticating. As a liberating process, it teaches people to be critical, autonomous thinkers; as a domesticating process, it pours facts into passive and unquestioning minds, reinforcing the status quo. He was very clear that a unity of theory and practice, *praxis*, is fundamental to understanding and transforming the power relations of everyday life. Freire believed that the feelings generated by critical consciousness would motivate community-based action; the emotion generated by seeing life more critically motivates people to act together for change. 'All education and development projects should start by identifying the issues which the local people speak about with excitement, hope, fear, anxiety or anger' (Hope and Timmel, 1984: 8). In cycles of action/reflection, this builds towards a critical *praxis*; a unity of action and reflection, of theory and practice:

> The insistence that the oppressed engage in reflection on their concrete situation is not a call to armchair revolution. On the contrary, reflection – true reflection – leads to action. On the other hand, when the situation calls for action, that action will constitute an authentic praxis only if its consequences become the object of critical reflection.... Otherwise, action is pure activism. (Freire, 1972: 41)

Freire, as Gramsci, believed that this process is not possible without a profound trust in the capacity of people to be able to think for themselves as autonomous subjects, and in doing so transcend their world and act together to recreate it. People, treated as objects, become *dehumanised*, unthinkingly and unquestioningly bound to their world in systems of power and control. Trapped by *false consciousness* in a *culture of silence*, they become passive, apathetic, resigned and devoid of hope.

The process of becoming critical is known as *conscientisation* in Freirean pedagogy. Questioning everyday experience, critical connections are made which expose the contradictions and injustices in social life. This is an empowering process that leads to collective action for change. In the process of concientisation, Freire identified three interlinking levels: *magical consciousness* (people are passive and unquestioning about the injustices in their lives); *naïve consciousness* (people individualise their problems and often blame themselves); and *critical consciousness* (connections are made with the structural nature of discrimination). These should be seen as partial, fluid and incomplete: we are never at one level or another, but always in a process of struggling to make sense of an ever-changing world. The process of conscientisation calls for us to transcend the forces of individualism, so powerfully embedded in western culture, and to see a world that is inextricably connected to an interacting whole. The *false consciousness* of individualism, the way in which we are detached from the whole and persuaded to accept life as it is, results in passive and pessimistic attitudes to life. 'Conscientization is the deepening of the coming of consciousness', and with it brings the hope and optimism that change is possible. But Freire warns that 'not all coming to consciousness extends necessarily into conscientization'; without curiosity, respect and humility expressed through *dialogue* it is not possible to reveal the 'truths hidden by ideologies' (Freire, 1993a: 109).

Problematising is a practical strategy in Freirean pedagogy. He refers to the issues that people identify with as relevant to their lives as *generative themes*: they generate a passion out of apathy, and this is an active energy for change. This is where we begin to see the emotions and intellect functioning together, an important aspect of understanding Freire. Issues that are part of everyday life are often taken for granted. People walk through empty precincts, with broken slabs and empty shops, past playgrounds that are not fit for play, not seeing the dereliction and degradation that surrounds them. I (Margaret) remember halting in my tracks in my early days as a community worker, questioning that there were more dogs roaming round in packs than people in that community. Those people that were out and about were heads down and disengaged from their surroundings. This will not always be the case, but is often found in the most marginalised communities, and it was this experience that linked an intellectual understanding of a *culture of silence* with

A culture of silence

the reality of the experience. It was Freire in action, and his conceptualisation enabled me to locate theory in everyday life, to live the concepts I understood intellectually as a praxis, a dynamic that builds theory in action.

In order to create a learning context in which people are not given answers but autonomously question this taken-for-grantedness, Freire used *codifications* to capture aspects of everyday experience in line drawings originally, but this approach lends itself equally to other ways of knowing through story, picture, music, photograph, drama and so on. By decontextualising the experience, we see life through fresh eyes, through a more critical and inquiring lens, and through a process of *dialogue*, the contradictions inherent in the codification become decodified.

Augusto Boal, influenced by Freire's ideas, developed *Theater of the oppressed* as a tool for *conscientisation* (Boal, 1979; 2008), the first edition of which was published in English in 1979). This has had an international impact on the use of drama to capture everyday experiences of oppression through forum theatre, an approach that does not use the spoken word, but works by enabling an observer to freeze the scene and substitute for a participant in order to create an interruption in the experience to see new ways of bringing about change. In this sense, dialogue can be speechless! You will find examples of Boal's influence on current practice in Chapter 6.

As we have shown, dialogue embodies the notion of human dignity and respect, encouraging people to relate to each other in ways that are mutual, reciprocal, trusting and cooperative. Dialogue 'strives for the emergence of consciousness and *critical intervention* in reality' (Freire, 1972: 54) by equalising power in relationships, placing everyone together as co-learners in the process of change, accepting that we all have as much to learn as we can teach. This is a precarious position for the practitioner; there is no hiding behind the power that comes from role status. The only protection we have comes from our own integrity, our belief that change is possible and our trust that all people have the capacity for *action and reflection*. It is a process which creates critical, inquiring and responsible citizens who 'carry both the seeds of radical change and the burden of oppression' (Popple, 1995: 64). The role of the animator/co-facilitator is one of teaching people to question through dialogue. We teach people 'to question answers rather than [...] answer questions' (Shor, 1993: 26), the antithesis of mainstream approaches to education.

As questions are raised, the practitioner responds with questions rather than answers, taking the questioning to a more critical level. Why? Where? How? Who? What? In whose interests? Successive questions probe deeper towards the source of the problem. It is a process that liberates the thinking of the participants as they become confident, analytic and creative in investigating the issue. They move towards a solution that is likely to be nearer to the root of the problem, and as they are active in the process of reflecting on the issue, they are more likely to engage in the action to transform it. It is a mutual process founded on reciprocity and humility that gets beyond the power imbalance of the traditional teacher–student relationship. This is the interface of praxis at which the knowledge and theory of the educator comes together with the everyday experience of the people, and this is discussed at some length in Chapter 6. Freire's pedagogy was never focused on methods without theory; he inserted theoretical questions of power, culture, oppression against pedagogical questions related to social agency, voice and democratic participation. 'In doing so, he reinforced the Frankfurt School's focus on theory and practice as imperative to the political struggles against exploitation and domination' (Darder et al, 2009: 5).

As Freire says, '*starting* with the "knowledge of experience had" in order to get beyond it is not *staying* in that knowledge' (Freire, 1995: 70). He demonstrated this by developing 'race', gender and ecological perspectives in his later work. An understanding of the relevance of epistemology and ontology is important here. The way we see the world is directly related to the way we act in the world. If we change the way we understand the world, our behaviour will alter as a consequence. As we extend our understanding into complex interrelationships, so we co-create a world based on multiple ways of knowing. We become inspired by hope that change for a better world is possible, and this change begins in grassroots communities.

In the process of empowerment, people often turn against each other in acts of *horizontal violence*. This refers to the way that top-down power models divide and rule politics: those who are working together in the struggle for freedom turn against each other, eroding solidarity by becoming 'sub-oppressors' (Freire, 1972: 27). Our thought has been so conditioned by the contradictions of the context in which we have been formed that we turn on our allies. This is characteristic in community development interventions, and is an experience we need to recognise as a natural stage of the equalising of power. The model of power in western thought is one of legitimising 'success' on the back of someone else's 'failure'. This is embodied in our education system, our economic system, our personal relationships and so forth. It is the essence of a competitive worldview, one based on arrogance rather than humility. When participation leads to an equalising of power, this can often lead to a desire to possess it and to abuse it, according to the dominant model that has formed us. This becomes an illusion of democracy, because although it is sited in community, it is not representative of shared power. It is destructive rather than liberating. This swing towards counter-oppression gradually stabilises if the horizontal process is eased towards mutual respect, dignity and equality. The process of *conscientisation* grows organically. Celia, a community activist in Hattersley, captured the process, "Since you and Paul have been working with us, Margaret, people have changed. They like being treated respectfully, and so they are gradually being respectful with each other." My heart sang when I heard her make this observation about the organic process of change. Early experiences in Hattersley had been punctuated by *horizontal violence* in the extreme, with petitions to get rid of me, confrontations, aggression and general abuse, not from all, but sufficient to destroy my optimism had I not understood the nature of this concept. It helped me to avoid taking attacks on me personally and sustained my hope that the process would equalise in time. I often say to people that had I not been equipped with a Freirean conceptual toolkit that helped me to make sense of the rawness of life in community development, I would not have survived! Another anecdote that comes to mind here is the way in which one of the tenants from the tower blocks came to complain to us about the residents' association denying them the right to become members. When we spoke to the well-established organisers of the residents' association, we were told that this was indeed the case, they would not permit the 'rabble' housed in the high-rise blocks to be part of their organisation. When we tried to negotiate a democratic right for all residents to be represented, the chair of the association walked out, attempting to organise a counter-group from the working men's club. Critical insights are vital in practice. In this case, understanding that a worldview based on competitive power will inevitably result in power being seized and wielded over others, a desirable commodity in powerless communities, helps to see an abuse of power as part of the process of change. Handing over power is a skilled and risky business. It will result in a swing of the pendulum until the process of critical education leads to a collective understanding that empowerment involves dignity and respect for all.

Freire saw the relevance but also the pitfalls of those who work in community as *traditional intellectuals* engaged in the process of change. The status and superiority that comes with the role can bring with it a lack of trust in people's ability to think and act for themselves. 'They talk about the people, but they do not trust them; and trusting the people is the indispensable precondition for revolutionary change' (Freire, 1972: 36). We are able to hear the influence of Gramsci on Freire's thought. The role of intellectuals is central to the process of transformative change, and despite its somewhat strange connotations, we can think of its function as that of uniting theory and practice to achieve a critical praxis. If, as Ira Shor does below, we consider this in relation to participatory practice, we begin to get a clearer idea of how the concept of the intellectual might be useful to our own roles:

> To be a critical, empowering educator is a choice to be what Henry Giroux has called a 'transformative intellectual'. Giroux's notion of 'civic courage' and a 'pedagogy of possibility' invite educators to become change-agents in schools and society, for critical thought and action, for democracy, equality, ecology and peace, against domination, manipulation, and the waste of human and natural resources. (Shor, 1993: 34)

Freire believed that it is not possible to achieve transformative practice without dialogue. So, vital to an understanding of *reflection* as a transformative concept is an understanding of its role as an integral component of dialogue. This is no mean feat, as Paula Allman says, it is not achieved easily. 'People enter into discussions in order to articulate what they already know or think.... Dialogue, in contrast and complete opposition, involves the critical investigation of knowledge or thinking.

Rather than focusing only on what we think, dialogue requires us to ask of each other and ourselves why we think what we do. In other words, it requires us to "problematise" knowledge' (Allman, 2009: 426). Liberating education begins in dialogue, in a trusting, collaborative process of reflection and action on everyday experience. Freire talks about *the word* as the very essence of dialogue, not just as a tool of communication, but having deeper 'constituent elements':

> Within the word we find two dimensions, reflection and action, in such radical interaction that if one is sacrificed — even in part — the other immediately suffers. There is no true word that is not at the same time a praxis. Thus, to speak a true word is to transform the world. (Freire, 1972: 60)

Reflection: Thinking in a doing world

Reflection leads us to the 'true word'; it is reflection that exposes the contradictions we live by. In the process of *conscientisation*, reflection helps us to make critical connections with the power relations that lead to subordination and domination, thus breaking through *magical* and *naïve* levels of consciousness that explain away the injustices of life as either fate or personal inadequacies. In dialectical relationship, reflection helps us to name the world, in other words, to question and become critical in the way we make sense of the world in order to act for change. Dialogue, a transformative, democratic communication between people, fosters relationships in which people build learning communities: 'they reflect on what they know, their lived experiences, and on how these impact the way they read their world … [and in doing so] they freely give voice to their thoughts, ideas, and perceptions about what they know and what they are attempting to understand, always within the context of a larger political project of emancipation' (Darder, 2002: 103). Reflection exposes the social contradictions that create injustices, and this new knowledge, in turn, leads to practice that is insightful, analytic and informed. One of the social contradictions from Chapter 2 that we may recall at this point is the strange phenomenon of child poverty in rich countries, with its critical connections to racism, sexism, truancy, educational failure, unemployment, childhood accidents, youth suicide, long-term ill health, premature death and more that lead to the erosion of life chances and the general destruction of hope. This not only provides a powerful source of reflection, but can in turn lead to ideas for problematising relevant, related issues with your community.

Freire considered praxis to be the essence of transformation, a dynamic interplay between theory and practice, action and reflection, which brings about personal and interpersonal transformation. It is a political discovery of who we are in the world. The process of action–reflection–transformative action is a dialectical process (Allman, 1999) as we have outlined earlier. It is at the core of the cycle model in Chapter 7. The process of reflection in praxis involves creating a distance between the context that we take for granted in order to be able to reflect more critically. Freire referred to his own exile in this way; it provided a critical distance from which he could reflect on his homeland more critically (Mayo, 2004). Similarly, our discussion of problematising in community groups using codifications to capture a relevant aspect of lived reality, offers the same critical distance from the life lived in context. This same notion could be applied to Giroux's concept of border crossing, 'To move away from "home" is to question in historical, semiotic and structural terms how the boundaries and meanings of "home" are constructed in self-evident ways often outside of criticism' (Giroux, 1993: 179).

Reflection is only a critical component of praxis when it is in dynamic with action. Freire was very clear that reflection without action results in verbalism, empty words not capable of transformation, 'actionless thought'; conversely, action without reflection results in mindless activism, or 'thoughtless action' (Johnston, cited in Shaw, 2004: 26) – action for action's sake, which destroys dialogue. The practice of critical reflection and action in the construction of new knowledge is the basis of transformative change. It is a process of transcending our reality in order to understand it and act together to change it.

Underpinning this whole process, we emphasise, are the values that frame the quality of the process. Praxis does not happen without respect, dignity, trust, reciprocity and mutuality, so much the essence of Freire's approach to humanisation. The creation of knowledge cannot happen if heart and mind are dichotomised: Freire's firm belief was that dialogue cannot exist without a profound love for the world. 'Love is at the same time the foundation of dialogue and dialogue itself' (Freire, 1972: 62). Neither can dialogue exist without humility; it cannot exist in relations of arrogance. So if we, as practitioners feel that we are somehow apart from the process, superior or not fully engaged in it, then dialogue as a respectful communication between people involved in a mutual search through action and reflection cannot exist. In Freirean terms, this becomes *anti-dialogue*, or *cultural invasion*, the imposition of one's own assumptions, values and perceptions of the world on others, silencing and disempowering, reinforcing domination and subordination. True dialogue is predicated on a profound belief in the capacity of people to transform the world. In this process of becoming more fully human, of claiming our humanity as subjects participating in the co-creation of the world, we reflect on the dehumanising aspects of life as it is, and we act together to transform the world into a living whole that is strengthened by its diversity. For these reasons, reflection is integral to praxis, is in dynamic with action as an integrated praxis and is the essence of the dialogical encounter. 'Only dialogue, which requires critical thinking, is also capable of generating critical thinking. Without dialogue there is no communication, and without communication there can be no true education' (Freire, 1972: 65). Beginning in every encounter, we find that true reflection leads to action: that consciousness is the basis of wider collective action for change. But that 'action is human only when it is not merely an occupation but also a preoccupation, that is, when it is not dichotomized from reflection' (Freire, 1972: 29).

Reflection has a past–present–future dimension in order to make sense of power structures in the world. Action, in response to the critical insights offered by reflection, develops progressively into wider contexts in order to bring about transformation: from personal to group, to project, to community, to alliance and movement for change. In these diverse contexts, reflection and action, in symbiotic movement, constantly reinforce the process of change from local to global. It is not a linear progression, but an organic and constantly evolving process that is mutually reinforcing through the dialogical process of action and reflection, in each context at each level. This is an approach to knowledge that is intellectual, practical, emotional and spiritual. It is a living process of inquiry into the co-creation of life as a mutual, respectful, flourishing experience that involves all aspects of being fully human in the world. As this process moves outwards, it reconnects our alienated world, and we feel the pain of all as our own pain:

My activism can never become dissociated from my theoretical work; on the contrary, the former has its tactics and strategies formulated on the latter. The moment we recognize that food production around the world could be sufficient to feed twice its population, it is desolating to realize the numbers of those who come into the world but do not stay, or those who do but are forced into early departure by hunger. My struggle against capitalism is founded on that – its intrinsic perversity, its antisolidarity nature. (Freire, 1998a: 88)

In cycles of action and reflection, we become increasingly critical, making connections with the alienating and destructive dimensions of life in order to explore alternatives, ways of seeing the world as an interconnected whole. The thread of humanity is held together by each individual, yet the quality of humanity is determined by collective responsibility to the whole. A commitment to liberation and justice requires new ways of thinking about social reality from a critical perspective that embraces both social and environmental justice: 'future participation will mean a very different experience of the self, an ecological self distinct yet not separate, a self rooted in environment and in community' (Reason, 1994: 37). But the process of change begins in reflection, in questioning, in conscientisation. '"In a process of enlightenment there can be only participants" (Habermas, 1974: 40). That is, others cannot do the enlightening for participants; in the end, they are or are not enlightened in their own terms' (Kemmis, 2001: 91).

Becoming a deliberative practitioner through evaluation

In *The deliberative practitioner* (1999) Forester demonstrates through the stories of planners (including community developers) how skilful participatory practice can facilitate and integrate the politically critical with the pragmatic. In the planners' stories we see how they encourage collective deliberation, listening, learning and acting. Thus they make participatory planning a reality rather than an empty ideal by intertwining reflection and deliberation, integrating vision, critique and practical reality and expanding democratic reflection as a tool for transformation. 'I see re-cognition as integral to deliberation in which parties learn together about fact, value and strategy all together' (Forester, 1999: 7). Forester shows how theoretical insight can support the process of working with the complexities of the political reality of inequalities in power, poverty, oppression and histories of silenced voices. Rather than providing a practical toolkit, a how–to–do–it, we learn from these stories not what to do but rather how to do it, in a range of complex circumstances: how to question, how to learn and how to act from a set of values and principles while being 'keenly and practically aware of the particulars that matter in the unique situations at hand' (Forester, 1999: 22). One of the important elements that emerges is the safe space which allows all participants, whether public servants or community members, to come together for critical reflection.

So, how can we create such spaces in a contemporary culture that shrinks the opportunities for critical public spaces, in which the main barriers to the process are embedded in the profit-dominated culture of our western times, referred to earlier in this book? The need to have outcomes or successes over short periods of time drives the content of actions in directions that fail to tackle fundamental issues and therefore skim the surface of deep-seated challenges. I (Jane) have stopped counting the project reports and papers I have read or written on initiatives to tackle some of the most intractable health and well-being inequalities, where a key variable has been the need for more time. Yet as far as I know, no one has looked systematically at its necessity as a component of, say, a health promotion programme, even if some attention has been paid to context and to diversity. In the collective consciousness, time is money or rather taking time costs money despite the fact that 'time sickness' actually costs more in the longer term in terms of health. The participatory mind sees these relationships. It recognises that a lack of balance in one dimension is not healthy for the whole. It also recognises that a narrow economic perspective driving perceived levels of efficiency and effectiveness may only lead to short-term fixes. To tackle inequalities in a sustainable way calls for a broader picture which reveals the complex interrelatedness between dimensions of poverty (Tomlinson et al, 2008).

A pragmatic way of doing or creating the space to reflect and learn is to use the current demand for evaluation as a space for integrating the pragmatic with the critical. The LEAP (learning, evaluation and planning) model developed by the Scottish Community Development Centre does just this (http://leap.scdc.org.uk/). Through embracing and advocating participation, and using the umbrella of evaluation, it is possible to create a small but expanding number of spaces for reflection which can be interwoven with story and dialogue based on the principles of emancipatory action research. Quite often in evaluation training workshops I (Jane) will ask participants why they think they should evaluate. Responses include such comments as: "so that we can get funding" and "because we have to". This is not surprising in view of the evidence-based mania, as Schwandt (2005) calls it, which promulgates instrumental rationality and within many contemporary practices seeks to impose ways of evaluating that ignore the realities of everyday life. However, many of those who have broken through their resistance to the notion of evaluation and engaged in self and participatory evaluation work have found the spaces and opportunities to develop systematic reflection empowering. It also involves a rare opportunity to have fun! Since you need to remember and describe an experience to reflect, reflecting together through creating a collage, painting a picture or creating a play are powerful fun processes at the collective level.

I (Jane) learnt the importance of fun when working with an experienced community trainer on a participatory evaluation in Netherton on Merseyside. The evaluation had been commissioned as a pilot by Merseyside Health Action Zone. They had written evaluation learning into their local strategy, although in practice found that this approach was constrained by the performance management approach of the Department of Health, with its focus on targets unconnected to local priorities. This pilot was an attempt to bring together 12 disparate projects funded by URBAN, all of which had the potential to impact on health and well-being. The idea was to work with local people and project workers on developing an evaluation of what they were doing. The community trainer, well known locally, would disappear at breaks in our work for a 'fag' with local people, building up a good rapport. However, it was in making what could have been quite tedious sessions on evaluation come alive that his skills came into their own. In getting people to think about indicators, he suggested that, rather than using such language, we ask: how will we celebrate the success of these projects in a year's time? This galvanised people and brought relevance into the evaluation project. As a result numbers swelled, and the community room we were using became too small when we met for our Monday lunch meeting. A year later, the fruits of their activity were demonstrated in a range of stalls for each project in the small square at the centre of the local small shopping centre. These stalls were showcasing what they had been doing, but behind that was a well-documented evaluation process (Springett and Dunkerton, 2001).

Participatory evaluation means coming together to listen to each other's stories, learning what other people have been doing in other places, but also collectively looking at statistical data, published accounts and scientific papers. Through participatory processes people can then agree joint indicators of change based on the values, principles and goals they have agreed. They can also decide who will share the task of collecting the agreed meaningful information and agree a time to come together to look at what is happening, whether things are on track and who else needs to be involved. Barriers to change, previously not recognised, are revealed and unexpected outcomes emerge. Small groups might follow the same process in their communities, taking the end of a formal meeting for the sharing of stories of significant change, recording or collecting them together. As we have seen, celebration is an important part of the community development process and successful events can be organised where people come together to share their experiences and at the same time invite others from other places to encourage a wider sharing and learning. From scrapbooks and graffiti boards to forum theatre, there are now a huge range of reflective tools available.

Numerical data can also be collected inclusively, whether it is the monitoring of pollution levels through citizen science initiatives for environmental health or local community health surveys through participatory rapid appraisals (PRAs). There are many such examples of this type of evaluative work throughout the world. The most famous is Sustainable Seattle's Indicators of Sustainable Community and its spin-offs across some cities and communities in the US and Canada.

In Wythenshawe an open space event was held where all community-based agencies, including the police, education, health and housing, came together with the community to develop joint indicators. In one of the iterative cycles, the question was asked, 'How would you know that you have made a difference in 10 years time?'. One of the answers that emerged from the groupwork was,

"People would look happier." After a democratic process, narrowing down the different indicators, this one remained. In the next cycle of dialogue, people were asked to discuss how they would collect information that would measure these selected indicators. In this particular case, the answer that emerged was: use the footage from CCTV cameras in the local centre to check whether people are looking happier ten years on!

In 1990, the Global Tomorrow Coalition organised a workshop in Seattle, in preparation for the Earth Summit that was held in Rio de Janeiro in 1992. It was the challenge of integrating economic, environmental and social values, and the opportunity to define new measurements of progress, that inspired Seattle citizens to create the civic movement that led to the founding of Sustainable Seattle. In 1992, Sustainable Seattle convened a panel of over 150 civic leaders – environmental groups, city and county government representatives, unions, the religious community, business leaders, educators, students and social activists – which developed the first set of draft indicators. In the following years, further indicators were developed culminating in a series of reports. They are currently engaged in a process at neighbourhood level.

> "We believe that the sustainable community will be promoted where many players in different roles and with differing interests and values are all provided with a flow of meaningful information, and where they have the opportunity for joint learning and innovative responses to this feedback from the environment and from other changes. It is this distributed intelligence which allows players in a community to anticipate and constructively address both individually and collectively the systemic problems the community continually faces and to deal with the threats and opportunities of natural and manmade disasters, the shifting global economy, and inequitable distributions of resources." (Judith Innes, available at www.sustainableseattle.org)

In the Sustainable Seattle model, citizen values and needs drive the process but scientific data and methods provide the foundation for indicators so that the selected metrics are understandable and valid. The process is iterative, with information moving among and being discussed by: (a) the general public, (b) a group of civic leaders and (c) a group of technical advisers.

The process of developing and selecting indicators is as important as publishing them. For example, Innes and Booher (2005: 230) believe that 'the process of debating the design of indicators shapes the players' thinking about the policies'. Innes and Booher also believe that if 'an indicator is to be useful, it must be clearly associated with a policy or set of possible actions … policy can be advanced by discussion of how to design suitable indicators'. Here we see how the local and the strategic can be integrated. Normally indicators are developed centrally and then handed down to the local level, where not only are priorities different but the actions are too. Moreover, indicators are often proxy tools bearing no relationship to what they are measuring, such as suicide rates as indicators of mental health or mortality (death rates) and morbidity (illness) as indicators of health. Health Action Zones suffered from this failure to link national policy to the local when the Department of Health introduced national indicators in relation to NHS goals that bore no relationship to the locally developed plans focusing on the social determinants of health. As a result, local evaluators spent more time trying to fit local actions into the predetermined targets than evaluating effectively. This was a particular problem for Merseyside, which had participatory evaluation as learning as a key local goal. If indicators are developed from the bottom up, then issues of relevant and appropriate policy can be debated as part of the dialogical process, and diverse and appropriate indicators developed to help all parties, strategic and local, to see how things that they see as important are changing. Participatory indicator and policy development presents a particular challenge to local and national politicians who are used to defining the agenda. In a recent conversation with a local councillor in Liverpool on the new requirements for community involvement, he observed that the change in role of the local politician to facilitator required a whole new set of skills, skills that would be difficult for some of his colleagues to grasp. This means the development of skills for participatory democracy, an issue we raise in the next chapter.

A participatory process has the added advantage of creating shared values and understanding among people who are working together through the process. Sustainable Seattle, with its participatory approach to development of indicators, is exceptional in that it fully involves the community in the development and updates of its indicators.

> Indicators a society chooses to report to itself about itself are surprisingly powerful. They reflect collective values and inform collective decisions. A nation that keeps a watchful eye on its salmon runs or the safety of its streets makes different choices than does a nation that is only paying attention to its GNP. The idea of citizens choosing their own indicators is something new under the sun – something intensely democratic. (Meadows, 1991: 5)

The first tentative steps to doing things differently, as shown by the experience from initiatives such as Seattle and Wythenshawe, emphasise how participatory democracy goes hand in hand with participatory indicator development. The social learning element alluded to earlier has increasingly come to the forefront of more recent initiatives (Holden, 2006). Rather than seeing evaluation and the development of measurement tools merely as the necessary integration of the technical with the participatory, effectively seeing the process as one in which people accept what scientists and statisticians say is the right measurement, it becomes a dialogical process whereby a social translation process takes place (Latour, 1999) through which political questions are translated into operational technical issues and vice versa. In fact, Callon and Latour (1986, cited in Hartz et al, 2008) were able to show through their research how this happens within science itself: so-called scientific facts, a product of previous knowledge and theory, measurement devices and social interpretations, are presented as concrete facts but are actually social constructions. The participatory process involves multiple perspectives widening the scope of the dialogue and enhancing the development of true measures of change. As a consequence, these are understood and accepted by all, not finite, but in a constant dynamic of re-evaluation of what is collectively seen as important.

Nevertheless, particular types of economic statistics still dominate the media and retain a hegemonic role in our society. "Why do we always have economic news on mainstream Swedish television every night?", a Swedish friend asked me. "I do not want to know what the Nasdaq or Dow Jones index is, or whether this stock is up or that is down. Why not have a measure of how many trees we have felled and not replaced, or social problems solved?"

Sweden comes well up the scale on the recent New Economics Foundation's (nef) 'National accounts of well-being' (Micealson et al, 2009). The work of nef on development of 'indicators that count' has questioned for many years the appropriateness of a GNP for measuring the state of the nation:

> National accounting indicators such as Gross Domestic Product (GDP) have only ever revealed a very narrow view of human welfare.... We now need to shift towards more meaningful measures of progress which capture the richness of people's lived experience. Do so and we also create a far more effective tool with which to guide policy. The Gross National Product counts air pollution and cigarette advertising, and ... the destruction of the redwood and the loss of our natural wonder in chaotic sprawl.... Yet [it] does not allow for the health of our children, the quality of their education, or the joy of their play ... the beauty of our poetry or the strength of our marriages ... it measures everything, in short, except that which makes life worthwhile. (Kennedy, 1968, cited in Micealson et al, 2009: 32)

A whole array of indicators has been developed by nef, building on its pioneering participatory indicator development in the 1990s.

Much further away in Kyrgyzstan, in the Community Health Action project that we introduced in Chapter 4, local health committees collect and analyse data focusing on specific health issues and actions they themselves have developed with the support of local health promotion workers. In local rayon (districts), representatives from all the local village committees look at the collective picture and encourage the taking of action on broader issues by local government. I (Jane) have personally witnessed one of these meetings and heard the enthusiasm, in what is a very poor part of the world, as people take control of their lives and seek change. Similarly, in Liverpool as part of the WHO Healthy Cities project local residents in Everton and Vauxhall collected air quality data to examine the pollution levels created by lorries from the docks, which they believed were contributing to increases in asthma. Equipment for measuring air quality tended to be located in open spaces, and the community was concerned with levels on the roadside. Supported by the local environmental health officer, Andy Hull, they collected the data that he then analysed. In a video created at the time a resident described her experience:

> "Everyone should be involved in research, people want to know what's going on and they are learning as well ... it helps to educate local people by letting them be in from the grass roots ... people should be involved from the beginning, not letting experts give it you on a plate so you don't know anything." (Resident, Vauxhall, Liverpool)

These are local examples of communities participating in collecting data. Other examples include the collection of data on birds in our gardens for the RSPB, providing core data for monitoring climate change. All these participatory processes are part of the cycle of learning and change that is core to a Freirean approach to transformation and underpins participatory evaluation, which starts with the experience of participants, and spirals out in ever-increasing circles to link local knowledge development with collective and global change.

Figure 8.1: Spiral of learning and action

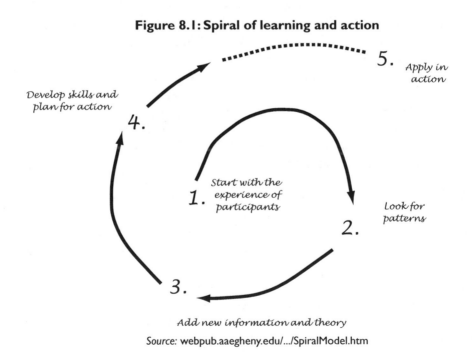

Source: webpub.aaegheny.edu/.../SpiralModel.htm

Meaning making

Heron (1996) has argued that in a cooperative inquiry process at least four different ways of knowing are used:

i.   *Experiential knowing*, that which emerges through direct face-to-face encounter with person, place or thing; it is knowing through empathy and resonance, and is almost impossible to put into words.
ii. *Presentational knowing*, that which emerges from experiential knowing, and finds expression in imagination through story, drawing, sculpture, movement, dance, etc.
iii. *Propositional knowing*, usually expressed through ideas and theories, associated with science or the academy.
iv. *Practical knowing* is about 'how to', and expressed in a skill or competence.

It seems axiomatic, therefore, if these four ways of knowing are congruent with each other (that is, knowing that is grounded in experience, expressed though stories and images, understood through theories which make sense and expressed in worthwhile action) that together they provide the basis for transformative practice in challenging and changing contexts.

A defining condition of becoming more fully human is that we have to understand the meaning of our experience. Making meaning is what critical reflection is about. Giddens (1991) argues that we live in a reflexive society in which we are continually making our own interpretations, rather than acting on the purposes, beliefs, judgements and feelings of others. Facilitating such understandings is the cardinal goal of critical reflection and contributes to transformative learning and change. Critical theory helps us make those interpretations by encouraging us to question what is taken for granted. It involves listening to other people's meaning makings and taking them seriously, a form of 'connected knowing' that calls us to suspend our own truth (Goldberger et al, 1996; Belenky et al, 1986/1997). The process is not just about reflecting on what has happened and what is, but also re-visioning what might be. In the latter, appreciative inquiry (Ludema et al, 2001) is useful. To be truly participative, focus not just on the personal or on individual projects or actions, but link them into the broader picture, the context, the whole. By engaging in true evaluation, that is, reflecting on and measuring action against a set of explicit values concerning social justice, dignity and respect, the last piece in the jigsaw of an emancipatory action research approach to community change for human well-being and sustainable development is put in place. In the next and final chapter we bring these ideas together in a single model.

NINE

Becoming whole

Ultimately we must ask ourselves what kind of a society we wish to
live in and what we are going to do to make our vision a reality ...
to find the courage and power to question and act in the interest of
a more democratic and just world. (Darder, 2002: 231)

Participation as reconnection to the whole

Participation is transformative. It is central to the purpose of community
development in striving for a just, healthy and sustainable world. This is our
enduring message. A participatory worldview, a world built on such values as
cooperation, equality, diversity and human dignity, frames the vision of participatory
practice. This practice begins in every encounter, building relations of trust and
integrity that heal the fractures created by our contemporary western worldview.
We think it useful to characterise the competitive western worldview as a top-
down, vertical perspective of life on earth that gives rise to relations of superiority
and inferiority, whereas a participatory worldview sees life from a horizontal
perspective, juxtaposing everything and everybody as a world in common, in all its
difference and diversity. Throughout this book we have explored real evidence of
the impact that neoliberal capitalism is having on the world as a living ecosystem,
as well as from a human rights perspective. The consequences of this market-driven
preoccupation with profit, which inevitably justifies human and environmental
exploitation, are social divisions and environmental degradation. New Right
politics, expressed through the Thatcher and Reagan regimes, demonised people
in poverty, the consequences of which Killeen (2008) presents as a human rights
issue. The persisting hold that the label of *undeserving poor* has had on popular
opinion has led to a reluctance on the part of the government to equalise wealth,
despite the overwhelming evidence of the impact social inequalities have on
health and well-being (Wilkinson and Pickett, 2006, 2009; WHO/CSDH, 2008),
giving rise to an added dimension of discrimination, that of *povertyism* (Killeen,
2008). Since the crisis of world capitalism in 2008, inequalities are being further
exacerbated by a recession that is hitting the poorest hardest.

Alienation, while disconnecting us from the whole, also obscures the
responsibility we have to ourselves, to each other and to the natural world as
an interdependent whole. In contrast, a participatory worldview is predicated
on human worth, not as some fanciful utopian dream, but as a component of
an ecosystem in fragile balance. This places humanity as a form of life that has
a responsibility to engage with biodiversity in symbiotic relationship with each
other and the earth. The system of life on earth flourishes in co-existence rather

than competition. This is not only respectful, but it is the only way to ensure a sustainable future for upcoming generations. Current times call for a practical utopia, one in which the alienating aspects of life as we live it today become healed and whole. In seeking to become whole, that is, to heal, we must strive for dynamic balance between chaos and order, as symbolised by this infinity sign, or lemniscate (see Figure 9.1).

Figure 9.1: Infinity – the harmony of opposites

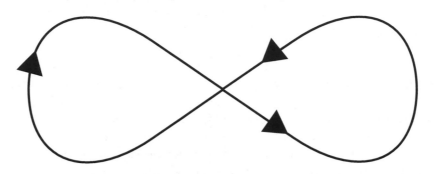

The notion of interconnectedness, of dynamic balance, fundamentally challenges dualism as a dominant view of the world that dichotomises existence into simplistic either/or forms: undeserving/deserving poor, Black/White, male/female, economy/environment, critique/consensus and so forth. We are seeking an understanding of reality that transcends neoliberalism, individualism and consumerism, so much the hallmark of current times. Here, the eastern symbol of the Tao is a useful metaphor. In ancient Chinese wisdom the world comprises two sets of energies, yin and yang (see Figure 9.2). This symbolises the balance of opposites in the whole of reality (Hope and Timmel, 1999). The energy of each is contained in the other, keeping the potential for and source of change in dynamic balance. It is an energy source that contains both positive and negative, and considered together can be transformative.

Figure 9.2: Tao – symbiotic balance of yin/yang

The challenge for community development is that of paradox, to hold onto both positive and negative at one and the same time. So in the process of becoming critical, these contradictions pose questions about the taken-for-grantedness of everyday life in order to identify a source of change. As we become more aware of the power imbalance in life, we begin to see some aspects as life-enhancing and some as life-restricting or even life-threatening. This idea can be explored both within and between cultures. So, for example, western cultures that do not honour older people create a way of life where older people are seen as dependent, feeble, the butt of jokes and a burden on society; at the same time, young people are diminished by adult generations who blame them for all social ills. By contrast, in eastern cultures older age is seen as synonymous with wisdom and is more likely to lead to flourishing rather than diminishing in later life. The notion of transformation through combining opposites is well illustrated by the intergenerational action research project that at the time of writing has been developed in Dovecot, Merseyside, an area of profound deprivation. Bringing young people, seen as the local 'problem', together with older people in dialogical and interactive spaces is beginning to transform not only relationships and understanding, but the older and younger people themselves. This is encapsulated in the pride of a young man previously marginalised being given responsibility for calling the bingo numbers for the older people's bingo game!

The use of metaphor is important in understanding our relationship to the whole. Hans Sarv (1997) offers the metaphor of the Formula 1 race as a way of seeing our local practice in relation to the bigger picture of society as a whole. He suggests that our practice interventions are a bit like a pit stop, a small intervention in relation to the whole system (see Figure 9.3). Yet, while this metaphor helps us place the context of our work in relation to the whole as practitioners in community, it becomes evident that we are only dealing with a fragment of the whole system, not the system as a whole.

To reach towards a transformative potential, we have to see our practice interventions at both specific and systemic levels and encourage the necessary spiral of connections. An example of what this means is shown in Figure 9.4, where local action becomes linked through reflection to a global whole, what Peat (2008) calls bringing forth creative change in a turbulent world through gentle action.

The way we see the world influences the way we act in the world: epistemologies and ontologies work in dynamic relationship. So, in making sense of

Figure 9.3: Practice as a pit stop – the specific within the systemic

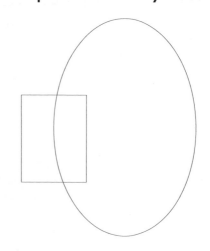

reality, we effectively co-create reality. When we explore the world from a more critical consciousness, we begin to act differently in the world. The very act of reality making is an act of change, part of the process of transformation.

Figure 9.4: New spiral of learning and action: connecting to the whole

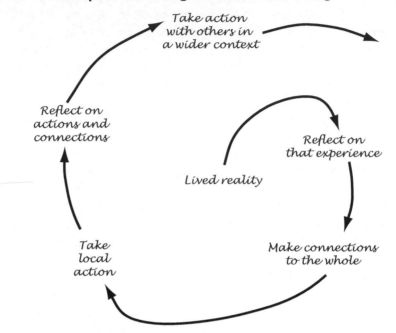

We have explored in some depth the values, principles and processes that are at the heart of participatory practice, that influence ways of thinking and acting, and that hold the key to the transformative process. Working with values, principles and processes is a very different way of working from one that comes from meeting targets, the rather war-like reference so often found in the utilitarian and instrumental approaches to work currently dominating the public sector. In each chapter, we have brought to the foreground an aspect of the process while interweaving it with the whole. Here, in conclusion, we want to bring those elements together as a whole, as a systemic approach to practice.

An individual's and a community's experience is a microcosm of the bigger picture. Our inner consciousness reflects our collective consciousness: we suggest that *conscientisation* is a process of connection to the whole, dialogue is a process of connection to the whole, story is a process of connection to the whole, and reflection is a process of connection to the whole. Once we start to acknowledge humanity's intimate connection to the wider ecosystem, we fit a missing piece in the jigsaw of social justice and sustainability, and we see our practice in a more holistic light (see Figure 9.5). So, while a community garden will not solve all the issues faced by a community, it is a 'pit stop', but it does have the potential to begin the process of change by connecting people with each other and with nature. However, for the process to be truly transformative, that is, to create the positive feedback talked about in systems theory, the act needs to be connected to other acts of participation, such as LETS, farmers' markets, credit unions, allotments, cooperative shops and other projects that contribute to a movement that integrates human well-being with environmental well-being, as shown in Figure 9.4. And as all aspects of life are interconnected, it is not only economics and the environment that benefit, but health, well-being, community and just about everything that concerns human flourishing. Too little change, to use the systems metaphor, and the system returns to the norm; too much change too quickly, and the system collapses. As the process unfolds, we need to develop practical theories that help us to understand the impact of what we are doing, to co-create a new knowledge in action that will help us to know where next to act. In these ways, we begin to piece together the fragments of the whole, to fit the pieces of the jigsaw together in a perfectly interconnected sum of the parts, as you can see in Figure 9.5 (Burns, 2007; Meadows and Lokey, 2009).

Figure 9.5: Practice as an interconnected sum of the parts

Bringing together different ways of knowing

Figure 9.6: Bringing together different ways of knowing

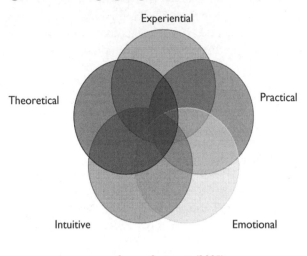

Source: Springett (2005)

One truth inevitably subordinates many truths, and so social differences based on class, 'race', gender, ethnicity, sexual preference and 'dis'ability become subordinated within dominant power and knowledge relations. Participatory practice is committed to working in democratic ways that equalise power and knowledge. In this respect, it is important to understand that dominant ways of knowing are expressed in a narrow interpretation of the intellect which has subordinated other, more holistic ways of making sense of the world that work beyond these narrow confines, see Figure 9.6.

There are many who have advocated education for democracy as an engagement with different ways of knowing. Peter Park, Paulo Freire, Jürgen Habermas, Stephen Kemmis, and others argue for an epistemological turn whereby all forms of knowing and experiencing the world are seen as interconnected, that our outer knowing is linked to our inner knowing in a dynamic way through consciousness. As Rozentuller and Talbott remind us:

> It can be desperately painful to let go of centuries-old habits of thought. When we do manage to transcend the great Cartesian divide, we will recognize how natural it is that our interior should give us the key to understanding the outer world. Consciousness is not something that merely goes on inside our own skulls; it is the inner aspect of the world. Just as our mathematical concepts belong not only to us, but to the world as well, so also more generally: our own interior is at the same time the world's interior. We are, after all, part of the world, not aliens from elsewhere. Is it really a surprise that where, in us, the

world wakes up to self-consciousness, this consciousness should find itself participating in, and capable of knowing, the world? Only a long history of artificially isolating the subject as knower from the world known could have made us think otherwise. (Rozentuller and Talbott, 2005:14)

Through engagement in knowing as thinking, feeling, sensory human beings, we participate in the world experientially through all our senses. Freire, for example was, from the outset, very clear that learning to read is not mechanistic, but an emotional and passionate way of knowing. He talks about dialogue as not only the way to question the status quo, but also as an expression of our being: dialogue is nurtured by love, humility, hope, faith and mutual trust – then, and only then, can this result in true communication (Freire, 1972). In the same way, Goethe argued that there was a close relationship between creativity and nature, for example the energy that grows a flower in the ground resembles the energy that grows a poem in a poet (Seamon and Zajonc 1998). Is not the use of an outer form to convey inner meaning the essence of all creative endeavour, and central to the expression of our knowing the world, reaching beyond the written word?

A participatory paradigm frames an emancipatory methodology, one that seeks to identify and change the causes not the symptoms of oppression. Within this methodology, methods of research are adopted which are consonant with underlying values of respect, dignity, mutuality and reciprocity, providing an ideological lens through which every stage of the process is validated. Dialogue 'becomes a potent method of integrating inquiry and intervention, and it can contribute to the intermingled processes of knowing and changing' (Tandon, 1981:293). All participants act in the interests of the whole, working together for change. It begins in everyday realities, and is a mutual process of discovery 'where the researcher and the researched both contribute to the expansion of the other's knowledge' (Opie, 1992: 66). Kemmis, influenced by Habermas's *theory of communicative action*, argues for 'a form of understanding beyond individual subjectivity – in an intersubjective space' (Habermas, 1984/87; Kemmis, 2006: 472). This involves paying attention to the 'huge silence' that is often not audible in White or male-dominated contexts, and involves:

> … identity politics, in particular, gender and 'whiteness' studies.…
> Who we are, what we think we know is also inherently connected
> to what we are not, what we do not and sometimes cannot know.
> (Noffke, 2005: 324)

This links closely to our emphasis on critical public spaces in which to develop critical dissent dialogue, across difference, in order to reach a mutual consensus on knowing a situation in order to act on it. It is a strategy for generating knowledge in action.

Reason defines three important, interrelated aspects of such a paradigmatic shift: 'the move to participatory and holistic knowing; to critical subjectivity; and to knowledge in action' (Reason, 1988: 10):

i. *Participatory and holistic knowing* is achieved through a critical engagement in and with the world.
ii. *Critical subjectivity* is the synthesis of naïve inquiry (a knowing based on feelings, emotions and experience) and scientific inquiry, bridging the subjective/objective divide to provide an approach to human inquiry that is objectively subjective. This offers a range of possible styles: from heuristic research, 'a process of internal search through which one discovers the nature and meaning of experience and develops methods and procedures for further investigation and analysis' (Moustakas, 1990: 9) to Heron's form of cooperative inquiry, which is based on different kinds of knowledge: *experiential* (direct encounter with people, places or things); *practical* (how to do something); *propositional* (theoretical knowledge about something); and *presentational* (symbolising the knowing which we cannot put into words in movement, sound, colour, shape, line, poetry, drama and story) (Reason, 1994: 42).
iii. Finally, *knowledge in action* is used to denote a transcending of the chasm between intellect and experience in which western consciousness has placed value on 'thinkers' at the expense of 'doers', dividing theory from practice. Knowledge in action is, therefore, engaged in the world rather than alienated from it.

We suggest that re-experiencing life from a participatory paradigm opens our minds to the notion of multiple truths and a more holistic way of making sense of the world. In the following section, we revisit the key elements that help the process along.

Dialogue: the first encounter, story and connected knowing

We have discussed the importance of empathy in becoming critical, particularly using story to develop a dialectical approach to dialogue, a connected knowing (Belenky et al, 1997), a way of being open to the experience of others as legitimate knowledge, and we will expand on this further in a moment. We see it as a crucial concept in working across difference and diversity to form alliances of trust for collective action. It offers a vital insight into the role of empathy in the process of transformation, and we see this as the basis of anti-sexist, anti-racist practice (Ledwith and Asgill, 2007), which engages with the power of White privilege, as addressed by people such as Michelle Fine, Margaret Ledwith, Joe Kincheloe, Richard Dyer, and others. Marion Dadds talks about *emotional validity* being 'the potential of the research ... to transform the emotional dispositions of people towards each other' (2008: 280). This important contribution helps us to understand emotional knowing more clearly, and to illuminate its transformative qualities, personally and interpersonally, leading to the deeper connected knowing that is at the heart of collective action. In a process of dialogue, everyone is brought together in a deeper connection with the lived realities of each other, and in so doing a greater trust and motivation for collective change is created. Dadds claims that this approach to research in practice changes the way people think and act together, 'contributing to developing empathetic understanding, kindness, respect and compassion [to] counteract human negativity on a localised or wider scale' (2008: 288).

The stories we tell are the stories through which we create our identities. These identity stories interpret perceptions of everyday life and become the filters through which we interact with the world. Telling and retelling our stories is central to the way we make sense of the world. So, as individual and collective storytellers, questioning our stories can provide interruptions in our everyday lives. Listening to the stories that people have to tell about their lives by suspending our own truth and hearing the truths forged from other experiences is the beginning of personal empowerment. Active listening, paying full attention with respect, creates a trusting encounter; taking people seriously builds self-esteem. This moves into a collective and mutual experience. The stories that we tell about who we are and how we make sense of the world around us can be told and retold as we learn to question given truths. Telling and retelling our stories in the context of group dialogue leads to new personal and collective insights with a past–present–future dynamic. From these beginnings, stories become collective narratives capable of influencing epistemological and ontological change. If you doubt this statement, think of second-wave feminism, which began with women in small groups in their communities sharing their life experiences – from the stories, collective narratives emerged that forged feminist theory in action, and in turn this quickly bourgeoned into a movement for change. We can draw on many examples of women's collective action for peace, equality and the environment, such as Women Against Pit Closures formed during the miners' strike of 1984–85, the Greenham Women's Peace Camp 1981–2000, the UN Beijing Conference of 1995, all of which had a global reach.

Creating the conditions for storytelling in dialogical groups calls for a consensus on what constitutes trust, dignity and respect in action. One way of beginning the process is to tell someone else's story, maybe something fictional. It is a way of developing the values that need to be honoured by the group. To trigger the process of critical consciousness, the stories need to be relevant to the everyday lives of the people in the group. As animator/co-facilitator of this process you will need to be confident in dealing with ethnocentric views and even bigotry. Remember that dialogue that sets out to explore racism, sexism or other power relations can prove painful, embarrassing or obtuse. The aim is to share the power, skills and knowledge by rotating or collectivising the roles that involve decision making and status, but creating a trusting context is a skill that calls for vigilant attention to the spoken word and noticing beyond the spoken word in order to maintain respectful relations. The process, as it unfolds, teaches to question what has previously remained unquestioned. Through the continued life of the group in ongoing dialogue participants begin to ask even deeper questions of themselves and each other; as confidence grows the group is co-facilitated, and deeper insights are made, leading to critical connections that reach from the specific to broader questions about life as a whole. Using story as voice, as reflection, as other ways of knowing, as creating collective narratives, as gaining insight into the nature of discrimination and of White, western, patriarchal privilege, the broader questions become part of the personal and specific. Moving beyond intellectual knowing, beyond the written word, intuition, feelings, emotions give more holistic, connected insights. These connections with bigger picture issues help us to identify common themes with historical, cultural, political and social dimensions. This can be illustrated by the consensus reached by global women at the UN Beijing Conference for a Platform for Action that identified just 12 issues that, acted on, would achieve justice for women globally.

Let us now return to the notion of connected knowing. Empathy across difference and diversity through suspending our own truth leads to 'connected knowing' (Belenky et al, 1997), a concept which helps us be open to difference and diversity as part of the living whole.

> The most trustworthy knowledge comes from personal experience rather than the pronouncements of authorities.... Since knowledge comes from experience, the only way to share the experience [is] seeing the other not in their own terms but in the other's terms. (Belenky et al, 1997: 112-13)

Connected knowing, in the process of dialogue, offers a way of suspending knowing, unlearning and re-learning by developing an openness to the experience of others. It offers the capacity to hear stories that tell other truths based on diverse lives, and in doing so offers the chance to re-tell little stories as collective narratives in the co-creation of a new world. In letting go of the need for a dominant truth, we open ourselves to a humanity based on diversity rather than domination.

Reflective knowledge (Park, 2001) is a vital dimension of personal transformation, without which the collective process will not evolve. Scrutinising our internal assumptions, prejudices and values is addressed in inner and outer arcs of attention (Marshall, 2001); as we begin to question everyday life, so we begin to question the ways in which we have made sense of our existence. This is always an uncomfortable process, and sometimes a distressing experience. It calls for an openness to unlearn what we have previously taken for granted as our truth, a truth that has helped us to explain our existence and to justify why it is so. It is our contention that without this preparedness, we cannot move into a collective process. If we are courageous enough to enter into this internal dialogue we open ourselves to the diversity of human experience and other ways of knowing the world. It is the foundation of other ways of knowing that are relational, engaged in dialogue with others, where our preparedness to suspend our own truth then enables us to listen with empathy. We drop the tendency to defend our position, an arrogant posturing, and we give our full attention to others in a process of trust and mutuality, a transcending of individualism in the search for a common good. This is the basis of personal transformation: a re-visioning of ourselves in relation to our world.

Beginning in the stories of people's everyday lives opens new ways of knowing (epistemology) and leads to action for new ways of being (ontology). A paradigm shift takes place as the dominant way of seeing the world is explored from a participatory worldview, a practical utopia. In these ways, the community group moves from issue to project, from project to community action, and through alliances and networks the action emanates beyond the boundaries of community, to connect collectively as movements for change.

Revisiting Freire is useful here: more than a strategy, he offers 'a way of living, loving, and interpreting the world', and when we embrace his pedagogy as a whole we find that we undergo 'a profound transformation of ourselves as human beings in our work with others' (Darder, 2002: 205-7). Freire talked of love as a love for all humanity: 'Love is an act of courage, not fear ... a commitment to others ... [and] to the cause of liberation' (1972: 78). His belief was that the process of dialogue, so central to the transformative project, could not exist 'in the absence of a profound love for the world and for people' (1993: 70).

Emancipatory action research as practical knowledge

Emancipatory action research must not be seen as an optional extra, but an integral component of any approach to participatory practice, offering an evolving dynamic between theory, policy and practice in an engagement with the ever-changing political context of our lives. It is an ongoing process of generating knowledge in action, going deeper into knowing in order to act more relevantly. Without this, practice lacks a cutting edge, and so loses its potential for bringing about change. Worse still, our practice becomes domesticating rather than liberating; we teach people to be silent and accepting of the status quo.

Emancipatory action research offers us the scope to develop a more critical praxis, a form of practice that is symbiotically creating knowledge in action and action as knowledge (Reason and Bradbury, 2001). In this way, different ways of knowing that have been effectively silenced in the positivist search for one truth are given voice.

> A primary purpose of action research is to produce practical knowledge that is useful to people in the everyday conduct of their lives. A wider purpose of action research is to contribute through this practical knowledge to the increased well-being – economic, political, psychological, spiritual – of human persons and communities, and to a more equitable and sustainable relations with the wider ecology of

the planet of which we are an intrinsic part. (Reason and Bradbury, 2001: 2)

Action research is emancipatory in essence. By this we mean that its intention is not only to generate practical knowledge relevant to change in the immediate context of people's everyday lives, but it also leads to new abilities to create new knowledge (Reason and Bradbury, 2001), new ways of knowing that extend the process beyond the specific and local to address the increased well-being of people, communities and the sustainability of the natural world. This demands that we pay attention to the economic, political, psychological and spiritual dimensions of life to find ways of healing the fractures that we have created by fragmenting life on earth. It is our belief that reconnection is possible within the frame of a participatory paradigm, an interconnected responsibility to the whole. This calls for local practice to extend beyond the immediate context to reach out collectively through alliances towards a movement for change. Each context is mutually and inextricably connected and evolving. The process is practical, based on cycles of action and reflection that lead to new epistemologies, new ways of seeing the world that lead to new ways of being in the world. This can be seen as research for practical knowledge that leads to liberating action through participation. The approach is based on the Freirean notion that all people have the right to be subjects in the world; agency and autonomy is restored through a mutual and reciprocal process that draws people together in relations of dignity and respect, as co-researchers in the process of change, questioning and making sense of the world in order to act together for a common good.

Emancipatory action research is founded on an ideology of participatory democracy, in harmony with the values, principles and practice of community development. In itself, it constitutes a participatory approach to practice, committed to working *with* not *on* people, with the explicit intention of equalising power relations and bringing about transformative change. Since the 1980s action research has gathered momentum for a worldwide movement for change, and has become increasingly critical with feminist influence on multiple truths, many ways of knowing, particularly in relation to the intersection of 'race', class and gender, as well as making connections 'between intellectual, emotional, practical, intuitive, sensory, imaginal' and other different ways of knowing (Marshall, 2001: 433). This enables us to become critical on a dimension between the inner, self-criticality and the outer, critical connection with the world in a process of 'inner and outer arcs of attention', questioning, dialoguing in cycles of action and reflection that integrate new knowledge, new ways of seeing the world, into action for change. These cycles are explored in relation to Rowan's cycle model in Chapter 7.

Emancipatory action research ensures that we pay attention to the interconnectedness of the whole. This practice operates at the levels of self, group, project, community, alliance and movement for change in an increasingly collective dynamic. To ensure that every stage of the process is true to what it claims, questions are set in consultation with everyone involved as a system of checks and balances.

Just because we state an aim, we cannot make the assumption that it is happening; we need to set quality and validity questions that check the experience is true to its word. If we believe that this is a mutual, reciprocal encounter, what evidence is there that all people across difference are giving voice to their experience and thoughts? What evidence is there that confidence and self-esteem are flourishing in everyone involved? What evidence is there that respect is received and given? What evidence is there of changes in decision making based on a sharing of power? The use of our values and principles as a frame for eliciting practical evidence, in this way, ensures that we are able to evaluate our impact.

Reason and Bradbury (2001) offer a useful framework for questioning the validity and quality of the practice.

1. *Practical outcomes:* What are the outcomes of the research? Does it work? What are the processes of inquiry? Are they authentic/life enhancing?
2. *Relationship outcomes:* How have the values of democracy been actualised in practice? What is the relationship between initiators and participants? What are the implications for infrastructure and political structures?
3. *Plural ways of knowing outcomes:* What dimensions of an extended epistemology are emphasised? Is this appropriate? What are the validity claims of different ways of knowing?
4. *Meaning and purpose outcomes:* What is worthwhile? What values have been actualised in the inquiry? At a wider level these lead to questions of spirituality and beauty for a world truly worthy of human aspiration.

This attention to quality and evaluation forms the basis of further cycles of action that move outwards towards transformative change in ongoing cycles of action/reflection, building on the knowledge gained in action.

Towards transformative practice

There are three key stages in the process of transformations: changing our selves, connecting with others and changing the world.

Changing our selves

In relation to changing the self, participation demands that we are part of the process; we cannot set ourselves outside the process of change. Engaging in participatory practice is engaging in our own transformation. How can we help others to become authentic if we are not open to challenge and to change ourselves? Maguire talks about her experience of participatory research:

> The participatory research process is invigorating, and likewise exhausting. But then that is the beauty of it. You will not be detached. You too, not merely the participants, will be rehumanised. Participatory

research is not only about trying to transform social structures 'out there' and 'the people', it is about being open to transforming ourselves and our relationship to others. Just as I examined the dilemmas and contradictions in participatory research, I was challenged daily to consider the dilemmas and contradictions of my own life choices. I was forced to question my part in the social construction and maintenance of large social structures, systems and relationships. And, relentlessly, I found myself asking, How am I choosing to be in the world? (Maguire, 1993: 174)

Figure 9.7: Towards transformative praxis

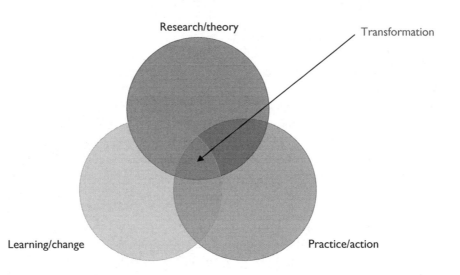

Personal change is connected to changing the world. This cannot be achieved without a unity of praxis in which theory, practice and change are integrated (see Figure 9.7). So, tools like reflective journals and the creation of critical dissent dialogue provide both inner and outer engagement with the process of being critical. If we are seeking balance and wholeness in community we need to hold a balance within ourselves, and be aware when that balance is challenged. We also need to understand the nature of relationship between ourselves and others. Self-reflection involves being aware of the relationship between our outer and our inner world.

The extent to which we human beings do not achieve our potential to be creative authors of our own vision is due to the tremendous set of socialised perceptions – Truths – which promote a limited consciousness and prevent the development of critical awareness of the natural phenomenon of which we are an integral part and the dynamic, dialectic interaction which defines the relationship with our environment. Our truths function, ultimately, to prevent our self actualisation as individuals and in groups. (Murphy, 1999: 180)

However, there is more to it than this. If we are a microcosm of the whole, then we have to seek balance and well-being within ourselves, since our own consciousness is interrelated to what is outside ourselves. So it is not just about re-visioning ourselves in relation to the whole, it is being whole in our self, in relation to the different parts of ourselves and the community of which we are a part. As we have previously said, it is about being critically reflexive and critically engaged in the world on an inner and outer dimension.

In these ways, we see a participatory worldview as not simply an approach to practice – it is a way of life. We cannot engage with people in our working relations in a mutual, equal way, only to be abusive or exploitative in other contexts of our lives. This is duplicitous and simply does not work. Our value base provides the foundation of our practice. For example, the concept of dialogue cannot be applied to practice without a profound understanding of the way that values of respect, dignity and human worth enable it to become an engagement that is mutual and reciprocal, one based on cooperation rather than competition, based on humility rather than arrogance. This may seem a simple idea, but consider the way that arrogance is a part of everyday life in the West, encouraged as a form of status in a competitive, top-down world. And arrogance is a form of bullying, an acting out of superiority that reflects dominant power relations. In order to ensure that superiority is not unconsciously acted out in dialogue as a form of power over others, we pay attention to, for example, the nature of Whiteness as an assumed superiority, often an intangible and poorly understood expression of power that diminishes those other than White. A self-reflexive approach to self-consciousness helps us to go deeper into an understanding of personal power: who am I, in my Whiteness, in my femaleness, in my middle classness, in my Englishness ... and how is this experienced by those who are other (Weiler, 2001)? An understanding of the way we express our values in relationships is vital to the process of liberation. Concepts of mutuality and reciprocity, for instance, are only possible if we relinquish power in the belief that others are fully capable autonomous beings who can join us as equals, as co-creators of change, in mutual, reciprocal engagement, in a process of search and re-search, of action and reflection. Partnerships cannot be mutual unless all parties believe they have as much to learn from each other as they have to give. In this sense, Freire saw mutuality in horizontal relations; co-learners, co-teachers, co-researchers working as true partners in the process of liberation.

Connecting with others

Healthier people do seem to feel a greater emotional sense of connection and belonging, and that sense of meaning and connection is a vital part of health. (Skinner, 1978: 203)

Connecting collectively is central to the community development process, and calls for us to work on a number of levels at the same time. In our participatory practice, not only should we be engaging with individuals, groups and projects within the community, but also with the organisations and people who connect with community or impact on it. This is about bringing to the surface those hidden connections. Our work is about connecting people at all levels in all contexts, from community groups to movements for change. Not only does this heal alienation, but it also creates a common purpose for a healthy world. Connections begin in less organised ways, for instance in the BBC film *Skint*, about the lives of children living in poverty on a Scottish estate, gang culture was rife throughout the year until Bonfire Night loomed, when the gangs would cooperate to collect material for the bonfire. For a brief period they were connected. Similar acts of connection can be seen in the Lantern Festival that is held every year in Ulverston and the Scarecrow Festival in Wray. Connecting people in celebratory activities like these is an important part of participatory practice and much is to be gained from the power of music, carnival, festival and celebration. Carnival, including all its unifying celebratory aspects, can also be used for protest, effectively presenting collective action in a non-confrontational form in accordance with the principles of participation. Lancaster Carnival of Culture is one such example where my granddaughter Grace (dressed as Belle) and I (Margaret, as her grandmother) joined the diversity of local voices on the streets, sharing music and fantasy with the common message that we want to preserve our local economy in the face of proposed corporate 'developments'.

Carnival as protest

Lancaster Carnival of Culture, 2008

As Peat (1986:62) says in *Blackfoot physics*, songs create and renew, they heal and make whole. He goes on to describe how in many societies sound, vibration and song are believed to be the 'creative generative forces within the cosmos'. This can be seen in the way that music making with the traumatised children of northern war-torn Uganda has worked as a collective, connected healing.

Making connections is also about ecological literacy. Sustainability involves modelling sustainable communities on nature's ecosystems as dynamic processes of co-evolution. As we saw in Chapter 3, living systems are self-generating networks open to continual flows of matter and energy. Ecosystems operate on six principles of ecology that are critical to sustainability, and to our health and well-being (see Capra, 2003; these principles are set out below). It calls for a critical pedagogy that puts an understanding of all life at its core.

Principles of ecology (based on Capra, 2003: 202)

Networks: at every level of the natural world, we find living systems nesting in other living systems – networks within networks. Their boundaries are not boundaries of separation, but boundaries of identity. All living systems communicate with one another and share resources across boundaries.

Cycles: all living systems must feed on a continual flow of matter and energy from their environment to stay alive, and all living systems continually produce waste. However, an ecosystem generates no net waste, waste being another species' food. Thus matter cycles continually through the web of life.

Solar energy: solar energy, transformed into chemical energy by the photosynthesis of green plants, drives ecological cycles.

Partnership: the exchanges of energy in the ecosystem are sustained by pervasive cooperation. Contrary to the received wisdom concerning the survival of the fittest, life did not take over the planet by combat but by cooperation, partnership and networking.

Diversity: ecosystems achieve stability and resilience through the richness and complexity of their ecological webs. The greater their biodiversity, the more resilient they are.

Dynamic balance: an ecosystem is a flexible, ever-fluctuating network. Its flexibility is the consequence of multiple feedback loops that keep the system in a state of dynamic balance. No single variable is maximised; all variables fluctuate around their optimum values.

Changing the world

We believe that the process of transformation often gets stuck at the personal, group or project stage. Yet we have shown in this book that if you think participatively and ecologically, everything is interconnected and stuckness is a failure to make key connections for energy to flow in the system with the necessary feedback processes. It is these processes that tip a system into a new way of being. We can engage in the dialogical, reflexive process within a community, but unless we extend that engagement to all who connect with that community, we are not opening up the valves for the process to become collective. We have to engage with communities of practice in ever-increasing cycles of reflection and action. As Popay (2006) has shown, the barriers to transformation lie within existing organisations and those working in them. In this way, our work involves the powerful as well as the powerless. In Chapter 4 there are many examples of stuckness, or what others have called 'the challenge of scaling up', of moving beyond the boundaries of community. This is directly related to collective critical consciousness, without which we stay local and specific.

From a practical perspective, there needs to be a commitment to continuous revolution, inner and outer. It involves linking people across systems, connecting with others. Castelloe et al (2002) argue that working participatively starts with 'putting the first last', working with those marginalised in society to create structures outside the existing ones, such as grassroots organisations, through which groups of people can come together to meet their own needs, on their own terms, as they gain the critical consciousness and collective power needed to shape systems to become more inclusive and participatory. Paulo Freire also emphasised that transformative change begins in grassroots communities, and it is the powerless who, in liberating themselves, are the ones who liberate the powerful (Freire, 1972). Community development is people development; people developing the power and self-worth to use their skills and knowledge to create positive change. It is about a transference of power to those local leaders that Gramsci conceptualised as *organic intellectuals* The work of the community practitioner is to create the context for developing the skills and knowledge for people to join together collectively to bring about change. As individual issues becomes shared, a group establishes a project, projects become organised under a community-wide umbrella, perhaps a community forum, this provides a level of organising that leads to alliances, and alliances unite as movements for change. This brings us back full circle to participatory democracy. Couto (2000) believes grassroots organisations encapsulate democracy in its most radical and people-centred form. So community development, while building grassroots groups which link together to form social movements, still retains local collective power to participate in decisions that improve local well-being. In this constant local–global dynamic, participatory democracy sustains a way of life on earth as a flourishing, mutual ecosystem.

Capra (2003) highlights the connection between patriarchy and the values accorded to material acquisition. He argues that the glorification of material consumption has deep ideological roots that go far beyond economics and politics. Its origins lie in the universal association of 'mankind' with material possessions in patriarchal cultures. He shows how the work of the anthropologist, Gilmore, found that across many cultures there is a recurring notion that 'real manhood' is different from simple biological maleness; it is something to be won. In the past manhood was associated with producing more than one's own needs, that is, serving the community as a whole and giving more than taking. However, over time, production for others shifted to production of material possessions for oneself, so associating maleness with material wealth as status. This association of our troubled times with patriarchy is echoed in Tarnas's book on the history of western thought:

> ... man [sic] faces the existential crisis of being a solitary and mortal conscious ego thrown into an ultimately meaningless and unknowable universe. And he faces the psychological and biological crisis of living in a world that has become to be shaped in such a way that it precisely matches his world view – ie in a man made environment that is increasingly mechanistic, atomised, soulless and self destructive. The crisis of modern man is essentially a masculine crisis. (Tarnas, 1991: 442)

A re-integration of the male/female divide, rebalancing the rational/relational and the detached/intuitive is represented below in Figure 9.8.

Figure 9.8: A matter of balance

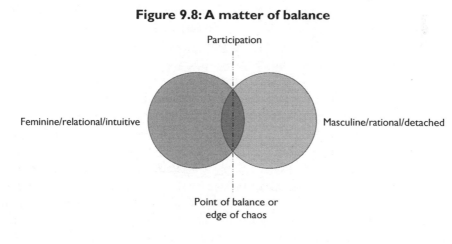

A transformative model for participatory practice

In Figure 9.9, we present you with a model of practice that captures the interconnectedness of the key components of transformative change. The image comprises five infinity symbols that represent key dimensions for transformation in interaction, capturing the potential of the whole to become a movement for change. If one dimension is weak or missing, the system is out of balance. The interactive balance of the whole combines to create the energy for change; in dialectical relation each component achieves synthesis, the energy for change. Broken lines denote the feedback loops vital to the functioning of the whole system, within which are related life-enhancing qualities that promote human and environmental flourishing. If you refer back to Figure 1.3 in Chapter 1 you can see that the elements of participation that formed the basis of our exploration throughout the book have evolved into the model of transformative practice that, in simple form, captures the complexity of these dimensions in practice. The succinct nature of the model offers an analysis that combines key concepts of practice in interactive, symbiotic balance, and it is this balance of the whole and an understanding of its interconnectedness that offers the potential for our work to become transformative in achieving its potential for change.

Without insight into the nature of power and powerlessness, and the way that this creates a system of dominance and subordination, we unconsciously fragment the whole. Take the story of the boy sleeping in the skip, for instance. Local residents complained, and the immediate practice response was to satisfy their demands by putting an ASBO (Anti-social Behaviour Order) on him. This is a surface-level reaction, which fails to see beyond the immediate. It was a youth worker who said to the multi-disciplinary team, "How is this going to help? This community is his lifeline, and now he is banned from coming near his home. At home, his family is living on the edge. There is no father. His mother has mental health issues that are linked to surviving poverty. He has brothers and sisters younger than him. What are we trying to do to them?". By questioning the purpose of practice, the youth worker offered another perspective beyond the personal. From there, emphasis was placed on working with the community, to support local activists with community-wide projects, and to emphasise the collective, connected community voice through a community forum. The forum offered a critical space for reflection on community issues, and a space for action. It also offered a more powerful collective voice that was heard in places of power, as well as connecting with campaigns, networks and alliances beyond the boundary of the community. By questioning, the youth worker problematised the boy's behaviour, captured a microcosm of the whole, and provided a catalyst in community development. From these beginnings, practice connects with the everyday lives of people and reaches out in collective action towards a global movement for change. It is not a linear process; it is cyclic and in dynamic balance. By this, we mean that practice keeps reaching from local to global, between action and reflection, in an inner

Figure 9.9: A transformative model for participatory practice

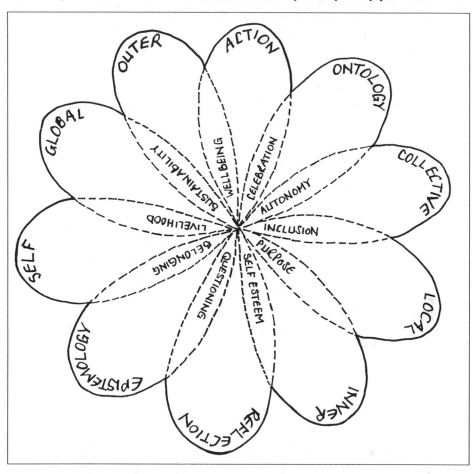

and outer process of consciousness, creating theory in action by exploring the way we make sense of the world in order to create well-being in the world.

How to use the model

1. The five intersecting infinity symbols each represent a pair of related key components of the symbiotic whole in dynamic interaction: action/reflection, ontology/epistemology, collective/self, local/global, and inner/outer consciousness. These capture the dimensions of participatory approaches to community development.

2. The broken lines indicate feedback loops containing qualities that lead to human and environmental flourishing. The concept of feedback loops is important in capturing the dynamic that is essential to the balance of the whole.

3. Each of the key components plays a fundamental role in the interconnectedness of the whole, and is therefore vital to the process of transformative change. The fulcrum of transformation is found in the centre of the model, where all components intersect.

The model is designed to aid reflection on the interconnectedness of key dimensions of practice. Taken apart, you would find that the five infinity symbols contain opposites that need to be considered in dynamic balance, which is also a source of transformation. Without this balance, the result is 'dis'-ease and fracture, and without a connection to the whole, it becomes fragmented and incomplete. The broken lines of the overlapping sections indicate feedback loops that contain a quality of practice particularly relevant to each position in the whole. The constant feedback maintains the whole in dynamic, cyclic interaction rather than a linear progression. It is necessary for this process to be maintained to keep practice relevant to its changing contexts. You could usefully consider this in relation to the excellent example of women's global action at the United Nations (UN) Beijing Conference (for a detailed discussion, see Ledwith, 2005). The Platform for Action was the culmination of years of grassroots activism connecting local groups to regional, national and continental networks in preparation for this unity of global action. Once governments pledge commitment, progress is monitored on a five-year basis, and action continues in a cyclic feedback loop through all stages, from local to global, to maintain momentum. It is only in this cyclic action/reflection process that change becomes sustainable. If the action was perceived as linear, it could become deflected and powerless at the global level.

Women's global action: women of the world unite

Beijing, 1995

In order to explore the model's interconnectedness, we will consider the ideas in the book in relation to each dimension.

Action/reflection

There is an inextricable link between social justice and environmental justice that has long been acknowledged as central to community development practice (see, for instance, statements from Community Development Exchange [CDX] at www.cdx.org.uk). It is not only unstable weather systems that have an impact on poor communities, but all aspects of environmental degradation put poor people at greater risk. This can operate in a number of ways. We know, for example, that access to 'green' spaces brings a significant improvement to health and well-being, physiologically and psychologically. Yet it is green spaces that are often absent in poor areas. At a neighbourhood level, take the issue of children's play, and compare the difference in what constitutes a children's playground in a poor neighbourhood and in a rich neighbourhood. You will find that poor children are exposed to much greater dangers from broken swings, broken glass, broken fences onto busy roads and a generally hazardous environment. In the most marginalised communities, playgrounds become whatever the environment offers, and this is often dangerous, toxic or a risk. This has to be understood in the context of overcrowded homes where there are no facilities for indoor play and no provision for outdoor play. Environmental degradation always impacts on poorest people first, not only as a safety hazard, but also destroying self-respect and dignity, and so destroying life chances. Reflection helps us to explore the connection between social justice and environmental injustice, and understand the implications this has for community development practice.

Issues of environmental degradation are often central to community concerns. Local action, perhaps in the form of a community garden, as discussed in Chapter 1, brings the community together and has a profound impact on the quality of community life. But, acting and reflecting on the issues from a local perspective will only give us part of the picture, not taking us under the surface to make broader connections. If we situate local manifestations of bigger issues within our reflective frame, we begin to get to the root sources of local problems. For instance, we have discussed the issue of biodiversity – the environment stays in balance when humanity behaves as part of the ecosystem, living with respect for nature and maintaining a healthy connection with the whole. This idea is essential to notions of sustainability. The escalation of global capitalism and the reification of the market, enhanced by individualism, has reached levels of consumption that have thrown the natural world into imbalance, creating a crisis of sustainability. At the same time, the escalation of globalisation has resulted in increased exploitation of people, resulting in greater human suffering. On a human level, we see such anomalies as the strange phenomenon of increasing social divisions in rich countries; on a physical level, we are faced with environmental concerns like the destruction of the ozone layer through carbon emissions. In our discussion of epistemology influencing ontology, or the way we see the world changing the way we behave in the world, we are concerned that western attitudes have permeated global cultures with the consequence that prejudiced attitudes that lead to structural discrimination against specific social groups in the West, discussed in depth in Chapter 2, are now evident on a global level. By making these connections, we see that the dominant western worldview operates at the interface of sustainability and social justice, exploiting both people and the environment for the benefit of the privileged.

Ontology/epistemology

These two concepts are important to practitioners because they capture the connection between the way that we make sense of the world (epistemology) and how this influences the way we act in the world (ontology). In other words, how we see the world affects our behaviour. This notion leads us to understand that if we alter the way we see the world, in turn our behaviour will change. Practitioners create the context for critical thinking through popular education, or *critical pedagogy*. Critical pedagogy is an approach to learning that develops critical thinking by teaching people to become critical about the circumstances of their everyday lives by questioning answers, rather than answering questions (Shor, 1993). It is a mutual approach to learning, where rather than teacher and taught, the process is one of teacher-learner/learner-teacher (Freire, 1972). A value base of respect, dignity, equality and reciprocity ensures that the experience fosters self-esteem, identity and autonomy, the prerequisites of transformative action. It is the form of learning that is threaded through the diverse practical projects that are initiated by community development practitioners in partnership with local people in order to break through the taken-for-grantedness of everyday life on the margins that encourages people to accept diminished life chances that deny them their full potential. Beginning in dialogue, and starting in the familiar circumstances of the everyday, Paulo Freire developed an approach to becoming critical that focused on capturing an aspect of life in a drawing. This provides the focus for a community group to begin exploring the drawing by questioning: Who is this? Where is this? What is happening and to whom? Through this simple form of problematising, which can be captured in a photograph, drama, poetry, music or story, the group begins to focus discussion on the issue rather than the 'code'. The key to the success of this method is that the code is relevant to the lives of the people concerned and will generate from its relevance to their lives the curiosity necessary for questioning. Listening respectfully, from the heart, to personal stories builds trust. The group share more deeply, and begin to empathise with different experiences and different ways of seeing the world. Empathy builds. Through dialogue, a more critical analysis of the political dimensions of personal stories emerges. As critical consciousness develops, a paradigm shift takes place, dislocating the dominant way of seeing the world, and re-visioning what is desirable and possible. The world we know changes when we see it in a different light; we engage with it in a different way. But transformation is active not passive; it calls for us to examine old ways of knowing and to explore new ways of knowing. Cycles of thinking and doing only become transformative when participants are fully engaged in the process; they see the need for transformation, and actively work together to bring about change for a happier, healthier and flourishing world.

Let us get practical at this point. A *problematising* or problem–posing approach involves identifying everyday aspects of life that capture an issue of discrimination and representing this in a decontextualised way in any form that will invite curiosity. This is a codification. In the process of *de-coding* (analysing the codifications), the animator encourages the group to question what is happening. Hope and Timmel (1984: 58) identify six stages that lead to critical consciousness, but based on our emphasis on connected knowing as a way of hearing the truths of others (see Chapter 6), we have inserted this important awareness of difference/diversity to make seven stages in total:

1. **Description:** what do you see? What is happening? Where is it happening?
2. **First analysis:** why is this happening? – 'why' questions move the process from observation to thinking
3. **Connected knowing:** how is this experienced differently by different people?
4. **Real life:** once the group in immersed in the issue, the next level is elicited by asking, does this happen in real life? Who is affected? In what way?
5. **Related problems:** if it seems appropriate, the next stage is to move laterally to related, connected issues – what does this lead to?
6. **Root causes:** this reaches out to much deeper connections with structural discrimination at the heart of critical consciousness – what are the causes/what has created this situation?
7. **Action planning:** what can we do about it?

Source: Developed from Hope and Timmel (1984)

Take a look at the photograph of the young Black man carrying a dog, and consider how this begins the process of questioning, eliciting answers that call for action, in this case revealing *the politics of disposability* witnessed by the world when Hurricane Katrina hit New Orleans, discussed in more detail in Chapter 2.

Paulo Freire profoundly influenced community development practice from the early 1970s onwards, resulting in a more critical approach to practice. This critical approach has not been so evident of recent years, with the advent of high levels of managerialism and bureaucracy, short-term funding and externally imposed political agendas. This has reduced the possibility for community development to achieve its transformative potential, and in consequence we are becoming increasingly policy-led. By reclaiming a critical approach to practice, we increase our chances of contributing to transformative change at a time when we need it more than ever. In this process of exploring different ways of seeing the world, a participatory

Problematising Hurricane Katrina

Source: Thomas Dworkin / Magnum

worldview becomes seen as a practical utopia, challenging the sense of a competitive worldview that inherently creates inequalities. We begin to see the connection between an altered epistemology and the practical possibilities for change.

Collective/self

The process of conscientisation, or becoming critical, is not liberating until it becomes a collective process.

> Liberating education is a social process of illumination…. Even when you individually feel yourself most free, if this feeling is not a social feeling, if you are not able to use your recent freedom to help others to be free by transforming the totality of society, then you are exercising only an individualist attitude towards empowerment or freedom. (Freire, in Shor and Freire, 1987: 109)

The collective process presents a real challenge to practitioners in an age of individualism that has resulted in disconnection, in less collective activity and responsibility for the whole. Layard and Dunn (2009) highlight this in their book on childhood, arguing that the tilt towards individualism has gone too far and what we require instead is a society based on the law of love. As humans we have basic affiliative needs and a fractured world reduces the satisfaction of those needs. It is not a case of loving ourselves so we can love others, but rather seeing that both are in need of the other. Unless we find ways to connect the self to the group, the group to the community, the community to alliances, and alliances to movements for change, we will fail in our transformative intention.

> Education, or the act of knowing as Freire calls it, is an ongoing research programme into aspects of people's experience and its relationship to wider social, economic and political factors. (Kirkwood, 1991: 103)

Local/global

Neoliberal capitalism operates at the interface of social justice and environmental justice, exploiting people and the planet for profit. We have evidenced ways in which this is presenting us with an unsustainable and divided world. This levels a challenge for community development practice. How do we put these insights into action? Every Action Counts is the result of a consortium of national organisations which, together with DEFRA (Department for Environment, Food and Rural Affairs), have developed a programme to support community groups to work on environmental issues to create greener, fairer and safer communities. By making connections with the whole, it becomes apparent that community workers and environmental activists need to work together at grassroots level. Collective connections increase when local practice keys into organisations that have a more global reach. Capacity Global, for instance, which is a London-based NGO (non-governmental organisation), supports local people to tackle urban issues of inclusion and environmental injustice as well as policy and campaigning worldwide (see www.capacity.org.uk). At a CDX conference, Maria Adebowale, Director of Capacity Global, a keynote speaker, said, 'Environmental justice encompasses the substantive right of all to a healthy environment' (CDX, 2009).

Similarly, nef (www.neweconomics.org) aims to improve the quality of life by putting people and the planet first. It works at every level in every context by supporting new ways of looking at practice that challenge mainstream thinking on the economy, environment and social issues. This is a holistic approach that supports practical, local economic initiatives at grassroots level as well as research, campaigning and policy debates. This combination of thinking and doing offers community development a bridge from local action to global influence. nef is also involved in developing indicators of well-being and environmental sustainability. In these ways, practitioners can link to organisations that provide structures with a local/global reach.

Inner/outer consciousness

The process of becoming critical has inner and outer dimensions; as Judi Marshall (2001) puts it, we need to use both inner and outer arcs of attention. Inner reflection allows us to reach levels of critical reflexivity, to reflect on our reflections in order to get deeper insights. This inner criticality is in symbiotic relationship with our outer perceptions, continually questioning and exploring meanings, possibilities and purpose in relation to life experience.

Practical tools for aiding the inner process of reflexivity include the practice of journal keeping. Reflecting on a critical incident, trying to make sense of an issue or an observation in practice, starts with the skill of capturing the essence of it in story, or diagram or drawing. We find it useful to use one page of a journal for this, and the facing page to record insights, reflections, ideas that lead to changed practice.

The outer process of consciousness is explored in groups where an issue, or in Freirean terms a 'generative theme', a situation from everyday life that will generate a passionate response out of everyday apathy, is the focus of dialogue. This can be done effectively through the use of stories about life experiences, but must always be carried out in a context of trust, respect and confidentiality. This is easier said than done. It calls for vigilance on the part of the animator, until these values are fully understood in action. For instance, an interruption, a comment, a sidelong glance can be imperceptible but deeply damaging to individuals in the group. It is our responsibility to maintain a culture of respect in a world that often rewards disrespect. Freirean approaches to problematising using drawings, cartoons or photographs or Boal's approach to forum theater are problematising approaches that form the group before the telling of personal experiences. While we emphasise the use of these participatory approaches to practice with community groups, these are also effective ways of focusing issues with policy makers, politicians and other powerful stakeholders. Conscientisation, or the processing of becoming critical, deepens through this practice and forms the basis for planning collective action.

After this brief introduction to the model, we invite you to explore the use of these ideas in different contexts, to expand them and apply them. We hope that this outline discussion within the framework of the model helps you to see ways in which all these ideas are inextricably interconnected with the whole. In these ways, this simple model offers you a framework for the planning and evaluation of your practice, extending it beyond the specific to its widest possible potential.

Towards a participatory democracy

In the end, this book has been about creating the conditions of learning for participatory democracy; a horizontal world based on co-existence and cooperation. We discussed this in some depth in Chapter 3, when we considered the implications of a participatory worldview. As we explore different ways of making sense of the world, we are able to see a different vision of what is possible, and this becomes our *practical utopia*, our vision for change.

It is our assertion that democracy is in crisis, and that it is time to re-engage activists in political action. Neoliberal globalisation has escalated, leading to times that are fast destroying the interconnectedness of life on earth. We explored the evidence for this in Chapter 2. Interconnectedness is not only a human need, but is the essence of biodiversity, essential for the survival of life on earth. Individualism runs counter to the flourishing of humanity, and the high levels of consumerism that it encourages result in not only human exploitation, but also exploitation of the earth's resources that are so vital to the survival of the whole.

The same top-down, authority-based processes have led to advanced levels of managerialism, bureaucracy and instrumentalism in the West. This gives rise to policies that are catapulted from on high and miss the needs of bottom-up, grassroots practice, the essence of participatory democracy. So, even when we are encouraged by policies that claim to be committed to change, we find that they make no difference at all because our transformative concepts have been applied with less than transformative intentions.

A major contribution to the process of re-engagement with democracy has emerged from the Learning for Democracy Group (2008). A large meeting of committed people came together in the Scottish Parliament in 2007 in response to an invitation to all those involved in community-based education across Scotland to discuss a widely circulated 'Open letter' written by Ian Martin, Mae Shaw and Jim Crowther of University of Edinburgh.

Open letter: Whatever happened to learning for democracy?

We see our work in community-based education as part of a broader democratic process. This is about enabling people to demand social justice and equality for themselves and others. There is now an historic opportunity to renew democracy in Scotland, and yet we are beginning to feel a profound sense of disappointment about the way in which both our own work and the lives of people in communities are being managed, regulated and controlled.... What is required, in the first instance, is a much more open, democratic and imaginative dialogue and debate about what kind of society we want to live in, and how we can begin to build it in Scotland today. Education and learning in communities can contribute to making this vision a reality, and they are a rich resource for tackling significant problems in society. Ordinary people need the opportunity to have their say, to be listened to and to talk back to the state. This is essentially a democratic process. It cannot simply be managed and measured; it has to be nurtured and cultivated in communities. It requires faith and trust in the people, and a valuing of genuinely democratic dialogue and debate.

The dialogue generated by this letter produced *Learning for democracy: Ten propositions and ten proposals*. We include these below as a valuable contribution to a new movement for democratic participation, a basis on which to develop practice.

Ten propositions

Democracy is about:

1. Freedom
Human flourishing is achieved through freedom to act individually and collectively, only constrained by due consideration for others.

2. Equality
All people are of the same moral worth and are obliged to mind the equality of others.

3. Justice
Justice and democracy are interdependent. An unjust society is an undemocratic society and an undemocratic society breeds injustice.

4. Solidarity
Shared aims and values arise from the pursuit of common purposes and mutually supportive ways of living.

5. Diversity
Dialogue between different cultures and identities can enrich society and help to build a common culture.

6. Accountability
The state is accountable to its citizens for providing the policy framework within which judgements about the common good are made and contested. Those who hold power are answerable to the people.

7. Dialogue
Democracy requires dialogue and the possibility of dissent. This means learning to argue, articulate beliefs, deliberate and come to collective decisions concerning what constitutes the good society.

8. Responsibility
Consistency and coherence between private and public behaviour are essential to the quality of democratic life.

9. Participation
Democracy is something to be negotiated from below rather than handed down from above. Citizens require the opportunity to talk back to the state.

10. Sustainability
A commitment to the environment and to future generations requires determined opposition to those forces which are wasteful and destructive.

We also include the proposals that inform practice for social justice.

Ten proposals

Learning for democracy means:

1. Taking sides

Educational workers are not merely enablers or facilitators. The claim to neutrality can reinforce and legitimise existing power relations. Practitioners need to be clear about what they stand for – and against.

2. Acting in solidarity

Practitioners should proactively seek opportunities to engage in a critical and committed way with communities and social movements for progressive social change.

3. Taking risks

Critical and creative learning is necessarily unpredictable and open-ended. Exploring official problem definitions and challenging taken-for-granted ways of thinking can be a liberating process.

4. Developing political literacy

Politics needs to be made more educational and education made more political. Learning to analyse, argue, cooperate, and take action on issues that matter requires a systematic educational process.

5. Working at the grassroots

Democracy lives through ordinary people's actions; it does not depend on state sanction. Practitioners should be in everyday contact with people on their own ground and on their own terms.

6. Listening to dissenting voices

Activating democracy is a process of creating spaces in which different interests are expressed and voices heard. Dissent should be valued rather than suppressed.

7. Cultivating awkwardness

Democracy is not necessarily best served by the conformist citizen. This means that the educational task is to create situations in which people can confront their circumstances, reflect critically on their experience and take action.

8. Educating for social change

Collective action can bring about progressive change. Learning for democracy can contribute to this process by linking personal experience with wider political explanations and processes.

9. Exploring alternatives

Learning for democracy can provide people with the opportunity to see that the status quo is not inevitable – that 'another world is possible'.

10. Exposing the power of language

The words used to describe the world influence how people think and act. Learning for democracy involves exploring how language frames attitudes, beliefs and values.

We are hopeful that this heralds a new era for community development that links to a world in movement. There are new democratic spaces opening up at local level, 'the critical challenge is how to deepen their inclusiveness and substance, especially in terms of how citizens engage within new democratic spaces, and how such participation delivers on meeting basic developmental and social needs' (Gaventa, 2007: xii). The propositions serve as a guide for dialogue and reflection; the proposals serve as a system of checks and balances to remind us whether we are truly applying in practice the principles that we claim to uphold, a reminder that working on the surface is not going to identify the root sources of oppression that are woven through the structures of society in such taken-for-granted ways that they are not questioned. The emergence of this call for 'learning for democracy' we see as the grassroots forerunner of a movement for change. A popular movement like this does not happen in isolation: the principles inherent in the call are central to other social movements, and thereby offer collective potential in alliance. In these ways, personal consciousness leads to a transformative autonomy that in turn leads to a collective autonomy, a precursor of transformative collective action (Doyal and Gough, 1991).

The process of transformative change

It has been our challenge to convey, in the written word , the essential nature of participatory practice without over- or under-stating its essence. The real challenge is for you, the reader, to put these ideas, principles and values into action – to experience is to understand. I (Margaret) clearly remember being introduced to the ideas of Freire and Gramsci, and the profound impact that they had on my understanding, but it was not until I experienced *hegemony, a culture of silence, horizontal violence* ... that I remember thinking to myself, "So this is what that feels like in action!". Just as I (Jane), having climbed out of my ivory tower and engaged with people in Netherton in a real participatory evaluation, realised what it felt like. The concepts came alive before our eyes, and that is what we describe as a 'living praxis':

> It's like trying to describe how to paint a Picasso. You can teach people about colour, you can teach them about form, you can teach them about structure and the paintbrush, and what bristles are like. And you can talk about different kinds of paper, and you can talk about what kind of music to play in the background to inspire them and you can talk about all sorts of things. But the bottom line is that when the image unfolds on the paper there is flowing of creativity from the wholeness of the person. (Lindsey and McGuinness, 1998: 1114)

Change involves different ways of seeing the world. When we start to think critically, we question everyday life, and we expose the contradictions we live by. As a consequence, we see different possibilities, we have different expectations and we begin to behave differently. Changed epistemologies lead to changed ontologies; the process of thinking and doing, of action and reflection in synergy lead to theory in action and action as theory (Reason and Bradbury, 2001). We begin to create new futures. However, teaching people to think critically is a dangerous occupation! The theory and practice developed by both Antonio Gramsci and Paulo Freire was grounded in participatory democracy – a worldview founded on participation – and, as a consquence, both of them were seen as threats to the status quo and imprisoned. If this makes you falter, remember that they have also had, together with feminism, the greatest impact on all forms of action for social justice since the late 1960s. There are others who remind us of the dangers of speaking out for justice, what Quakers call 'speaking truth to power', and what Stephen Kemmis (2006) calls 'speaking unwelcome truths'. Some suggest practical strategies for our individual survival: Mo Griffiths (2003) talks of 'ducking and weaving' and Peter Mayo (2009) recommends 'flying below the radar'. We suggest that the safest strategy to challenge structural violence is to work collectively, in alliance with others.

Clearly, action for change is a risky business, as Brian Murphy writes:

> Growth is entirely dependent on our willingness to risk. Risk is the process of growth. Human life without constant risk is morbid, degenerative, less than human. Risk is a venture into the unknown, to make it known. It is walking over the horizon to create new horizons…. (Murphy, 1999: 26)

Risk taking is also part of storytelling. The stories that have made sense of our world have offered security, however false, and the dismantling of them can mean loss of identity and connection. This co-creation process has implications for those who work with communities. We need to be aware of the sensitivity of the process and our part in the story making. But most of all, we need to change the story, for in changing the story we change the world.

References

Abma, T. (2006) 'The practice of responsive evaluation', *American Journal of Evaluation*, vol 27, no 1, pp 31–43.

Adebowale, M. (2008) 'Understanding environmental justice: making the connection between sustainable development and social justice', in G. Craig, T. Burchardt and D. Gordon (eds) *Social justice and public policy: Seeking fairness in diverse societies*, Bristol: The Policy Press, pp 271–55.

Adorno, T.W. and Horkheimer, M. (1972) *The dialectic of the enlightenment*, New York, NY: Herder and Herder.

Agnew, J. (1998) *Revisioning world politics*, London: Routledge.

Allen, S. (2003) *Audit of art and health projects in Cumbria*, Eden District, Cumbria: Cumbria Arts and Health Group.

Allman, P. (1999) *Revolutionary social transformation: Democratic hopes, political possibilities and critical education*, London: Bergin & Garvey.

Allman, P. (2009) 'Paulo Freire's contributions to radical adult education' in A. Darder, M. Baltodano and R. Torres (eds) *The critical pedagogy reader* (2nd edn), London and New York: Routledge, pp 417–30.

Altpeter, M., Earp, J.A., Bishop, C. and Eng, E. (1999) 'Lay health advisor activity levels: definitions from the field', *Health Education and Behaviour*, vol 26, no 4, pp 495–512.

Angus, J. (2002) *A review of evidence in community based arts in health*, London: Health Development Agency.

Angus, J. and White, M. (2003) *A literature review of arts and adult mental health*, London: Social Inclusion Unit.

Ansari, W.E.I., Phillips, C.J. and Zwi, A.B. (2002) 'Narrowing the gap between academic professional wisdom and community lay knowledge: perceptions from partnerships', *Public Health*, vol 116, pp 151–9.

Antonovsky, A. (1979) *Stress, health and coping: New perspectives on mental and physical wellbeing*, San Francisco, CA: Jossey-Bass.

Antonovsky, A. (1996) 'The salutogenic model as a theory to guide health promotions', *Health Promotion International*, vol 11, no 1, pp 11–18.

Archbishop of Canterbury's Advisory Group on Urban Priority Areas (1985) *Faith in the city*, London: Church House.

Argyris, C. and Schön, D. (1978) *Organisational learning: A theory of action perspective*, San Francisco, CA: Jossey-Bass.

Arnstein, S. (1969) 'A ladder of participation', *Journal of the American Planning Association*, vol 35, no 4, pp 216–24.

Baker, E.A., Bouldin, N., Durham, M., Lowell, M.E., Gonzalez, M., Jodaitis, N., Cruz, L.N., Torres, I., Torres, M. and Adams, S.T. (1997) 'The Latino Health Advocacy Programme: a collaborative lay health advisor approach', *Health Education and Behaviour*, vol 24, no 4, pp 495–509.

Bakhtin, M. (1984) *Problems of Dostoevsky's poetics* (edited and translated by Caryl Emerson), Minneapolis, MN: University of Minnesota.

Barnes, M. (2007) 'Whose spaces? Contestations and negotiations in health and community regeneration forums in England', in A. Cornwall and V.S.P. Coelho (eds) *Spaces for change? The politics of citizen participation in new democratic arenas*, London: Zed Books, pp 240–59.

Barnett, R. (1997) *Towards a higher education for a new century*, London: Institute of Education, University of London.

Barr, A. and Hashagen, S. (2000) *ABCD handbook: A framework for evaluating community development*, London: Community Development Foundation.

Bateson, G. (1972) *Steps to an ecology of mind: Collected essays in anthropology, psychiatry, evolution, and epistemology*, San Francisco, CA: Chandler Publishing Company.

Bateson, G. (1979) *Mind and nature: A necessary unity*, New York, NY: E.P. Dutton.

Belenky, M.F., Clinchy, B.M., Goldberger, N.R. and Tarule, J.M. (eds) (1986) *Women's ways of knowing*, New York, NY: Basic Books.

Belenky, M.F., Clinchy, B.M., Goldberger, N.R. and Tarule, J.M. (1997) *Women's ways of knowing: The development of self, voice and mind* (10th anniversary edn), New York, NY: Basic Books.

Benhabib, S. (1992) *Situating the self: Gender, community and postmodernism in contemporary ethics*, Cambridge: Polity Press.

Berger, P.L. (1963) *Invitation to sociology*, Garden City, NY: Doubleday.

Berger, R. and Quinney, R. (eds) (2005) *Storytelling sociology: Narrative as social inquiry*, Boulder, CO: Lynne Rienner Publishers.

Berkeley, D. and Springett, J. (2006) 'From rhetoric to reality: a systemic approach to understanding the constraints faced by Health For All initiatives in England', *Social Science and Medicine*, vol 63, no 11, pp 2877–89.

Berner, E. and Phillips, B. (2005) 'Left to their own devices? Community self-help between alternative development and neoliberalism', *Community Development Journal*, vol 40, no 1, January, pp 17–29.

Beveridge, Sir W. (1942) *Social insurance and allied services*, London: Inter-departmental Committee on Social Insurance and Allied Services.

Bing, V. and Trotman Reid, P. (1996) 'Unknown women and knowing research: consequences of color and class in feminist psychology', in N.R. Goldberger, J.M. Tarule, B.M. Clinchy and M.F. Belenky (eds) *Knowledge, difference, and power: Essays inspired by women's ways of knowing*, New York, NY: Basic Books., pp 175–204.

Bird, R.J. (2003) *Chaos and life: Complexity and order in evolution and thought*, New York: Columbia University Press.

Blackman, T. (2006) *Placing health: Neighbourhood renewal, health improvement and complexity*, Bristol: The Policy Press.

Blair, T. (1998) *The third way: New politics for the new century*, London: The Fabian Society.

Boal, A. (1979) *Theater of the oppressed*, New York, NY: Urizen Books.

Boal, A. (translated by A. Jackson) (1994) *The rainbow of desire: The Boal method of theatre and therapy,* London and New York: Routledge.

Boal, A. (2008) *Theater of the oppressed: Get political* (new edn), London: Pluto.

Bohm, D. (1980) *Wholeness and the implicate order,* London: Routledge.

Bohm, D. (1996) *On dialogue* (edited by Lee Nichol), London: Routledge.

Bolam, B., Gleeson, K. and Murphy, S. (2003) 'Lay person or health expert? Exploring theoretical and practical aspects of reflexivity', *Qualitative Health Research Forum: Qualitative Sozialforschung,* May, vol 4, no 2, available at www.qualitative-research.net/index.php/fgs/article/view/699, accessed 12 June 2009.

Bolton, G. (2005) *Reflective practice: Writing and professional development* (2nd edn), London: Sage Publications.

Borg, C. and Mayo, P. (2006) *Learning and social difference: Challenges for public education and critical pedagogy,* Boulder, CO: Paradigm Publishers.

Bortoft, H. (1996) *The wholeness of nature: Goethe's way of science,* Edinburgh: Floris.

Boud, D., Keogh, R. and Walker, D. (1985) 'Promoting reflection in learning: a mode', in D. Boud, R. Keogh and D. Walker (eds) *Reflection: Turning experience into learning,* London: Kogan Page.

Bourne, J. (1999) 'Racism, postmodernism and the flight from class', in D. Hill, P. McLaren, M. Cole and G. Rikowski (eds) *Postmodernism in educational theory: Education and the politics of human resistance,* London: Tufnell Press, pp 131–46.

Boyd, R.D. and Myers, J.G. (1988) 'Transformative education', *International Journal of Lifelong Education,* vol 7, no 4, pp 261–84.

Bray, J., Lee, J., Smith, L. and Yorks, L. (2000) *Collaborative inquiry in practice,* London: Sage Publications.

Brewer, M., Browne, J., Joyce, R. and Sutherland, H. (2009) *Micro-simulating child poverty in 2010 and 2020,* London: Institute for Fiscal Studies.

Brookfield, S. (1987) *Developing critical thinkers: Challenging adults to explore alternative ways of thinking and acting,* San Francisco, CA: Jossey-Bass.

Bruce, N., Springett, J., Hotchkiss, J. and Scott Samuel, A. (eds) (1995) *Research and change in urban community health,* Aldershot: Avebury.

Buber, M. (1948) *Israel and the world: Essays in a time of crisis,* New York, NY: Schoeter Books.

Bühler, U. (2004) *Participation 'with justice and dignity' beyond the 'new tyranny',* Research Paper, Bradford: Department of Peace Studies, Bradford University.

Burns, D. (2007) *Systemic action research: A strategy for whole system change,* Bristol: The Policy Press.

Calaprice, A. (ed) (2005) *The new quotable Einstein,* Princeton, NJ: Princeton University Press.

Cannan, C. (2000) 'The environmental crisis, Greens and community development', *Community Development Journal,* vol 35, no 4, October, pp 365–76.

Capra, F. (1996) *The web of life: A new synthesis of mind and matter,* New York, NY: HarperCollins.

Capra, F. (1982) *The turning point: Science, society and the rising culture*, New York, NY: Simon and Schuster.

Capra, F. (2003) *Hidden connections: A science for sustainable living*, New York, NY: Flamingo.

Castelloe, P., Watson, T. and White, C. (2002) 'Participatory change: an innovative approach to community practice', *Journal of Community Practice*, vol 10, no 4, pp 7-32.

Cavanagh, C. (2004) *Comeuppance: Storytelling and social justice*, Toronto, Canada: Catalyst Centre.

Cavanagh, C. (2007) 'Popular education, social movements and story telling: interview with Chris Cavanagh', in C. Borg and P. Mayo, *Public intellectuals, radical democracy and social movements: A book of interviews*, New York, NY: Peter Lang Publishing, pp 41-8.

Cave, B., Molyneux, P. and Coutts, A. (2004) *Healthy sustainable communities: What works?*, Milton Keynes and South Midlands Health and Social Care Group.

CDX (2009) conference report: *Making connections: Community development and environmental justice*, available from www.cdx.org.uk

Chambers, R. (1997) *Whose reality counts? Putting the first last*, London: ITDG.

Chesterman, J., Judge, K., Bauld, L., Pound, E. and Coleman, T. (2002) *Effectiveness of smoking cessation services. An analysis of outcomes at health authority level*, London: Department of Health.

Chia, R. (2003) 'From knowledge creation to perfecting action: Tao, Basho and pure experience as the ultimate spiral of knowing', *Human Relations*, vol 56, no 8, pp 953-81.

Clandinin, J. and Connelly, M. (2000) *Narrative inquiry: Experience and story in qualitative research*, San Francisco, CA: Wiley.

Cohen, R., Ferres, G., Hollins, C., Long, G., Smith, R. and Bennett, F. (eds) (1996) *Out of pocket: Failure of the Social Fund*, London: The Children's Society.

Collins, S.B. (2005) 'An understanding of poverty from those who are poor', *Action Research*, vol 3, no 1, pp 9-31.

Community Pride Initiative and Oxfam (2005) *Breathing life into democracy: The power of participatory budgeting*, London: Oxfam.

Cooke, B. and Kothari, U. (eds) (2001) *Participation: The new tyranny*, London: Zed Books.

Cooperrider, D.L., Whitney, D. and Stavros, J. (2007 *The appreciative inquiry handbook* (2nd edn), San Francisco: Berrett-Koehler.

Cornwall, A. and Coelho, V.S.P. (eds) (2007) *Spaces for change? The politics of citizen participation in new democratic arenas*, London: Zed Books.

Cornwall, A. and Jewkes, R. (1995) 'What is participatory research?', *Social Science and Medicine*, vol 41, issue 12, pp 1667-76.

Couto, R.A. (2000) 'Community health as social justice: lessons in leadership' in *Family and Community Health*, vol 23, no 1, pp 1-17.

CPAG (Child Poverty Action Group) (2008) *Child poverty: The stats: Analysis of the latest poverty statistics*, London: CPAG.

Craig, G. (2008) 'The limits of compromise? Social justice, "race" and multiculturalism' in G. Craig, T. Burchardt and D. Gordon (eds) *Social justice and public policy: Seeking fairness in diverse societies*, Bristol: The Policy Press, pp 231–50.

Craig, G. and Taylor, M. (2002) 'Dangerous liaisons: local government and the voluntary and community sectors', in C. Glendinning, M. Powell and K. Rummery (eds) *Partnerships, New Labour and the governance of welfare*, Bristol: The Policy Press, pp 131–48.

Craig, G., Burchardt, T. and Gordon, D. (2008) *Social justice and public policy: Seeking fairness in diverse societies*, Bristol: The Policy Press.

CSDH (Commission on Social Determinants of Health) (2008) *Closing the gap in a generation: Health equity through action on the social determinants of health*, Final report of CSDH, Geneva: World Health Organization.

Cuijpers, P. (2002) 'Peer-led and adult-led school drug prevention: a meta analytical comparison', *Journal of Drug Education*, vol 32, no 2, pp 107–19.

Cupitt, D. (2005) interviewed by Neville Glasgow, BBC Radio 4, 8 September, cited in G. Bolton (2005) *Reflective practice: Writing and professional development* (2nd edn), London: Sage Publications.

Dadds, M. (2008) 'Empathetic validity in practitioner research', *Educational Action Research*, vol 16, no 2, pp 279–90.

Danaher, G., Schirato, T. and Webb, J. (2000) *Understanding Foucault*, London: Sage Publications.

Darder, A. (2002) *Reinventing Paulo Freire: A pedagogy of love*, Boulder, CO and Oxford, UK: Westview Press.

Darder, A., Baltodano, M.P. and Torres, R.D. (eds) (2009) *The critical pedagogy reader* (2nd edn), London: Routledge.

Dewey, J. (1925) *Experience and nature*, Chicago, IL: Open Court Publishing Co (republished in 1958, New York, NY: Dover Publications).

DH (Department of Health) (2008) *A dialogue of equals: The Pacesetters programme community engagement guide*, London: DH (www.dh.gov.uk/en/Publicationsandstatistics/Publications/PublicationsPolicyandGuidance/DH_082382).

Dimasio, A. (1994) *Descartes: Error, emotion, reason and human brain*, New York, NY: Putnam.

Dixon, J., Levine, M. and McAuley, R. (2006) 'Locating impropriety: street drinking, moral order and the ideological dilemma', *Political Psychology*, vol 27, no 2, pp 187–206.

Doniger, W. (1998) *The implied spider: Politics and theology in myth*, New York, NY: Columbia University Press.

Donnision, D. (1998) *Policies for a just society*, Basingstoke: Macmillan.

Dooris, M. (2006) 'Healthy settings: challenges to generating evidence of effectiveness', *Health Promotion International*, vol 21, no 1, pp 55–65.

Dorman, P. (2008) 'The welfare state at 60', *Poverty*, issue 130, Summer, p 130.

Douglas, N.W., Whitty, G. and Aggleton, P. (2000) 'Vital youth: evaluating a theatre in education project', *Health Education*, vol 100, pp 207-15.

Dowler, E., Turner, S. and Dobson, B. (2001) *Poverty bites: Food, health and poor families*, London: Child Poverty Action Group.

Doyal, L. and Gough, I. (1991) *A theory of human need*, Basingstoke: Macmillan.

Dwelly, T. (2001) *Creative regeneration: Lessons from 10 community arts projects*, York: Joseph Rowntree Foundation.

Elbow, P. (1998) *Writing with power: Techniques for mastering the writing process*, New York, NY: Oxford University Press.

Elliott, J. (2005) 'Becoming critical: the failure to connect', *Educational Action Research*, vol 13, no 3, pp 359-73.

Fay, B. (1987) *Critical social science*, Ithaca, NY: Cornell University Press.

Fisher, W.F. and Ponniah, T. (2003) *Another world is possible: Popular alternatives to globalization at the World Social Forum*, London: Zed Books.

Flaherty, J., Veit-Wilson, J. and Dornan, P. (2004) *Poverty: The facts* (5th edn), London: Child Poverty Action Group.

Foresight (2007) *Tackling obesities: Future choices* (2nd edn), London: Government Office for Science.

Forester, J. (1999) *The deliberative practitioner: Encouraging participatory planning processes*, Cambridge, MA: MIT Press.

Forgacs, D. (ed) (1988) *A Gramsci reader*, London: Lawrence and Wishart.

Foucault, M. (1980) *Power/knowledge: Selected interviews and other writings*, Brighton: Harvester Wheatsheaf.

Freire, P. (1972) *Pedagogy of the oppressed*, Harmondsworth: Penguin.

Freire, P (1985) *The politics of education: Culture, power and liberation*, London: Macmillan.

Freire, P. (1993a) *Pedagogy of the city*, New York, NY: Continuum.

Freire, P. (1993b) 'Foreword' in P. McLaren and P. Leonard (eds) *Paulo Freire: A critical encounter*, London and New York: Routledge, pp ix-xii.

Freire, P. (1995) *Pedagogy of hope*, New York, NY: Continuum.

Freire, P (1998a) *Pedagogy of the heart*, New York, NY: Continuum

Freire, P. (1998b) *Teachers as cultural workers: Letters to those who dare to teach*, Boulder, CO: Westview Press.

Freire, P. (2005) *Pedagogy of indignation*, Boulder, CO: Paradigm Publishers.

Freire, P. and Faundez, A. (1989) *Learning to question: A pedagogy of liberation*, New York, NY: Continuum.

Gardiner, M. (2000) *Critiques of everyday life*, London: Routledge.

Gaventa, J (2004) 'Strengthening participatory approaches to local governance: learning lessons from abroad', *Civic Review*, vol 93, no 4, pp 16-27.

Gaventa, J. (2006) 'Finding spaces for change: a power analysis', *IDS Bulletin*, vol 37, no 6, pp 26-33.

Gaventa, J. (2007) 'Foreword', in A. Cornwall and V.S.P. Coelho, *Spaces for change? The politics of citizen participation in new democratic arenas*, London: Zed Books, pp x-xviii.

Giddens, A. (1987) *Social theory and modern sociology*, Cambridge: Polity Press.

Giddens, A. (1991) *Modernity and self-identity: Self and society in the late modern age*, Cambridge: Polity Press.

Giddens, A. (1998) *The third way: The renewal of social democracy*, Cambridge: Polity Press.

Giddens, A. (2000) *The third way and its critics*, Cambridge: Polity Press.

Giroux, H. (1993) 'Paulo Freire and the politics of postcolonialism', in P. McLaren and P. Leonard (eds) *Paulo Freire: A critical encounter*, London and New York: Routledge.

Giroux, H. (2006a) *Stormy weather: Katrina and the politics of disposability*, Boulder, CO: Paradigm Publishers.

Giroux, H. (2006b) 'Katrina and the politics of disposability', *In These Times*, 14 September (www.inthesetimes.com/article/2822, accessed 2 April 2008).

Giroux, H. (2009) 'Critical theory and educational practice', in A. Darder, M.P. Baltodano and R.D. Torres (eds) *The critical pedagogy reader* (2nd edn), London: Routledge, pp 27-51.

Giroux, H. and McLaren, P. (1996) *Between borders: Pedagogy and the politics of cultural studies*, London: Routledge.

Goguen, J. and Myin, A. (2000) 'Art and the brain: 11 investigations into the science of art', *Journal of Consciousness Research: Controversies in Science and the Humanities*, vol 12, no 7, pp 7-16.

Goldbard, A. (2006) *New creative community: The art of cultural development*, Oakland, CA: New Village Press.

Goldberger, N.R., Tarule, J.M., Clinchy, B.M. and Belenky, M.F. (eds) (1996) *Knowledge, difference, and power: Essays inspired by women's ways of knowing*, New York, NY: Basic Books.

Goldsmith, E. and Allan, R. (1972) 'A blueprint for survival', *The Ecologist*, vol 2, pp 1-22.

Goodson, I. (2007) 'All the lonely people: the struggle for private meaning and public purpose in education', *Critical Studies in Education*, vol 48, no 1, pp 131-48.

Goodwin, B. (2007) *Nature's due: Healing our fragmented culture*, Edinburgh: Floris Books.

Gordon, D. (2008) 'Children, policy and social justice', in G. Craig, T. Burchardt and D. Gordon, *Social justice and public policy: Seeking fairness in diverse societies*, Bristol: The Policy Press, pp 157-79.

Grabov, V. (1997) 'The many facets of transformative learning theory and practice', in P. Cranton (ed) *Transformative learning in action: Insights from practice*, New Directions for Adult and Continuing Education, no 74, pp 89-96, San Francisco, CA: Jossey-Bass, Summer.

Gramsci, A. (1971) *Selections from prison notebooks*, London: Lawrence and Wishart.

Gray, J. (2007) *Enlightenment's wake*, London: Routledge.

Green, L.W. and Mercer, S.L. (2001) 'Community-based participatory research: can public health researchers and agencies reconcile the push from funding bodies and the pull from communities?', *American Journal of Public Health*, vol 91, pp 1926-9.

Griffiths, M. (2003) *Action for social justice in education: Fairly different*, Maidenhead: Open University Press.

Habermas, J. (translated by J. Viertel) (1974) *Theory and practice*, London: Heinemann.

Habermas, J. (1984) (translated by T. McCarthy) *The theory of communicative action, vol 1: Reason and the rationalisation of society*, Cambridge: Polity Press.

Habermas, J. (translated by T. McCarthy) (1987) *The theory of communicative action, vol 2: Lifeworld and the system*, Cambridge: Polity Press.

Habermas, J. (1994) 'Struggles for recognition in the democratic constitutional state', in C. Taylor (ed) *Multiculturalism. Examining the politics of recognition*, Princeton, NJ: Princeton University Press, pp 105-7.

Habermas, J. (translated by B. Fultner) (2003) *Truth and justification*, Cambridge, MA: MIT Press.

Hague, C. and Jenkins, P. (2005) *Place identity, participation and planning*, London: Routledge.

Haila, Y. and Dyke, C. (eds) (2006) *How nature speaks: The dynamics of the human ecological condition*, Durham, NC: Duke University Press.

Hancock, T. (1993) 'Health, human development and the community ecosystem: three ecological models', *Health Promotion International*, vol 8, pp 41-7.

Hancock, T. and Perkins, F. (1985) 'The mandala of health: a conceptual model and teaching tool', *Health Education*, vol 23, pp 8-10.

Hartz, Z.M.A., Denis, J.-L., Moreira, E. and Matida, A. (2008) 'From knowledge to action: challenges and opportunities for increasing the use of evaluation in health promotion policies and practices', in L. Potvin and D. McQueen (eds) *Health promotion: Evaluation practices in the Americas, values and research*, New York, NY: Springer.

Hawkins, P. (1992) 'Organisational learning: taking stock and facing the challenge', *Management Learning*, vol 25, no 1, pp 71-82.

Heidegger, M. (translated by J. Glenn Gray) (1963) *What is called thinking?*, London: HarperCollins.

Henkel, P. and Stirrat, S. (2001) 'Participation as spiritual duty: empowerment as secular subjection', in B. Cooke and U. Kothari (eds) *Participation: The new tyranny*, London: Zed Books, pp 168-84.

Heron, J. (1992) *Feeling and personhood: Psychology in another key*, London: Sage Publications.

Heron, J. (1996) *Cooperative inquiry: Research into the human condition*, London: Sage Publications.

Heron, J. (2001) 'Transpersonal co-operative inquiry', in P. Reason and H. Bradbury (eds) *Handbook of action research: Participative inquiry and practice*, London: Sage, pp 333-9.

Heron, J. (2005) *Spiritual inquiry: A handbook of radical practice*, Kaukapakapa, New Zealand: South Pacific Centre for Human Inquiry.

Hill Collins, P. (1990) *Black feminist thought: Knowledge, consciousness, and the politics of empowerment*, London: Routledge.

Hines, C. (2000) *Localization: A global manifesto*, London: Earthscan.

Holden, M. (2006) 'Urban indicators and the integrative ideals of cities', *Cities*, vol 23, no 3, pp 170–83.

hooks, b (1989) *Talking back: Thinking feminist, thinking black*, Boston, MA: South End Press.

hooks, b (1993) 'bell hooks speaking about Paulo Freire – the man, his work', in P. McLaren and P. Leonard (eds) *Paulo Freire: A critical encounter*, London: Routledge, pp 145-52.

Hope, A. and Timmel, S. (1984) *Training for transformation: A handbook for community workers*, Zimbabwe: Mambo Press.

Hope, A. and Timmel, S. (1999) *Training for transformation: A handbook for community workers, Book 4*, London: ITDG Publishing.

Horton, M. (1998) *The long haul: An autobiography*, New York: Teachers College Press.

Howarth, C., Kenway, P., Palmer, G. and Miorelli, R. (1999) *Monitoring poverty and social exclusion, 1999*, York/London: Joseph Rowntree Foundation/New Policy Institute.

Husserl, E.A.G. (1989) *Ideas pertaining to a pure phenomenology and to a phenomenological philosophy: First book general introduction to pure phenomenology* (translated by F. Kerstein), Boston, MA: Kluwer Academic Publishers.

Hustedde, R. and King, B. (2002) 'Rituals, emotions, community faith in soul and the messiness of life', *Community Development Journal*, vol 37, pp 338-48.

Innes, J.E. and Booher, D.E. (2005) 'Reframing public participation: Strategies for the 21st century', *Planning Theory and Practice*, vol 5, no 4, pp 419-36.

Irish, S. (2004) 'Tenant to tenant: the art of talking to strangers', *Places, Forum of Design for the Public Realm*, vol 16, no 3, pp 61-7.

Isaacs, W. (1999) *Dialogue: The art of thinking together*, New York, NY: Broadway Business.

Jackson, E.T. and Kassam, Y. (1998) *Knowledge shared: Participatory evaluation in development cooperation*, West Hartford, CT: Kumarian Press.

Jacobs, G.C. (2006) 'Imagining the flowers, but working the rich and heavy clay: participation and empowerment in action research for health', *Educational Action Research*, vol 14, no 4, pp 569-81.

Jacobs, G.C. (2008) 'The development of critical being? Reflection and reflexivity in an action learning programme for health promotion practitioners in the Netherlands', *Action Learning: Research and Practice*, vol 5, no 3, pp 221-35.

Jarvis, M.J. and Wardle, M. (1999) 'Social patterning in health behaviours: the case of cigarette smoking', in M. Marmot and R. Wilkinson (eds) *Social determinants of health*, Oxford: Oxford University Press, pp 224-37.

Johnston, R. (2008) 'Making space for social purpose adult education within civil society', Paper presented to the 38th Annual SCUTREA (Standing Conference on University Teaching and Research in the Education of Adults), University of Edinburgh, 2-4 July.

Kane, L. (2008) 'The World Bank, community development and education for social justice', *Community Development Journal*, vol 43, no 2, April, pp 194-209.

Kemmis, S. (2001) 'Exploring the relevance of critical theory for action research: emancipatory action research in the footsteps of Jurgen Habermas', in P. Reason and H. Bradbury (eds) *Handbook of action research: Participative inquiry and practice*, London: Sage, pp 91-102.

Kemmis, S. (2006) 'Participatory action research and the public sphere', *Educational Action Research*, vol 14, no 4, pp 459-76.

Kenway, J. (2001) 'Remembering and regenerating Gramsci', in K. Weiler (ed) *Feminist engagements: Reading, resisting, and revisioning male theorists in education and cultural studies*, London and New York: Routledge, pp 47-66.

Killeen, D. (2008) 'Is poverty in the UK a denial of people's human rights?', York: Joseph Rowntree Foundation (also available at www.jrf.org.uk).

Kirkwood, C. (1991) 'Freire methodology in practice', in *Roots and branches* (series of occasional papers), vol 1: Community Development and Health Education, Milton Keynes: Open University Health Education Unit.

Kolb, D.A. (1984) *Experiential learning: Experience as the source of learning and development*, Englewood Cliffs, NJ: Prentice-Hall.

Kothari, U. (2001) 'Power, knowledge and social control in participatory development', in B. Cook and U. Kothari (eds) *Participation: The new tyranny*, London: Zed Books, pp 139-52.

Kravagna, C. (1998) *Working on communities: A model of participatory praxis* (translated by Aileen Derig), Bonn, Germany: European Institute for Programme Cultural Policy, available at www.radicalart.org (check Jane)

Labonte, R. (1993) 'Community development and partnerships', *Canadian Journal of Public Health*, vol 84, pp 237-40.

Labonte, R. (1993a) *Community health and empowerment,* Toronto: Centre for Health Promotion.

Labonte, R. (1994) 'Health promotion and empowerment: reflections on professional practice', *Health Education and Behaviour*, vol 21, no 2, pp 253-68.

Labonte, R. and Feather, J. (1996) *Handbook on using stories in health promotion practice*, Saskatoon, Saskatchewan, Canada: Prairie Region Health Promotion Research Centre.

Lacey, L., Tukes, S., Manferdi, C. and Warnecke, R.B. (1991) 'Use of lay health educators for smoking cessation in a hard to reach community', *Journal of Community Health*, vol 16, pp 269-82.

Laclau, E. and Mouffe, C. (2001) *Hegemony and socialist strategy: Towards a radical democratic politics* (2nd edn), London: Verso.

Lansens, L. (2007) *The girls*, London: Virago Press Ltd.

Latour, B. (1999) *Pandora's hope: An essay on the reality of science studies,* Boston: MA: Harvard University Press.

Lawlor, D.A., Frankel, S., Shaw, M., Ebrahim, S. and Davey-Smith, G. (2003) 'Smoking and ill health: does lay epidemiology explain the failure of smoking cessation programs among deprived populations?', *American Journal of Public Health,* vol 93, no 2, pp 266-70.

Layard, R. and Dunn, J. (2009) *A good childhood: Searching for values in a competitive age,* Harmondsworth: Penguin.

Learning for Democracy Group (2008) *Learning for democracy: Ten propositions and ten proposals,* available at http://www.scutrea.ac.uk/library/Wallchart%20pdf.pdf

Ledwith, M. (2005) *Community development: A critical approach,* Bristol: The Policy Press.

Ledwith, M. (2009) 'Antonio Gramsci and feminism: the elusive nature of power', *Educational Philosophy and Theory,* vol 41, no 6, pp 684-97.

Ledwith, M. and Asgill, P. (2000) 'Critical alliance: black and white women working together for social justice', *Community Development Journal,* vol 35, no 3, July, pp 290-9.

Ledwith, M. and Asgill, P. (2007) 'Feminist, anti-racist community work: critical alliance – local to global', in L. Dominelli (ed) *Revitalising communities in a globalising world,* Aldershot: Ashgate, pp 107-22.

Lindsey, M. and McGuinness, L. (1998) 'Significant elements of community involvement in participatory action research: evidence from a community project', *Journal of Advanced Nursing,* vol 28, no 5, pp 1106-14.

Lister, R. (2008) 'Recognition and voice: the challenge for social justice', in G. Craig, T. Burchardt and D. Gordon (eds) *Social justice and public policy: Seeking fairness in diverse societies,* Bristol: The Policy Press, pp 105-22.

Ludema, J., Cooperrider, D. and Barrett, F. (2001) 'Appreciative inquiry: the power of the unconditional positive question', in P. Reason and H. Bradbury (eds) *Action research: Participative inquiry and practice,* London: Sage.

Ludwig, D.S. and Kabat-Zim, J. (2008) 'Mindfullness in medicine', *JAMA,* vol 300, no 11, pp 1350-2.

McAdams, D (1993) *The stories we live by: Personal myths and the making of the self,* New York: Guilford Press.

McAdams, D., Josselson, R. and Lieblich, A. (2006) *Identity and story: Creating self in narrative,* Washington, DC: American Psychological Association.

McGill, I. and Brockbank, A. (2004) *The action learning handbook,* London: Routledge.

McLaren, P. (1995) *Critical pedagogy and predatory culture,* London: Routledge.

McLaren, P. (2000) *Che Guevara, Paulo Freire, and the pedagogy of revolution,* Oxford: Rowman & Littlefield.

McLaren, P. (2009) 'Critical pedagogy: a look at the major concepts', in A. Darder, M.P. Baltodano and R.D. Torres (eds) *The critical pedagogy reader* (2nd edn), London: Routledge, pp 61-83.

McLaren, P. and Jaramillo, N.E. (2007) *Pedagogy and praxis in the age of empire: Towards a new humanism*, Boston, MA: Sense Publishers.

McLaren, P. and Leonard, P. (1993) *Paulo Freire: A critical encounter*, New York: Routledge.

McMahon, C. (2007) *The rose of Sebastapol*, London: Phoenix.

Mack, J. and Lansley, S. (1985) *Poor Britain*, London: George Allen & Unwin.

Maguire, P. (1993) 'Challenges, contradictions and celebration: attempting participatory research', in P. Park, M. Brydon-Miller, B. Hall and T. Jackson (eds) *Voices of change: Participatory research in the US and Canada*, Westport, CT: Bergin and Garvey, pp 157-76.

March, J.G. and Simon, H.A. (1993) *Organisations* (2nd edn), Harmondsworth: Penguin.

Marshall, J. (2001) 'Self-reflective inquiry practices', in P. Reason and H. Bradbury (eds) *Handbook of action research: Participative inquiry and practice*, London: Sage Publications, pp 433-39.

Marshall, J. (2004) 'Living systemic thinking: exploring quality in first person action research', *Action Research*, vol 12, no 3, pp 305-35.

Martin, I. (2008) 'Whither adult education in the learning paradigm: some personal reflections', Keynote speech presented to the 38th Annual SCUTREA (Standing Conference on University Teaching and Research in the Education of Adults), University of Edinburgh, 2-4 July.

Maslow, A.H. (1969) *The psychology of science*, Chicago, IL: Henry Regnery Company.

Maturana, H.R. and Varela, F. (1987) *The tree of knowledge: The biological tools of human understanding*, Boston, MA: Shambhala Publications.

Mayo, P. (1999) *Gramsci, Freire and adult education: Possibilities for transformative action*, London: Zed Books.

Mayo, P. (2004) *Liberating praxis: Paulo Freire's legacy for radical education and politics*, Westport, CT: Praeger Publishers

Mayo, P. (2009) 'Flying below the radar: critical approaches to adult education', in M.W. Apple, W. Au and L. Gandin, *The Routledge international handbook of critical education*, London and New York: Routledge, pp 269-80.

Meadows, D. (1991) *The global citizen*, Boston: Island Press.

Meadows, D. and Lokey, E. (2009) *Thinking in systems: A primer*, London: Earthscan/James and James.

Melucci, A. and Avritzer, L. (2000) 'Complexity, cultural pluralism and democracy: collective action in the public space', *Social Science Information*, vol 39, no 4, pp 507-27.

Merleau-Ponty, M. (1962) *Phenomenology of perception* (translated by Colin Smith), New York, NY: Humanities Press.

Mezirow, J. & Associates (1990) *Fostering critical reflection in adulthood: A guide to transformational and emancipatory learning*, San Francisco, CA: Jossey-Bass.

Micealson, J., Abdallah, S., Steuer, N., Thompson, S. and Marks, N. (2009) *National accounts of wellbeing: Bringing real wealth into the account sheet*, London: New Economics Foundation.

Milne, S. (2004) *The enemy within: Thatcher's secret war against the miners* (3rd edn), London: Verso.

Minkler, M. and Hancock, T. (2008) 'Community driven asset identification and issue selection', in M. Minkler and N. Wallenstein (eds) *Community-based participatory research for health: From process to outcomes* (2nd edn), San Francisco, CA: Jossey-Bass.

Minkler, M. and Wallerstein, N. (eds) (2008) *Community-based participatory research for health: From process to outcomes* (2nd edn), San Francisco, CA: Jossey-Bass.

Moore, R.O. (2007) 'Social theory, social policy and sustainable communities', in S. Cropper, A. Porter, G. Williams, S. Carlisle, R.O. Moore, M. Neill, C. Roberts and H. Snooks (eds) *Community health and wellbeing: Action research on health inequalities*, Bristol: The Policy Press.

Mouffe, C (2005) *On the political: Thinking in action*, London: Routledge

Moustakas, C.E. (1990) *Heuristic research: Design, methodology and applications*, Newbury Park, CA: Sage Publications.

Murphy, B. (1999) *Transforming ourselves, transforming the world: An open conspiracy for social change*, London: Zed Books.

nef (New Economics Foundation) (2009) 'National accounts of well-being' (www.nationalaccountsofwellbeing.org/).

Noffke, S. (2005) 'Are we critical yet? Some thoughts on reading, rereading, and becoming critical', *Educational Action Research*, vol 13, no 3, pp 321-7.

Novak, T. (1988) *Poverty and the state*, Milton Keynes: Open University Press.

Obama, B. (2007) *Dreams from my father: A story of race and inheritance*, London: Canongate.

O'Donohue, J. (2004) *Beauty, the invisible embrace: Rediscovering the true sources of compassion, serenity and hope*, New York, NY: HarperCollins.

Ong, A. (1997) 'Chinese modernities: narratives of nature and capitalism', in A. Ong and D. Nonini, *Ungrounded empire: The cultural politics of modern Chinese transnationalism*, London: Routledge.

Opie, A. (1992) 'Qualitative research, appropriation of the "other" and empowerment', *Feminist Review*, no 40, Spring, pp 52-69

Oppenheim, C. (2007) 'Child Poverty in London', *Poverty*, Issue 126, Winter, pp 15-17.

Oppenheim, C. and Harker, L. (1996) *Poverty: The facts*, London: Child Poverty Action Group.

Owen, H. (1997) *Open space technology: A user's guide* (3rd edn), San Francisco, CA: Berrett-Koehler.

Park, P. (2001) 'Knowledge and participatory research', in P. Reason and H. Bradbury (eds) *Handbook of action research: Participative inquiry and practice*, London: Sage Publications: pp 81-90.

Pascale, R., Millerman, M. and Gioja, L. (2000) *Changing the way we change*, Boston, MA: Harvard Business School Press.

Peat, F.D. (1986) *Blackfoot physics: A journey into the Native American universe*, New York, NY: Fourth Estate.

Peat, F.D. (2008) *Gentle action: Bringing creative change to a turbulent world* (new edn), Pari, Italy: Pari Publishing.

Peck, M.S. (2002) *The road less travelled: A new psychology of love, traditional values and spiritual growth* (25th anniversary edn), New York, NY: Simon & Schuster.

Pert, C.B. (1999) *Molecules of emotion: The science between mind and body medicine*, Los Angeles, CA: Scribner.

Peters, M. and Lankshear, P. (1996) 'Postmodern counternarratives', in H. Giroux, C. Lankshear, P. McLaren and M. Peters (eds) *Counternarratives: Cultural studies and critical pedagogies in postmodern spaces*, New York, NY: Routledge, pp 1-39.

Petersson, P., Blömqvist, K. and Springett, J. (forthcoming) *Old wine in new bottles? Närsjukvård and the Swedish health care system*, Research Platform for Narsjukvard, Kristianstad: Kristianstad University.

Piachaud, D. (2008) 'Social justice and public policy: a social policy perspective', in G. Craig, T. Burchardt and D. Gordon (eds) *Social justice and public policy: Seeking fairness in diverse societies*, Bristol: The Policy Press, pp 33-51.

Pirsig, R. (1974) *Zen and the art of motorcycle maintenance: An inquiry into values*, New York, NY: William Morrow.

Pitchford, M. with Henderson, P. (2008) *Making spaces for community development*, Bristol: The Policy Press.

Polanyi, M. (1958/1974) *Personal knowledge: Towards a post critical philosophy*, Chicago, IL: University of Chicago Press.

Popay, J. (2006) *Community engagement and community development and health improvement: A background paper for NICE*, London: NICE.

Popay, J., Thomas, C., Williams, G., Bennett, S., Gatrell, A. and Bostock, L. (2003) 'A proper place to live: health inequalities, agency and the normative dimensions of space', *Social Science and Medicine*, vol 57, pp 55-69.

Popple, K. (1995) *Analysing community work: Its theory and practice*, Milton Keynes: Open University Press.

Potvin, L. and McQueen, D. (eds) (2008) *Health promotion: Evaluation practices in the Americas, values and research*, New York, NY: Springer.

Prigogine, I. (1997) *The end of certainty*, London: Simon & Schuster.

Pyrch, T. and Castillo, M. (2001) 'The sights and sounds of indigenous knowledge', in P. Reason and H. Bradbury (eds) *Handbook of action research: Participative inquiry and practice*, London: Sage Publications, pp 379-85.

Quinney, R. (1998) *For the time being: Ethnography of everyday life*, New York, NY: State University of New York Press.

Ramazanoglu, C. and Holland, J. (2002) *Feminist methodology: Challenges and choices*, London: Sage Publications.

Reason, P. (1988) *Human inquiry in action: Developments in new paradigm research*, London: Sage Publications.

Reason, P. (1994) *Participation in human inquiry: Research with people*, London: Sage Publications.

Reason, P. (1998) 'Political, epistemological, ecological and spiritual dimensions of participation', *Studies in Cultures, Organizations and Societies*, vol 4 (edited by C. Gorden), New York, NY: Pantheon.

Reason, P. (2000) 'Action research as spiritual practice', University of Surrey Learning Community Conference, 4–5 May (http://people.bath.ac.uk/mnspwr/Thoughtpieces/ARspritiualpractice.htm).

Reason, P. (2002) 'Justice, sustainability and participation', Inaugural Lecture (www.bath.ac.uk/~mnspwr/).

Reason, P. (2005) 'Living as part of the whole: the implications of participation', *Journal of Curriculum and Pedagogy*, vol 2, no 2, August, pp 35–41.

Reason, P. and Bradbury, H. (eds) (2001) *Handbook of action research: Participative inquiry and practice*, London: Sage Publications.

Reason, P. and Rowan, J. (eds) (1981) *Human inquiry: A sourcebook of new paradigm research*, Chichester: Wiley.

Richards, H., Reid, M. and Watt, G. (2003) 'Victim blaming revisited: a qualitative study of beliefs about illness causation and responses to chest pain', *Family Practice*, vol 20, no 6, pp 711–16.

Ridge, T. (2004) 'Putting the children first: addressing the needs and concerns of children who are poor', in P. Dornan (ed) *Ending child poverty by 2020: The first five years*, London: Child Poverty Action Group, pp 4–11.

Rodgers, D. (2007) 'Subverting the spaces of invitation?', Local politics and participatory budgeting in post–crisis Buenos Aires', in A. Cornwall and V.S.P. Coelho, *Spaces for change? The politics of citizen participation in new democratic arenas*, London: Zed Books, pp 180–201.

Rosenberg, J.D. (ed) (1998) *The genius of John Ruskin: Selections from his writings*, London: University Press of Virginia.

Rowan, J. (1981) 'A dialectical paradigm for research', in P. Reason and J. Rowan (eds) *Human inquiry: A sourcebook of new paradigm research*, Chichester: Wiley.

Rowbotham, S. (1977) *Hidden from history: 300 years of women's oppression and the fight against it*, (3rd edn), London: Pluto Press.

Roy, A. (2004) *The chequebook and the cruise missile*, London: Harper Collins.

Rozentuller, V. and Talbott, S. (2005) 'From two cultures to one: on the relation between science and art', *The Nature Institute,* no 13, Spring, pp 13–18 (available at www.natureinstitute.org).

Ruskin, J. (1862) *Unto this last,* London: Smith Elder

Sarv, H. (1997) *Kompetens att utveckla: Om den lärande organisationens utmaningar* (*Skills for development: If the organisation dares to learn*), Stockholm, Sweden: Liber AB.

Sawicki, J. (1991) *Disciplining Foucault: Feminism, power and the body* (Thinking gender), London: Routledge.

Scholte, J.A. (2000) *Globalization: A critical introduction*, Basingstoke: Palgrave Macmillan.

Schön, D. (1983) *The reflective practitioner: How professionals think in action*, London: Maurice Temple Smith Ltd.

Schwandt, T. (2005) 'The centrality of practice to evaluation', *American Journal of Evaluation*, vol 26, no 1, pp 95–105.

Scott-Samuel, A. and Springett, J. (2007) 'Hegemony or health promotion? Prospects for reviving England's lost discipline', *Journal of the Royal Society of Health*, vol 127, no 5, pp 210–13.

Seabrook, J. (2003) *The no-nonsense guide to world poverty*, Oxford: New Internationist Publications.

Senge, P. (1990) *The fifth discipline: The art and practice of the learning organisation*, London: Random House.

Senge, P., Scharmer, C.O., Jaworski, J. and Flowers, B.S. (2005) *Presence: Exploring profound change in people, organisations and society*, London: Nicholas Brealey Publishing.

Shaw, M. (2004) *Community work: Policy, politics and practice*, Working Papers in Social Sciences and Policy, Hull and Edinburgh: Universities of Hull and Edinburgh.

Shaw, M. and Martin, I. (2000) 'Community work, citizenship and democracy: re-making the connections', *Community Development Journal*, vol 35, no 4, pp 401–13.

Shor, I. (1992) *Empowering education: Critical teaching for social change*, London/Chicago, IL: University of Chicago Press.

Shor, I. (1993) 'Education is politics: Paulo Freire's critical pedagogy' in P. McLaren and P. Leonard (eds) *Paulo Freire: A critical encounter*, London and New York: Routledge, pp 8–24.

Shor, I. and Freire, P. (1987) *A pedagogy for liberation: Dialogues on transforming education*, London: Bergin & Garvey.

Shotter, J. (2001) 'Inside dialogical realities: from an abstract-systematic to a participatory-holistic understanding of communication', *Southern Journal of Communication*, vol 65, pp 119–92.

Shotter, J. (2005) 'Goethe and the refiguring of intellectual inquiry: from "aboutness" thinking to "withness" thinking in everyday life', *Janus Head*, vol 8, no 1, pp 132–58.

Shotter, J. (2006) 'Understanding process from within: an argument for "withness"-thinking', *Organization Studies*, vol 27, no 4, pp 585–604.

Shotter, J. and Katz, A.M. (1998) '"Living moments" in dialogical exchanges', *Human Systems*, vol 9, pp 81–93.

Sinfield, A. (2009) 'Recession: a major threat to tackling poverty', *Poverty*, issue 132, Winter, pp 6–9.

Skinner, B.F. (ed) (1978) *Reflections on behaviorism and society*, Englewood Cliffs, NJ: Prentice Hall.

Skolimowski, H. (1994) *The participatory mind*, London: Arkana.

Smart, B. (2002) *Michel Foucault*, London: Routledge.

Smith, N. and Middleton, S. (2007) *A review of poverty dynamics research in the UK*, York: Joseph Rowntree Foundation.

Smuts, J.C. (1926) *Holism and evolution*, New York, NY: The Macmillan Company.

Spivak, G.C. (1990) *The post-colonial critic: Interviews, strategies, dialogues* (edited by S. Harasyn), London: Routledge.

Spretnak, C. (1993) *The resurgence of the real: Body, nature and place in a hypermodern world*, Harlow: Addison-Wesley.

Springett, J. (2005) 'Transformation through action research', Keynote address to the Swedish Association of Local Authorities Annual Conference, Lund.

Springett, J. (2009) 'Kultur: att införliva den holistika och mänskliga' ['The arts: putting the human back into public health'], in G. Ejlertsson and I. Andersson, *Folkhäls som tvärvetenskap* [*Interdisciplinary public health*], Lund: Studentlitteratur.

Springett, J. and Dunkerton, L. (2001) *Evaluating together*, Liverpool Institute for Health: Liverpool John Moores University.

Springett, J., Owens, C. and Callaghan, J. (2007) 'The challenge of combining "lay" knowledge with "evidence-based" practice in health promotion: Fag Ends Smoking Cessation Service', *Critical Public Health*, vol 17, no 3, pp 243-56.

Stacey, R. (1996) *Complexity and creativity in organizations*, San Francisco, CA: Berrett-Koehler.

Steedman, C. (2000) *Landscape for a good woman: A story of two lives* (2nd edn), London: Virago.

Stevenson, H.M. and Burke, M. (1991) 'Bureaucratic logic in new social movement clothing: the limits of health promotion research', *Health Promotion International*, vol 6, no 4, pp 281-9.

Storr, A. (1974) *The essential Jung: Selected writings*, London: Fontana.

Stringer, E.T. (2007) *Action research* (3rd edn), London: Sage Publications.

Sullivan, J. (2005) *El teatro y lucha de salud del barrio* (*Theatre and environmental health in Texas*) (available at: www.communityarts.org).

Tandon, R. (1981) 'Dialogue as inquiry and intervention', in P. Reason and J. Rowan (eds) *Human inquiry: A sourcebook of new paradigm research*, Chichester: Wiley.

Tandon, R. (2008) 'Participation, citizenship and democracy: reflections on 25 years of PRIA', *Community Development Journal*, vol 43, no 3, pp 284-96.

Tarnas, R. (1991) *The passion of the western mind: Understanding the ideas that have shaped our world view*, London: Random House.

Taylor, P. and Mayo, M. (2008) Editorial to special issue: 'Participatory approaches in community development: transition and transformation', *Community Development Journal*, vol 43, no 3, July, pp 263-8.

Thompson, N. (2003) *Promoting equality: Challenging discrimination and oppression in the human services* (2nd edn), Basingstoke: Macmillan.

Thompson, N. (2006) *Anti-discriminatory practice* (4th edn), Basingstoke: Palgrave Macmillan.

Tiller, W.A. (1997) *Science and human transformation: Subtle energies, intentionality and consciousness*, Walnut Creek, CA: Pavior Publishing.

Timmins, N. (1996) *The five giants: A biography of the welfare state*, London: Fontana.

Tomlinson, M. and Walker, R. (2009) *Coping with complexity: Child and adult poverty*, London: Child Poverty Action Group.

Tomlinson, M., Walker, R. and Williams, G. (2008) 'Child poverty and well-being in the here and now', *Poverty*, issue 129, Winter, pp 11–17.

Torbert, W. (2001) 'The practice of action inquiry', in P. Reason and H. Bradbury (eds) *Handbook of action research: Participative inquiry and practice*, London: Sage Publications, pp 250–60.

Townsend, P. (1995) 'Poverty: home and away', *Poverty*, no 91, Summer.

Treleaven, L. (2001) 'The turn to action and the linguistic turn: towards an integrated methodology', in P. Reason and H. Bradbury (eds) *Handbook of action research: Participative inquiry and practice*, London: Sage Publications.

UNICEF (2005) *State of the world's children 2005: Childhood under threat*, Wetherby: UNICEF Publications.

UNICEF (2007) *Child poverty in perspective: An overview of child well-being in rich countries*, Innocenti Report Card 7 (www.unicef.org.uk).

Weiler, K. (1994) 'Freire and a feminist pedagogy of difference', in P. McLaren and C. Lankshear (eds) *Politics of liberation: Paths from Freire*, London: Routledge.

Weiler, K. (ed) (2001) *Feminist engagements: Reading, resisting, and revisioning male theorists in education and cultural studies*, London: Routledge.

WEN (Women's Environmental Network)/Sustain (2008) *Growing round the house: Briefing*, London: WEN/Sustain.

Wenger, E. (1998) *Communities of practice: Learning meaning and identity*, Cambridge: Cambridge University Press.

Westerman, W. (2009) 'Folk schools, popular education, and a pedagogy of community action', in A. Darder, M. Baltodano and R. Torres (eds) *The critical pedagogy reader* (2nd edn), New York and London: Routledge.

White, S. and Pettit, J. (2004) *Participatory approaches and the measurement of human wellbeing*, UN University–World Institute for Development Economics Research (UNU-WIDER) Research Paper no 2004/57, Helsinki, Finland: UNU-WIDER.

Whitehead, J. and McNiff, J. (2006) *Action research: Living theory*, London: Sage Publications.

WHO (World Health Organization)/CSDH (Commission on Social Determinants of Health) (2008) *Closing the gap in a generation: Health equity through action on the social determinants of health*, Final report of CSDH, Geneva: WHO.

Wilber, K., Patten, T., Leonard, A. and Morelli, M. (2008) *Integral life practice: A 21st century blueprint for physical health, emotional balance, mental clarity and spiritual awakening*, Boston: Integral Publishing.

Wilkinson, R. and Pickett, K.E. (2006) 'Income inequality and population health: a review and explanation of the evidence', *Social Science & Medicine*, vol 62, pp 1768–84.

Wilkinson, R. and Pickett, K.E. (2009) *Spirit level: Why more equal societies almost always do better*, Harmondsworth: Penguin Allen Lane.

Willats. S. (1976) *Art and social function: Three projects*, London: Latimer.

Williams, F. (1989) *Social policy: A critical introduction*, Cambridge: Polity Press.

Wilson, M. (1975) *Health is for people*, London: Darton, Longman and Todd.

Wink, J. (1997) *Critical pedagogy: Notes from the real world*, Harlow: Longman.

Winter, R., Sobiechowska, P. and Buck, A. (eds) (1999) *Professional experience and the investigative imagination: The art of reflective writing*, London: Routledge.

Wood, B. (2007) *Personal health-imagery: Explorations in health promotion*, unpublished doctoral thesis, Liverpool: John Moores University.

Young, A. (1990) *Femininity in dissent*, London: Routledge.

Zeki, S. (1999) *Inner vision: An exploration of art and the brain*, Oxford: Oxford University Press.

Index